THE CAVE OF THE HEART

By the same author

The Cave of the Heart

The Life of Swami Abhishiktananda

SHIRLEY DU BOULAY

OM

Where no longer is any place
where no longer is any time
where no longer is any thought
where no longer is any word
in the Silence
from where proceeds the Word
the Supreme gathering place
the highest step of the Lord
full of honey.

> —Abhishiktananda
> (Inscribed in a copy of his book
> *Hindu-Christian Meeting Point:*
> *Within the Cave of the Heart.*)

ORBIS BOOKS

Maryknoll, New York 10545

Founded in 1970, Orbis Books endeavors to publish works that enlighten the mind, nourish the spirit, and challenge the conscience. The publishing arm of the Maryknoll Fathers and Brothers, Orbis seeks to explore the global dimensions of the Christian faith and mission, to invite dialogue with diverse cultures and religious traditions, and to serve the cause of reconciliation and peace. The books published reflect the views of their authors and do not represent the official position of the Maryknoll Society. To learn more about Maryknoll and Orbis Books, please visit our website at www.maryknoll.org.

Photos are used with the permission of the Abhishiktananda Society.

Grateful acknowledgment is made to the Abhishiktananda Society and to the following publishers for permission to quote from works by Swami Abhishiktananda: ISPCK (New Delhi, India), for *Hindu-Christian Meeting Point: Within the Cave of the Heart* (1993), *The Mountain of the Lord: Pilgrimage to Gangotri* (New ed., 1990), *Saccinanda: A Christian Approach to Advaitic Experience* (1974, rev. 1984); the Christian Literature Society (Madras, India) for *The Church in India: An Essay in Christian Self-Criticism* (Madras, 1969); Dimension Books (Starruca, PA) for *The Eyes of Light* (1983); Les Editions du Cerf (Paris) for *Henri le Saux: Lettres d'un sannyasi chrétien à Joseph Lemarié* (1999).

Additional acknowledgment is made to the following publishers for permission to quote from copyrighted materials: ISPCK (New Delhi) for Sten Rodhe, *Jules Monchanin: Pioneer in Christian-Hindu Dialogue* (1993); the Christian Literature Society (Bangalore, India) for *All India Seminar: The Church in India Today*; Samuel Weiser, Inc. (York Beach, ME) for Arthur Osborne, *Ramana Maharshi & the Path of Self-Knowledge* (1970); T.N. Venkataraman (Tiruvannamalai) for *Talks with Sri Ramana Maharshi*, 3 vols. (1972); Editions Presence (Paris) for *Interiorité et revelation: Essais theologiques* (1982) and *Initiation à la Spiritualité des Upanishads*.

Manufactured in the United States of America.

Du Boulay, Shirley.
    The cave of the heart : the life of Swami Abhishiktananda / by Shirley du Boulay.
        p. cm.
    Includes bibliographical references and index.
    ISBN 13 : 978-1-57075-610-8 (pbk)
        1. Abhishiktananda, Swami, 1910-1973.   2. Monks—India—Biography.
    3. Hinduism—Relations—Christianity.   4. Catholic Church—Relations
    —Hinduism.   I. Title
    BX4705.A214D83 2005
    261.2'45'092—dc22
    [B]
                                                                2005011412

For Murray Rogers

Contents

Acknowledgments

I WOULD LIKE TO THANK the following libraries and collections for giving me access to papers and letters concerning Swami Abhishiktananda: archives of the Abhishiktananda Society, Kergonan Archives, Rennes Diocesan Archives, private collection of Father Murray Rogers, family letters held by Mme. Agnès Le Bris.

I am greatly indebted to the Le Saux family: Renée Le Fur, Annie-Louise Guguen, Sister Thérèse, (Henri's sisters); Louis Montagnon (nephew) and his wife, Véronique, for sharing their memories and showing me round St. Briac. Special thanks are due to Agnès Le Bris (niece) and her husband, Jean-Pierre, for their generosity and help in giving me photocopies of letters from the collection of her mother Louise, Henri's eldest sister (deceased), also to Father Joseph Duré, archivist of the Diocese of Rennes.

I would also like to thank the nuns of St. Michel de Kergonan for their hospitality and the monks of l'Abbaye Sainte-Anne de Kergonan for sharing their memories of Dom Le Saux with me, especially the abbot, Robert Le Gall, Father Emmanuel d'Argent, Father Yves Boucher, Father Jean-Gabriel Gelineau, Brother Jimmy Buzaré, Brother Yves le Floch, and Brother Robert Williamson. I also received welcome help and support from Father Victor Broekart, the librarian of St. André de Bruges, Françoise Jacquin, Father Joseph Lemarié, Father Maurus, prior of Asirvanam Monastery, Father Gispert-Sauch, S.J., Dr. Elvira Bernariggi and André Poutier. Special thanks are due to Vicky Clouston for help with translations from the French, to Kate Davies for stalwart support in the final stages of the preparation of the manuscript, and to Robert Ellsberg of Orbis Books, a strong and reliable support throughout every stage of the writing.

I am much indebted to the generosity of three scholars, Edward Ulrich, Christian Hackbarth-Johnson, and Judson Trapnell, who shared papers and knowledge with great kindness. Especial gratitude is due to Judson Trapnell, who read the first six chapters and made valuable comments, but who died tragically young in 2003.

The greatest debt of all goes to three close friends of Abhishiktananda: Murray Rogers, who suggested that I should write the biography and who shared his memories and supported me so greatly during its writing; Professor Bettina Bäumer, who read the finished draft and shared insights gained from her years in India and her personal knowledge of Swami Abhishiktananda; and James Stuart, whose magnificent and scrupulously edited collection of Abhishiktananda's correspondence, *Swami Abhishi-tananda: His Life Told through His Letters*, provided a vital part of this book, as it will of any biographies yet to be written.

Foreword

Raimon Panikkar

Dear Abhishikta!

Two years after your total resurrection I wrote a long letter to you.* You were alive for me then. Tonight (or rather, early this morning, because I spent most of the night reading the fascinating book by Shirley du Boulay) I will attempt another stammering epistle, for thirty years later you are living in me still.

Most probably I was one of your best friends. We never disagreed, so we didn't need to make "virtuous" efforts to overcome divergence of opinions, as you had to do with most people. It now dawns on me that one of the reasons for our spontaneous friendship was that you never needed to play any role with me—or rather, there was no role to play between us. I remember my rendering of that Gospel passage: "The kingdom is (neither within nor among but) *between* you." I took you as you were and you took me as I was. We created a *between*, a communion.

I wish the author of your biography had never asked me to write a foreword to her brilliant book. To speak about the ineffable is not an easy task. Shirley du Boulay has described your character in a wonderful manner, and I can only endorse what she has written. But I am not the one to write an introduction to your life. I lack the necessary "objectivity," for you are not an object for me. After reading this manuscript I am . . . I cannot just say overwhelmed, impressed, or moved. Perhaps I shouldn't have left the previous sentence dangling, but ended it simply with the "I am" so dear to you.

Through the author's vivid narrative I have relived a bit of my life. Her engaging description almost made me nostalgic for what could have become my life, if you yourself had not "rescued" me. As you so well described in our pilgrimage to Gangotri, the vocation of the monk is not that of the priest. Shirley du Boulay's description rekindled so many

---

*A shorter English version of the original French text appeared in *Studies in Formative Spirituality* (1982).

memories and made me reenact the conversations of two passionate people, each convinced that we should deepen our lives (where the "kingdom" is), because with mere "cosmetics" we would not contribute to the radical *metanoia* needed both for Hinduism and Christianity—as well as for the world at large.

How you struggled and suffered to express your intuitions! It sounds strange, almost preposterous, to confess that everything you said now sounds so self-evident to me that I wonder if it does not simply come from a higher source. In any case, the force of our vision and commitment was the same—even if our language was slightly different.

In 1973 you wrote to me from the nursing home in Indore saying that, once you recovered, you would come to Banares (now known as Varanasi) and stay with me. We had to catch up with each other after so long an absence. Alas, it was not possible. You left this body—and here I still remain. You may understand my feelings. Our relationship was *advaita* (nonduality), and that is why I cannot just write a foreword to your biography. I need to converse with you. Anything else would appear artificial to me. Shirley will understand.

I shall not repeat what I wrote in that first letter to you of thirty years ago. I will only underline a few aspects of your life, just to add some minor strokes to the biography. For now, with the hindsight of these past decades, I better understand the significance of your stubborn existence. From your early youth you had but one single aim: to be *ekāgratā*, as we say in India, or "God intoxicated," as some people might put it. India was just a symbol. The *ātman* within was "calling" you.

"If the grain of wheat does not fall into the ground and die. . . ." You died to yourself, but the earth has received you and the fruits are visible. The changes you dreamed of for the church are not yet all fulfilled, but at least they no longer appear odd or impossible. New "winds" are blowing, in spite of passing backlashes. Nobody today raises an eyebrow on hearing that the church is not identical with the catholic government in Rome. The self-given title of the church, repeated again in the Second Vatican Council, is precisely *sacramentum mundi,* which in the original language of the first fathers sounds even better and deeper: *mysterion tou kosmou,* the mystery of the cosmos. To that *mysterium* we gave our loyalty.

Abhishikta! I have fond memories of our conversations. I recall how skeptical you were about my optimism. I was saying, for instance, that grammar was on my side when I claimed that the word "monk" is the substantive and the words "Hindu" or "Christian" are adjectives. Thus, it did no violence to say "Christian monk" or "Hindu monk," whereas it would be forcing the language to say "a Hindu Jesuit" or "a Buddhist Salesian."

You yourself wrote that you felt you were much too French and even Cartesian in your spontaneous approach to reality. That was simply normal—a proof that you were never rootless. We are all the fruit of our culture. You were aware of this and it helped you to overcome some of your "scruples." But you were not aware of how much you remained (like most Westerners) a disciple of Parmenides: reality could not be contradictory. And here was the source of your anguish at finding yourself to be at the same time Christian and Hindu, monotheist and *advaitin*. For me this was no problem at all, not only because I see no contradiction but also because I do not identify reality with rationality. The real is not obliged to obey Parmenides, and we do not fall into irrationality if we are aware of it. I think that the issue of "double belonging," of which Shirley writes, is still a false problem. I am as much the son of my father as of my mother. Nowadays to be French and European would no longer be considered a "double belonging." Your anguish came out of a dialectical thinking. Your greatness was that you overcame dialectical thinking not by another way of thinking but through painful and excruciating experience. That experience was enormously fruitful. You remained loyal to two dialectically opposed worldviews. For this, we are grateful to you.

Dear Swamiji! I cannot write about you. I can only write to you. I was not able to assuage your suffering. I was unable to convince you because you felt I was making it too easy. Now you do not need my words, but still we profit from your struggles.

The obstacles lie on both sides. This should make us very humble. "Fundamentalism" (a word that we didn't use) lies hidden in most religions. There is no point in discussing ideas, as you rightly said. What has immense value is your life. And you lived yours to the full.

Let me now fulfill my task of prefacing this beautiful biography. Shirley du Boulay magnificently describes your doubts and your inconsistencies: you wanted solitude, but even when you could get it you went traveling here and there; you dreamed of a pure *sannyāsa*, yet you fell short of the ideal; you wanted to get rid of all books, but you could not dispense with them.

Certainly you were inconsistent with your ideas. But let me defend you. They were *your* ideas, and you sensed time and again that what are paramount are not ideas but life, experienced life. Your "inconsistencies" were the most consistent praxis of your experience. You allowed yourself to be led not by your ideas, nor even by your ideals, but by the Spirit that "blows" where, when, and *how* she "wills." To that in-spiration you were loyal. Your greatness was that you were not conscious of it. Let me offer here a clue, a "hermeneutical" key the philosophers would say, to evaluate your inconsistencies. To qualify the metaphor, the Spirit is a wind that blew and directed you where she found least resistance— that is, toward your weaker flanks. I understand why you became so cross at Dr. Cuttat's critical remarks when he said the danger of a certain *advaita* is that it does not give enough weight to love. He was theoretically right. But this was the weakness of a certain *advaita* and not your weakness.

You discovered your *bhakti* (love of God) not as a theological reflection on the incarnation but as a lived and revolutionary experience in your encounter with Marc, your beloved disciple. With Marc your love knew no barriers. As I wrote to you in my first letter, with Marc you "discovered a fundamental human dimension: *paternity.*" That love made you whole.

I was then not much younger than you, but now I am much older than you ever were; perhaps this entitles me to bear witness to your life. I know most of the persons Shirley du Boulay mentions in this biography. Many of them are no longer alive. Her book is of an immense value because it describes you as you were: a man of flesh and blood, an incarnated man, and not just a "thinking reed." Writing about you she also describes not only the situation of the church in India but, indirectly at least, of the world at large.

Swamiji, your struggles and sufferings have not been in vain. You are becoming a symbol for spiritual survival. Was this not the message of Christ?

RAIMON PANIKKAR
LENT 2005

Preface

THIS IS A STORY OF TRANSFORMATION. It tells how a country boy, Henri Le Saux, eldest son of a large and loving Breton family, became a Benedictine monk who, even before he made his final profession, was taken over by a passionate longing to go to India. In 1948 he achieved his ambition, the monk became a *sannyāsi*, an Indian holy man, and Dom Henri became Swami Abhishiktananda. He helped to found an ashram, feeling completely at home in the saffron robes worn by Hindu ascetics, sometimes—though at first he was deeply embarrassed by doing this—going out with a begging bowl for a little rice. He who had once been master of ceremonies for his monastery, famous for his liturgical strictness, came to celebrate Mass sitting cross-legged on the banks of the Ganges, a *dhoti* taking the place of his priestly robes, a stone from the river roaring past doing service as an altar. For the last years of his life he lived largely as a hermit, high in the Himalayas, spending months at a time in solitude. So the devout Roman Catholic struggled with the enchantment of Hinduism, and the Benedictine monk, initially a typical product of French Catholicism before the Second Vatican Council, found himself at the cutting edge of twentieth-century spirituality. It is the story of a man searching for God, prepared to give up everything and to risk all in the search.

It is also the story of a man caught in contradiction. Passionately French, he took Indian nationality so wholeheartedly that he never left the country from the moment he arrived in 1948; devoted though he was to his family in Brittany, he never returned to France or saw them again. He was a man who longed for silence and yet loved to talk, a man who rejoiced in solitude yet had countless friends, a man who reveled in books and writing yet preferred the direct teachings of lived experience. Most of all was the contradiction between the irresistible attraction he felt toward *advaita*, the nondual experience of Hinduism, and his inborn love of his Catholic faith.

And here lies the heart of his anguish and his crowning consummation. The monk who for the first half of his life worshiped only what Catholics then thought of as the "Christian" God, who was nurtured in the strictest form of French Roman Catholicism before the Second Vatican Council, was, in midlife, drawn to Hinduism, in particular to *advaita*, by so strong a magnet that he had no option but to respond to the call. He was not a man who did anything by halves, so he immersed himself in every aspect of India, traveling the length and breadth of the subcontinent, going on pilgrimage, meeting people of every nationality and every faith, living in caves in the holy mountain of Arunachala, and following teachings unacceptable to most orthodox Christians in the 1950s, sitting with joy, for instance, at the feet of a famous Hindu guru.

For years he was in anguish, feeling that there were two men inside him, one a Hindu, the other a Western Christian. He was torn apart in his efforts to be loyal to both, finding that "Easter is the great passing over to the pure reality at the very heart of *advaita*. But how agonizing it is to be perched on the knife-edge between the opposite slopes of Hinduism and Christianity."[1] He knew that the world needed what he called "bridges" and that he, indeed, had become one, but he was all too aware that the danger of living as a bridge is the risk of belonging to neither side, whereas, "however harrowing it may be, our duty is precisely to belong wholly to both sides. This can only be done in the mystery of God."[2]

Abhishiktananda was a pioneer in interreligious dialogue, in the tradition of the Jesuit missionary Roberto de Nobili, who lived as a *sannyāsi* in the early seventeenth century, yet forging his own path, always true to his own way. When he was given permission to leave his monastery and go to India, he joined the French priest Father Jules Monchanin in founding Shantivanam Ashram. Soon after he arrived, they went together to visit the great sage Ramana Maharshi, a meeting that turned out to be, for Abhishiktananda, "a call which pierced through everything, rent it in pieces and opened a mighty abyss."[3] From that moment he endured the greatest pain and anguish as he was caught between the nonduality he found in Hinduism and the Western Christianity in which he had been nurtured. He was pulled between two traditions, caught in "double-belonging," something that would almost have amounted to heresy at the time.

For years it was a crucifixion, but eventually he found peace and reconciliation; found that there is, as he had hoped, an *advaita* that is in no way opposed to Christianity, that it was possible to have a "sense of Christ beyond all forms."[4] So too he learned the blessed art of living in the present and came to live himself what he called his "one sermon"—"Realize who you are at this very moment."[5] His constant search was for enlightenment, or what he more often called awakening. In one of his last letters, just two weeks before he died, he wrote, "The Awakening alone is what counts."[6] Slowly and painfully he learned to reconcile the two traditions, to find the truth beyond the opposites. But it took a serious heart attack to break all barriers and release the full radiance that had increasingly been emanating from him. Even after his death people could "still feel the 'vibes of holiness' that were around at the time from even mentioning his name."[7]

He tried—and to a large measure succeeded—in expressing himself theologically, but his legacy is not so much theological as experiential, and he came to see his most important books as those that reflect how he lived and what he had done, rather than those that tried to express his thought theologically. Immensely courageous, he insisted on living everything about which he wrote, whether it was the experience of having a guru, climbing to the sources of the Ganges, living as the poorest of the poor, worshipping with people of other faiths at a time when this was not only unusual but could risk his standing as a Christian monk. He dived into the experience of Hinduism and swam in its waters with a joy tempered only by constant worry that he was being untrue to his Christianity.

By the end of his life he was widely perceived as a holy man, an enlightened being. Shigeto Oshida, a Japanese Dominican monk who became a close friend, wrote of an occasion when, in a group celebrating Bara Din, the great feast of the Nativity, his "double-belongingness" was transcended as his inborn French Catholicism met his beloved Hinduism. A Catholic girl began to sing of the feast in Gregorian chant, accompanied by one of the Hindus. It was too much for Abhishiktananda, who for twenty-five years had cut himself off from his motherland and his monastic brothers: "Stop, please stop," he cried out explosively. "It's tearing me apart." At this point the two traditions must have met in Abhishiktananda as never before, for a Hindu friend, his eyes on Abhishiktananda, said, "Christ is here. I am looking at him."[8]

So was he, as has been suggested, "a weird and crazy monk," or was he a man who, in his courage in enduring the anguish of being split between two great traditions, reached unusual heights of spiritual greatness and who, over thirty years after his death, is a beacon to those striving to remain faithful to one tradition while being open to the truths of others—a man who is, in fact, a Christian for today, able to transcend differences between religions and live in the transcendent truth?

Chronology

1910	August 30. Born in Saint Briac, Brittany
1921	Entered minor seminary at Châteaugiron
1924	Mother nearly died in childbirth
1926	Entered major seminary at Rennes
1929	October 15. Entered l'Abbaye Sainte-Anne de Kergonan
1930	May 13. Began his year as a novice
1931	May 17. Profession of simple vows
1935	May 30. Final profession
	December 21. Ordained priest
1939	September. Outbreak of World War II. Henri called up for military service
1940	July. Captured, escaped, returned to monastery
1944	Death of his mother
1948	July 26. Left France for India
	August 15. Arrived at Colombo
	August 17. Joined Fr. Monchanin in Kulittalai
1949	First visit to Sri Ramana Maharshi at Arunachala
1950	March 21. Inauguration of Shantivanam Ashram
	Took new name and became Abhishikteshvarananda
1952	Long periods at Arunachala
1953	Met Harilal (Poonja)
1954	November. Sudden death of his father
1955	July to January 1956. Spiritual crisis. Met Dr. Mehta
1956	February. Met Sri Gnanananda
	September. Five weeks of silence in Mauna Mandir
1957	May. Met Raimon Panikkar
	October 10. Death of Fr. Monchanin
1957/1958	Theological conferences at Shantivanam
1958	January. Granted indefinite renewal of his edict of exclaustration
1959	First visit to the Himalayas. Met Jyotiniketan Community

1

Roots in Brittany

1910–1929

I am terribly, terribly, French.[1]

Is it fanciful to make an association between someone's birthplace and the life that lies ahead of them? Probably. Nevertheless, to wander around Saint Briac, the small town in the region of Ille et Vilaine on the north coast of Brittany where Henri Le Saux was born, is to be filled with thoughts not so much of his outer life as of the deepest needs and urges that were eventually to dominate his life. A gull, caught in the slipstream of the wind and drifting across the sky, at one with all around it, the epitome of unity. The sea beneath, symbol of the deep unconscious, the arena of turbulent activity and primal passions, reminder of the old proverb, "The Bretons are born with the waters of the sea flowing around their hearts." To walk on the Pointe de la Garde-Guérin, the local beach where the family played as children, to wander around the town and savor its quiet peace, its stone buildings built to last, is to taste the longing simply *to be* that was to dominate the life of the boy who was born here as Henri Le Saux and died as Swami Abhishiktananda, a hermit living in the Himalayas in silence and solitude. A man who, in his fifties, on the twenty-ninth anniversary of his first solemn communion at Saint Briac, was to write in his diary, "Whether you like it or not, it is always around childhood impressions that everything else later on gets collected. The impressions of a child are absolutes: school, family etc. . . ."[2]

The Le Saux family came originally from Britain, leaving Wales in the twelfth century and coming to Brittany—in fact, the name Le Saux in the Breton language means "the Saxons." (The normal pronunciation is "So," but one of Henri's sisters remembers, with some scorn, a branch of the family who insisted on pronouncing it "Le Socks.") Alfred Le Saux

1

was of seafaring stock, but his mother had lost her father, her brother, two husbands, and a son at sea; one can understand her reluctance to encourage another son to go to sea, and Alfred did not take much persuading to find a job on land.

He married Louise Sonnefraüd, whose family had lived in Alsace. Her father came originally from Austria, but during the Franco-Prussian war of 1870 he had somehow found his way through enemy lines and joined the French army. Eventually he left his family in Alsace and settled in Saint Briac, his daughter Louise marrying Alfred Le Saux in 1905.

Alfred and Louise started a shop, selling groceries. It was a corner shop, with a colorful mosaic over the door with its name, À LA PROVI-DENCE DE DIEU, stylishly inscribed over the shop front. (The shop still exists today, using the same name, though it is now a gift shop.) Though they were very dependent on the summer season, the shop was a success and Alfred became one of the richest men in town, replacing his horse and cart with a Ford car long before it was commonplace and being the first in the town to have a telephone. He was gassed and wounded in the legs in the First World War, so on his return home his physical activity was limited and he walked with sticks. He was convinced that he would have been killed, were it not that in his knapsack was a piece of palm from the recent Palm Sunday celebration. The French traditionally use something more shrubby and substantial than the thin piece of palm leaf frond used in Britain, so this could have been more than a devout speculation. Alfred would drive the car and make the deliveries while Louise ran the shop. Women were beginning to have a more significant role in society, even replacing the men who were at war, but this would have been less noticeable in Brittany, as even in normal times so many of the men were at sea. Between them, Alfred and Louise sold groceries, wine, whiskey, cheese, a few vegetables—"all the good stuff" as his daughters proudly remember. Some of their best customers were English, for at the time many people who had worked with the Indian civil service retired to Saint Briac, taking advantage of the weak franc and strong pound that prevailed at the time. So the background of Henri's later asceticism was a large shop full of gastronomic delights—salamis hanging from the ceiling, bottles of wine and cognac on the shelves, and, pervading everything, the aroma of good coffee.

The shop is on the corner of a long, well-built, and beautifully proportioned stone house, the windows outlined in brick, running the length of a short street called Le Passage de la Coulée. It is in the center of town, behind the post office, and for many years it was home to the Le Saux family. Nearly a hundred years later it is still there, the only outward change being a small additional house at the far end. And it still belongs to the Le Saux family, divided into sections to give various members a degree of independence from each other. Sometimes as many as four members of the family have lived here at the same time, each with their respective spouses and children. Louis Montagnon, one of Louise and Alfred's grandchildren, remarked with a mixture of pride and wry amusement, "It was a clan. They were a real clan—the Le Saux at Briac. A big family, that's one thing—it can explode, fall apart. But a clan . . . Never!"[3] They lived the life of the extended family, today in Europe something more talked about than practiced.

And they are Bretons—that should never be forgotten. Louis and his wife, Véronique, live in Saint Briac, and like many of the family their children all have Breton names, Noalig, Gwennenn and Tugdual. Though there is said to be little difference between being French and being Breton, pride and national consciousness creep in, perhaps almost unconsciously. For instance, twelve-year-old Tugdual, when asked the difference between the French and the Bretons, replied, only half jokingly, "The Bretons are much more intelligent." Even his more restrained father admits, "We are a people with a certain culture—a culture which has been crushed to some extent, but which is anyway quite rich. Now the French State is more tolerant and lets us live in harmony with our surroundings. It's not a question of a passport, but a feeling of belonging to a people. It's like Wales and the Welsh. In fact the national song of Brittany is the same as the Welsh National Anthem."[4] His wife, Véronique, feels that in a way France has colonized Brittany and she recalls the statue that used to be opposite the town hall in Rennes, the regional capital of Brittany; it represented Brittany kneeling humbly before France. Just before the Second World War, to the delight of many patriotic Bretons, it was blown up.

Just a minute's walk from the house belonging to the Le Saux clan is the great stone church, most of which was built in the nineteenth century. The original seventeenth-century church was paid for by the local fishermen, something we are reminded of by the carved fishes on plaques around the outside of the church, and by a dramatically placed boat that used to hang above the entrance door. It was eventually moved, lest it fell on someone's head, and now hangs less conspicuously in the north aisle. Just as fishing, the main trade of the town, is in evidence, so is the fact that we are in Brittany, for on one side of the altar stands a statue of St. Tugdual, one of the seven founders of Brittany; on the other is his disciple, St. Briac, whose life is depicted in the stained glass of the windows.

Today the church is still well used, and most Saturdays a wedding is celebrated there—though not always between locals—Parisians consider it *très chic* to be married in Brittany.

ALFRED AND LOUISE HAD WAITED five years for their first child; they were to wait many more for their second, so the birth of this boy was an event of even more than usual significance. He was born on August 30, 1910, and taken the very same day to the local church, where he was christened Henri Hyacinthe Joseph Marie. For seven years he was the only child, forming a relationship with his mother of an intimacy that was gentle and touching and, perhaps unusually in such a very close mother–son relationship, gave no evidence of being anything but entirely healthy. Henri and his father got on well enough, but Alfred comes off as a shadowy figure, a good man and remembered by Henri's sister Rénée as "not at all hard on us, no, not at all."

One of the remarkable things about Henri's early life was his relationships with his family. In 1917, a girl was born, named Louise after her mother but known as Louisette, and over the next thirteen years the family grew to seven, the last child, Marie-Thérèse, being born in 1930 when Louise was forty-five years old. In between were three more girls—Rénée, Marie-Josèphe, and Anne-Louise—and in 1920 another boy, Hyacinthe, who seems to be something of a mystery. The family is reluctant to talk about him, saying only, "He was a bit bizarre, a bit different—a bit disturbed if you like. It's better not to talk about him—it was a bit of a saga in the family." His mother, however, thought it would be a pity if he changed, as he had such a nice nature.

Henri was a lively and intelligent boy. When he was five he went to the local school, L'Ecole de Sainte-Anne, and was in many ways a typical boy, sometimes a paragon of a son, looking after his younger sisters and brother, helping in the shop, churning the butter on Saturdays; sometimes behaving like any young boy, off with his local friends, climbing the Sailor's Cross at the top of the hill. Being the eldest by seven years—and nineteen when Marie-Thérèse was born—almost inevitably he became in effect a model for his siblings. As they grew up he taught them to swim and played games with them; above all he taught them to sing. He had a harmonium in his room, and, according to Rénée, they would gather around and "he used to make us sing and sing." They sang Breton songs and Marie-Thérèse still treasures the book they used—Botrel's *Chansons en Sabots*, though Henri may not have realized that Botrel, though a Breton, was a singer from Paris presenting the music from a Parisian perspective. (Ironically the Breton music heard today is, for the most part, more traditional, not less.) In the light of Henri's long absence from France, some of the songs have a particular poignancy.

> Adieu donc, cher petit Parson!
> Adieu, pays de mon Enfance!
> Adieu donc, cher petit Parson,
> Vieux amis et vieille maison!
> Votre gâs, demain, s'en vie
> En exil, au pays de France,*
> Votre gâs, demain, s'en ira;
> Seul, Dieu sait quand il reviendra!†

Despite the years spent away from the place of his birth—though it could have been a case of absence making the heart grow fonder—the family is agreed that of all the Le Saux family it was Henri who was the most proud of his national identity. Perhaps this indicated a rebellious streak in him, for in his youth Breton culture was not encouraged—it was even suppressed, though not as fiercely as in, for instance, Finistère. At school the Bretons were mildly despised, and the boys were forbidden to speak the Breton language; those who did risked being made to wear a clog or a wooden plaque as punishment. While his mother and his siblings were fairly indifferent to their Breton blood, Henri was deeply attached to it, joining the celebrations when the monument in Rennes, so humiliating to Brittany, was blown up. Even in his sixties, when Agnès and her fiancé went to see him in India, she remembers him telling her the dates of the joining of Brittany to France. (The agreement was finally ratified in 1532.) Up to the end of his life he was moved beyond words by the music of Brittany. Once he was asked if he would "sing us a song of your dandy youth" by someone who began to hum a Breton sea-song;

---

*Before Brittany was united to France, France would have seemed like another country.

†Farewell then, dear little person!
Farewell, country of my childhood!
Farewell then, dear little
Old friends and old house!
To-morrow your little lad leaves,
Exiled to the country of France.
Your little lad, to-morrow, goes,
Alone. God knows when he will return!
(From Théodore Botrel, *Chansons en Sabots* [Paris: Editions de la Lyre Chansonnière, 1943])

he broke down in tears and pleaded with the singer to stop—he could not bear it. As he admitted to his great friend, Murray Rogers, despite everything that he experienced, despite the totality of his immersion in India, he remained "terribly, terribly, French." There may be some who feel he should have said that he remained "terribly, terribly, Breton."

He carried out his unsought position as role model for his younger siblings with great love and, one might say, skill, if that were not to imply a degree of calculation that was not in his nature. His sister Rénée still remembers, "If we wanted to confide in someone, it was to Henri we turned rather than our father. So if Henri was not at home, we would write to him."[5] This feeling extended to the next generation, who never met him but who heard about their "legendary uncle." His niece Agnès was so captivated by what she heard that many years later not only did she and her fiancé go to see him in India, but she became the careful and meticulous guardian of the family correspondence, one of those who managed to decipher his often almost indecipherable handwriting. So too it extends to her brother Louis, who during his life wrote to his uncle every month, even though they had never met, to his children, and to his wife, Véronique, who humbly calls herself "only a relation by extension" but who knows as much about him as anyone in the family.

In fact, everyone in the family remembers their "Oncle Henri"—Louis, whose physical likeness to his uncle is so great that Henri's friend and biographer, James Stuart, was "bowled over"—says that each of them felt they had a privileged relationship with him. "I think each one had a feeling that they had a special relationship with him, and each relationship was different, one from another. He knew how to respect the personalities of each of my aunts. He never showed any preference for one over the other."[6] One sister, however, admits to a "slightly ambiguous" relationship with her brother, recalling how "the son dominated the father"—a curious remark about someone as apparently undominating and gentle as Henri, adding that "once he became a curé he had every right, but. . . ." Her silence is eloquent; Henri's growing dominance of his family occasionally attracted resentment, especially after they married. "Henri was a priest so he could do anything he liked and tell the entire family what to do. . . . Well we had our own home and we had our own lives to lead."[7] But small resentments apart, he was devoted to his family, loving and being loved and keeping up with them all his life, writing regularly from wherever he was and, though thousands of miles away, helping them with the various situations they found themselves in. For instance when Louis' parents were disappointed that he did not pursue the religious calling they had hoped for him, it was Henri who helped them to accept it and allow their son to follow his own path. Louis feels that Henri was neither a saint nor an eccentric, but was "definitely someone from a higher place, so to speak."

THE BEGINNING OF THE TWENTIETH CENTURY was a time when a huge percentage of the population of Brittany was Roman Catholic, weekly church attendance was compulsory, and to go to Mass daily not unusual. Yet even in such a climate the Le Saux family were exceptionally devout, above all Alfred. In fact Alfred was considered to be ostentatious about his faith and was known rather mockingly in the town as "Le petit Jésus"; more kindly he was dubbed "the saint" by a small boy noticing how frequently he went to church—three times on Sundays. He even had a prie-dieu in the church with his name on it—a traditional custom for the pious rich. Their devoutness extended into every detail of their lives, even though they were too busy running the shop to go to Mass every day. The name of the shop was almost certainly meant to imply *A la Providence de Dieu* and "when they had gâteaux on Sundays, there was always, always, a bit put aside for the poor. It was part of sharing. There was always a bit left uneaten, just in case someone came."[8] So too the weather was in the hands of God. One year there was a terrible drought, so the curé held special services to intercede for rain, expressing penitence and admitting the sinfulness of the people of Saint Briac by singing Psalm 51, the *Miserere*, with its guilt-ridden lines, more appealing to Christians a hundred years ago than now—"For I acknowledge my transgression; and my sin is ever before me. . . . Behold I was shapen in inquity and in sin did my mother conceive me." The intercessions were all too successful and there was so much rain that Saint Briac was badly flooded and poor little Hyacinthe sobbed "it's all the Miserere's fault."

The great festivals of the church marked their lives as clearly as they marked the seasons, and the family would also attend mission services in the parish church. On the feast of Corpus Christi the children used to walk in the procession, Henri donning a sheepskin and becoming, for a few hours, John the Baptist. And every year on August 15, the feast of the Assumption of the Blessed Virgin Mary, there was a pilgrimage from Saint Briac to the nearby Chapelle de l'Epine; the entire congregation would walk there, singing, all the way from the church. The little stone chapel, in the middle of a field, was built on the spot where a peasant had found a statue of the virgin in a thornbush. Tradition has it that he took the statue home for the night, but it disappeared and was found again the following day, back in the thornbush.

Then, of course, there were the *Pardons*, the local manifestations of popular fervor, which are thought to be as much as a thousand years old. The faithful—in those days almost the entire population—walked, sometimes for miles, to seek forgiveness, fulfill a vow, or beg for grace. The great *Pardons* can be very impressive, but often it is the smaller ones that are the most fervent—like one at Beg-Miel, where the procession goes down to the seashore and sails away in little boats. Tourists tend to hope that they will see traditional Breton dress being worn, and sometimes they will, especially in the regions of Finistère and Morbihan. Saint Briac used to have its own costume, with a headdress known as "the cock" which Henri's grandmother wore at his parents' wedding, but by Henri's time it was no longer worn. In fact there is now a sneaking suspicion that wearing traditional dress is cultivated as a tourist attraction.

The Le Saux's were a close family, on the whole loving each other and looking back on what was, by any standards, a happy childhood. It comes as no surprise to discover that, fifty years later, Henri wrote to his friend Anne-Marie, "It seems only yesterday that we were ten, eleven years old—that wonderful age! And everything else seems to have overlaid it, like a cloak that you have put on for a long journey."[9]

WHEN HE WAS JUST FIVE, Henri went to the local school, the École de Sainte-Anne, just half a mile from the Le Saux family house. (It still serves as the local primary school.) Signs of his calling to the priesthood must have begun to show early, for in October 1921, when he was eleven, his parents sent him to the Petit Séminaire de Châteaugiron, a beautiful old town twenty-five kilometers southeast of Rennes. The seminary took children from ten to eighteen years old, and at this stage there was no assumption that they would enter the priesthood, but the option was there—perhaps even a gentle expectation—and the syllabus included the appropriate studies.[10]

Already it is clear that Henri was an outstanding pupil, always among the top pupils of his class, and in June 1926 he passed the first part of the baccalauréat, for which the boys had to study a minimum of nine subjects. In order to go on to the Grand Séminaire there were certain criteria the boys had to fulfill, and two of the comments listed in Henri's files shed an interesting light on him as a teenager. Under the heading "Judgment" the entry reads, "Good, with a tendency to paradox"; and under "Character," again "Good," but surprisingly, given the huge family he grew up with, there is the addition "but very shy."

Perhaps he was not so much shy as unhappy and homesick. Years later he wrote to his family to dissuade them from sending his nephew Louis to the seminary, or at least to keep him at home until he was twelve:

I still have wretched memories of Châteaugiron. Even apart from being separated from St Briac, it was so old-fashioned. Not even a room for showers (whereas here, anyone who does not take a daily bath is simply disgusting!), such a narrow training (one year, the order came that our shorts should cover the knees!—our dear professors probably had bad thoughts from seeing our knees), etc. However, if I had not been there, should I have kept my vocation?[11]

Throughout his life he became more and more opposed to "this 'ghetto' education which has done such damage to the Church"[12] and in a later letter about his nephew he wrote: "The trouble with these seminaries is that the future priests are terribly cut off from reality. The day when they go for military service or are sent to parishes, they are absolutely 'lost.'" And writing to a nun friend he admitted, "Personally I needed years to free myself (if indeed I have done so even now) from the infantilism and the lack of a sense of personal responsibility, which was effectively instilled into me on the pretext of obedience."[13]

While he was at the minor seminary something happened that seems to have been one of the determining events in his young life. His mother nearly died giving birth to a child, the sixth, which itself did not survive. A year later another child was expected and Henri, devoted to his mother as he was, was terrified that this time she might actually die. So terrified was he that his prayers for her would end with the promise that, if she were to survive, he would dedicate his life to the service of the Lord and would go wherever he was sent, even to the most distant mission. (James Stuart suggests that he was thinking here of his uncle, his mother's brother, Henri Sonnefraüd, who as a member of the Foreign Missionary Society of Paris, was sent to China in 1923.) Rénée remembers, "You felt that he had given over his life because he was so frightened of losing Maman. He loved Maman so much and he was so frightened of losing her —so he sacrificed himself."

The feeling that he had a vocation to the priesthood, already flickering in his consciousness, was fanned by this experience; he had fulfilled the necessary criteria for entry to the seminary. So in September 1926, at only sixteen the youngest of the thirty-nine new pupils, he took the next step in the direction of the priesthood by entering the major seminary at Rennes. (A reflection on the changing times—in Henri's time his group of thirty-nine joined about 150 seminarians already there; today there is a total of ten.)

First he had to complete the last year of his baccalauréat, and in July 1927 he passed with the second prize in science, honorable mentions in philosophy and history, and a report that noted that he was a very good pupil though, without any explanation for the criticism, it complained that he "behaved badly in the refectory." Curiously, these apparently distinguished marks were only awarded an overall *Assez Bien*—the equivalent of little more than a pass.

In those days life as a seminarian was hard. The day began at five o'clock in the morning with a time of personal prayer, and Mass was celebrated at six o'clock. They started studying at the curiously precise time of 7:25, and lessons began at eight o'clock, with lunch taken at noon, in silence. It was a time when the regular admission of sin was part of religious life, and every day, as they returned to the chapel after lunch, they sang the *Miserere*, the great penitential psalm that little Hyacinthe was convinced had caused the flooding of Saint Briac. And so the day went on with studies and lessons from 1:30 to 6:55, when they all gathered to recite the rosary and listen to a lecture on some spiritual subject before the evening meal. Night prayer was at 8:35 and lights had to be out by nine o'clock.

By today's standards—indeed by any standards—it was a hard and exacting life for a sixteen-year-old boy, yet clearly Henri was happy at the major seminary, far happier than he had been at Châteaugiron. His teachers commented on the great change in him, noting that he was drawn more to piety than to rules and that he was a little critical. They also commented on his defective pronunciation, something that persisted throughout his life and was probably caused by a slight harelip; his friends would affectionately divide themselves into those who could hear him better if they were sitting opposite him and those who preferred to sit slightly to one side.

The second year the seminarians' studies were concentrated on philosophy; the third and last was the year of apologetics. In the light of the direction in which his spirituality was to go, this has an ironic twist, for the study of apologetics, the defense of the Christian faith on intellectual grounds, traditionally falls into three parts: to show that it is reasonable to have a religion, to prove that Christianity is the most rational of all the religions, and to demonstrate that orthodox Christianity is the best of all its various forms. Religious competitiveness was to become so foreign to Henri Le Saux that it is curious to imagine him having to study it.

In his final year he won the first prize in history, scripture, and theology and second in liturgy, coming second overall among his contemporaries. In fact he did so well that there was pressure for him to continue his studies in Rome. By then his mind was made up, and his file notes laconically, "très bon séminariste, esprit bien meilleur, va entrer chez les

Bénédictins" (very good seminarian, much better attitude, going to become a Benedictine).

BUT IT WASN'T AS SIMPLE as those easily written words imply; for nearly two years the subject of Henri's vocation was to become a battleground among many forces. It was a big decision, one of the most important of his life, and ranged against him were his family, the archbishop of his diocese, the abbot of his chosen monastery, and, most of all, his own initial ambivalence.

Though the seed had been sown when he was only fourteen years old, when he had vowed that he would dedicate himself to the Lord's service if his mother survived her seventh pregnancy, the probability was that at that stage he was thinking in terms of becoming a diocesan priest, with the likelihood of remaining near Saint Briac and his beloved family. But two years later, at the major seminary, he struck up a close friendship with a fellow seminarist whose great desire was to become a Benedictine monk. Shortly after sharing these thoughts with Henri, his friend unexpectedly died, leaving Henri convinced that he had inherited his friend's vocation to become a monk.

In the autumn of 1928 he visited the Benedictine Abbey of Sainte-Anne of Kergonan, on the south side of Brittany, nearly two hundred kilometers from Saint Briac. Three months later, he wrote to the novice master the first of six letters that survive, though possibly in draft form.

He tells the novice master that his director at the seminary seemed to agree that he should follow his feeling that he had a vocation to the cloister, though he did not say so explicitly, suggesting that the end of the year would be the time for a decision. This advice was exactly the same as he had received from the novice master when he visited the monastery. By December 1928 the time for a decision had come.

Overflowing with youthful idealism and drawn to the hope of finding the presence of God more fully in the cloister than anywhere else, Henri was filled with joy at the thought. And yet . . . and yet . . . often he felt downcast and worried at the thought of the pains of monastic life. Most of all he dreaded leaving home and was realistic about the full implications of poverty: "I like to have things of my own, to have things which in some sense complete my 'I,' but in the monastery I have to feel that none of the things that I use belongs to me."[14] So too, sociable by nature, he dreaded the prospect of having to avoid human society and was apprehensive at the thought of the monotony with which one day would follow another, almost identical.

He felt an irresistible call, yet he was realistic, seeing how much there is in the monastic life that is hard to bear. It is touching to see him struggle, asking the novice master "to repeat for me your original judgement,"[15] showing that he was still at the stage of decision making where confirmation from outside was needed, the inner voice not yet strong enough to make up its own mind. "I have need to be persuaded myself; however much I act as one who must soon follow the call of God, it seems to me so incredible that I should soon become a monk, that I dare not accept the idea."[16]

Soon after writing this letter he made his decision and, at Christmas, he told his parents. They were devout; they had brought him up to be devout and had sent him to the minor seminary, which carried a strong possibility of leading to the religious life—surely they would be delighted? They were not. "They were in despair . . . the blow has been terrible. They were in such a state of depression and anguish when I left them yesterday morning I had to give them hope that I would wait."[17] They were distressed not only at the thought of losing their eldest son but that there would be no one to look after their young family if they were to be sick or to die before their time. Louisette, the eldest, was only eleven; there were the youngest three, and Marie-Thérèse was not even born. (If the implications about Hyacinthe are true, he would not have been able to cope, even when he was old enough, and he was only nine at the time.)

Other problems emerged, though much milder and less emotional—mere pebbles by comparison to the great boulders of family grief. It turned out that the archbishop did not like his seminarists to become monks until they had served the diocese for several years as priests, and the abbot of Kergonan preferred his novices to do their military service before they entered the novitiate. At the end of January 1929, he wrote to the novice master again. The surviving letter, almost certainly a draft and even harder to read than normal, indicates that he had agreed to wait for seven years, until his sister was old enough to take responsibility for the family in the event of their parents' death; in the meanwhile he could satisfy the abbot's wishes by doing his military service during this time. His great dread was that this long delay might result in his losing his vocation—something he could only have feared if his mind was not completely made up.

Henri's acceptance of his fate seems to have softened the opposition, as one by one the barriers were lifted. His parents became resigned to the thought of their eldest son becoming a monk, placated partly by his promise that in his first five years at the monastery he could, if they needed him, revert to the secular ministry and move nearer home. The archbishop gave him permission to leave the diocese, and the abbot of Kergonan relaxed his restrictions on military service. Henri's sister Rénée remembers that his mother's disapproval was softened partly by her fear that her son's great intelligence might lead him to pride and arrogance. She prayed hard that he would stay out of the limelight and might have thought her prayers were answered; after all, as his sister reflected years later, "Well you know, a monk at Kergonan, he's not going to get very famous is he?"

Through all these exchanges about his vocation runs Henri's piety, expressed in the language of his day and undoubtedly sincere: for instance, he is grateful for "the touching solicitude with which the good God binds up our wounds and gently inclines the soul to his holy will."[18] So too does his idealism color every thought. In his first letter to the novice master he writes: "I have a very ambitious spirit—and this is permissible, is it not? when it is a matter of seeking God—and I hope I shall not be disappointed."[19] Already he has noted that to be a monk is not necessarily to be virtuous, and he is thinking in terms of raising the standards of monastic life: "In becoming a monk I have a great ambition; and the way that God has used me to bring me to this had been above all the sight of the mediocrity into which so many priests lapse after a few years in the ministery, and which at all costs I want to avoid."[20] Looking back on the course of his vocation, and showing a remarkable maturity for his years, he marveled at the way, in facing the problems that presented themselves, he became slowly detached from any natural attachment to the cloister and came to see in entering the religious life nothing but the naked will of God:

> In all this I seem to be so much like a pawn, so to speak, and to be living in a kind of dream. I didn't understand—and less than ever do I now understand—all the steps that I am taking. I can neither convince myself, nor can I even imagine, that I shall end this year in a monastery, and this idea seems to my natural mind both horrible and futile; but I feel myself driven by something which does not allow me to draw back or turn aside, and compels me, almost in spite of myself, to throw myself into the unknown which I see opening before me.[21]

His sisters had seen how hard it was for him to accept his vocation, one of them remembering him in his room, at the harmonium, clenching his fists and saying, "My God, you can't possibly ask that of me!" But once he had made his decision, he set about his new way of life with utter singlemindedness and dedication. Indeed, Murray Rogers, who knew him well in later life, says that his singlemindedness is as much a key to his character as the fact that he was "terribly French."

It had taken nearly two years, but at last all obstacles were removed and he was free to follow his vocation. But as Oscar Wilde is said to have remarked, "There is only one thing worse than not getting what you want and that is getting it." Just as he had found it hard to accept his vocation —though harder still to deny it—so now he found it hard to accept the pain his decision was causing to his parents and friends. He so dreaded having to talk to his parents about his imminent departure to the monastery that on one visit home he admitted that a fire in the shop was a welcome diversion, preoccupying the family and freeing him from the need to discuss his future. He wrote to Raymond Macé, a friend he had made at the seminary who was to become canon of Rennes, of his sorrow:

> Believe me, that is the worst sorrow of those who go away: to abandon parents and friends, to give up an easy life, is hard and at times extremely painful, but even so in fact the sacrifice is easy to make. . . . Only when it is a question of imposing the sacrifice on those who are dear to us! Can anything be worse than that?[22]

By the summer his mother was pregnant again, which may have taken her mind a little from her sadness. But her grief was still so great that Marie-Thérèse, the child who was to be born four months later, wondered, years later, as an elderly religious sister, if she had felt its repercussions and that perhaps her vocation was born in that unhappy womb? So Henri's last holiday at home was painful and depressing, and the time for his departure to Kergonan must have come with some relief. On October 18, 1929,[23] just nineteen years old, he entered the Benedictine monastery at Kergonan.

2

An Irresistible Call

Kergonan 1929–1939

*A monk cannot accept mediocrity,
only extremes are appropriate for him.*[1]

T HE NEW ARRIVAL AT A BENEDICTINE MONASTERY is, for the first few days, treated as a guest. This both stresses that great Benedictine characteristic, hospitality, and also symbolizes that the newcomer is free to go— he is not imprisoned. Nevertheless, for a young man to arrive at one of these big, often imposing buildings, assuming that he will rarely leave it again, must be a daunting experience.

Father le Boucher, at the turn of the millennium ninety-three years old and still a monk of Kergonan, remembers all those years ago when he was a novice, deputed to prepare Henri's room in the house used at the time for the novitiate. A tiny incident revealed, he felt, something important about Henri and his attitude to the monastic life. Father le Boucher made up the bed, set out two towels and some soap, and looked around for a mirror, in those days always provided. He could not find one and had to make do with a little piece of glass, the size of a man's hand and broken. With a slight feeling of shame he put it in place.

Years later Henri told Father le Boucher that, on arriving at the monastery, his greatest joy was this broken mirror. He saw it as a promise of the austere way of life that he longed to live; confirmation that he would not be encumbered with material possessions but would live in bareness and simplicity. His early fear that he might want to have possessions "which in some sense complete my 'I'" had finally and completely gone as he embraced poverty willingly, indeed eagerly. On this issue he was never to change.

The reason that he chose the Abbey of Sainte-Anne of Kergonan is not hard to seek. It is in Brittany, near the small village of Plouharnel and a short distance from the old town of Vannes. It is also only a few hours' train journey from Saint Briac, so was not too far from home. The only recorded reason for his choice of the Benedictines over any other religious order was his friendship with the seminarian who died young, leaving his vocation unfulfilled.

There are, of course, important differences between the religious orders, so what was Henry opting for in choosing the Benedictines? He was casting his lot with one of the oldest religious orders, founded in the sixth century by St. Benedict of Nursia, who has come to be known as the Father of Western Monasticism. St. Benedict is one of the giants of Christianity. His famous Rule, only nine thousand words long, is still regarded as one of its great treasures. In A.D. 500 he retired to a cave near Subiaco and attracted so many people that a community grew around him. Eventually he founded twelve monasteries. Unlike the other great religious orders, the Benedictines do not, strictly speaking, constitute a single order, but are a confederation of many congregations,* alike only in that they all follow, respect, and treasure the Rule of St. Benedict. At present there are twenty-one congregations with a total of over twenty-five thousand monks and nuns.

In joining the Kergonan community Henri was becoming both a Benedictine and a member of the Congregation of Solesmes, founded in 1010. At the end of the eighteenth century, when anticlericalism became an active political force in France, Benedictine life was for a while forbidden, and the recent history of Solesmes dates from 1833, when Dom Prosper Guéranger settled there with five other priests and an ambition to reestablish the Benedictine order in France; four years later it was raised to the rank of abbey, and Dom Guéranger became its first abbot. He was of the ultramontane persuasion, wanting French Catholicism to be firmly controlled by Rome; and under his influence Solesmes became a center of the liturgical movement in France, its singing of Gregorian chant famous throughout the world. The new abbey also became the mother house of a new congregation, and nine daughter houses were founded, the last being Sainte-Anne of Kergonan, founded in the parish of Plouharnel in 1897.

So when Henri arrived in 1929 Sainte-Anne's was relatively young, and the young novice could not have realized that he was joining a monastery that was liturgically strict, well to the right in churchmanship and already acquiring enough of Solesmes' excellence at what Henri

---

*A congregation is a group of monasteries united by ties of doctrine and discipline.

always called "the Gregorian" to be challenging their mother house. By the end of the century they were making their mark in the CD lists.

Outwardly the life of a monk is uneventful, hidden, even from the outside rather boring. Yet the inner journey carries as much drama and excitement as the outer, and Henri was embarking on the most adventurous and exciting journey, whose goal was nothing less than God himself. Henri's friend Murray Rogers said of him, "He felt that God asked for everything. He knew that you can't half love God, you can't be a part time Christian. He was madly in love with God."[2]

Had Henri Le Saux stayed in the secular world, he might well have been an ambitious man—and who is to say that ambition is left outside the monastery door? His letters are peppered with references to his ambition—not, it should be said, for power or for high monastic office, but quite simply for God. Only days after his arrival, dazed by his good fortune, he wrote to his friend of the wonders of this life, perfectly suited to the pursuit of holiness:

> Of course it needs guts to become a holy monk, but despite its difficulty, I feel one is bound to aim high. A monk cannot accept mediocrity, only extremes are appropriate for him. The richness of the monastic life I have only begun to glimpse now that I have entered it for good; and I still feel myself as if inundated, dazzled by it; it is too vast for one to be able to grasp it all at once.[3]

The details of the Benedictine timetable change over the years and from country to country, but the broad principles remain the same, one of St. Benedict's great legacies being the division of the monastic day into regular periods of prayer, work, and study. When Henri was first at Kergonan, as now, some seventy-five years later, the monks spent at least four hours every day in chapel, in addition to the hours of preparation. Father Joseph Lemarié, who was to become one of Henri's closest friends, entered in 1936 and remembers the daily timetable at the time, which he thinks was the same as when Henri had arrived in 1929.

The great bell sounded at four in the morning, and everyone dressed quickly and went to the chapel for the Office of Matins. This was followed by private Masses, each ordained monk celebrating, either on his own or perhaps served by juniors and the lay monks. Then there was breakfast followed by the Office of Prime, and at ten o'clock the whole community came together for Sung Mass. No monk could take communion more than once in the day, so at this High Mass it is possible that the only communicant would be the celebrant, who would not have said a private Mass earlier.

After a period of study, the midday meal would be preceded by the Hour of Sexte and followed by None. In the late afternoon there would be Vespers and last thing at night, as it grew dark, Compline would be sung, ending with a Marian hymn, usually the infinitely moving "Salve Regina," the monks pouring out their longing for the feminine, so absent from their lives and entirely symbolized by the figure of the Mother of God to whom they sang. Then the great silence would envelope the monastery and its inhabitants until the following morning. "You see," Henri wrote to his sister Louisette, "I pass my time praying to the Good God, and I do not feel the time spent in this way is wasted in any way."[4] So long hours were spent in chapel, doing what Benedictines still call the Divine Office, the "Opus Dei," the work of God, always held to be the monk's first duty and responsibility.

These hours of prayer were beautifully balanced by work and study. During the morning the master of novices taught the young monks the Rule of St. Benedict, and for those preparing for the priesthood there were periods of theology, moral philosophy, biblical exegesis, and the study of liturgy. Father Lemarié is not sure of the level of these studies, but he does remember that the teachers had no university qualifications.[5]

In the afternoon there was manual work between two and four o'clock, and three times a week there were classes in plainchant, which Henri loved with an abiding passion. The monks had little free time and little opportunity for conversation, though there was an hour's recreation in the afternoon.

It was a strict and unrelenting program and a far cry from the freedom of Saint Briac, but for some years it was to suit Henri well. He was not unaware of the insidious possibilities of boredom, and he admitted that his nature did complain from time to time. After seven months, writing to his friend Raymond Macé, he enclosed a copy of the timetable and the daily program, reminding him that it was the same every week, every month, every year, only the changes of liturgical season and the religious feasts offering variety.

His fellow monks were very impressed by Henri's intellectual ability. Father le Boucher had heard that he had got a "Très bien" in his baccalauréat, which was unusual in those days, and that his superiors had wanted him to continue his studies in Rome, had he not felt the call to the monastery. One monk, taking the new arrival to the small library specially intended for the novices (the novices could only take a book from the main library by asking one of the senior monks to find it for them) was deeply impressed when Henri immediately chose an ancient collection of St. Thomas Aquinas, the famous twelfth-century theologian. No one had previously looked at these works; they were considered too difficult and intelligible only to someone well versed in the Latin of the time of Aquinas. So Henri's taking the books out one by one filled his young contemporaries with awe. They were impressed also by his yearly contribution to the written offering made every year to the abbot on his feast day. Seventy years later Father le Boucher remembers that Henri's essay was always "most unusual."

And silence pervaded all. The only time the monks were allowed to talk to each other was during the two half-hour periods of recreation and in the kitchen, as they washed the dishes after lunch and after supper. Later he came to love silence with a deep passion: there is no record of how he found this first experience of it.

AND WHAT OF HIS FAMILY? How much could he correspond with them, visit them, be visited by them? He was such an eager letter writer, and when one surveys the treasured piles of letters—some published* but many more in private hands—it seems as if he could never have been out of touch for long. Yet at this stage of his life there cannot have been contact enough for such a loving young nineteen-year-old, for they were allowed to receive only one letter a month, and each letter they wrote had to be individually negotiated with the abbot. During Advent, Lent, and periods of retreat they could write no letters at all. The gaps must have felt interminable and very lonely.

As for his mother—how hard she struggled to come to terms with losing her beloved son to God. Soon after he left for Kergonan she wrote:

> I understand, my Henri, yes, I understand your happiness since you are there, where the good God wishes you to be. You understand too that your poor mother is only a poor woman who for 19 years did her utmost to spoil her little one and her eldest son as I have often said to you but for me my little one has gone . . . and will only come back so rarely.[6]

As so often, grief took the form of guilt. If she were a better Christian, she felt, she would resign herself more quickly—she hopes that acceptance will come.

---

*Notably *Swami Abhishiktananda: His Life Told through His Letters,* ed. James Stuart (Delhi: ISPCK, 1989); and *Henri Le Saux: Lettres d'un sannyāsi chrétien à Joseph Lemarié* (Paris: Cerf, 1999).

You are going to pray so much for us, my little one, that God will
certainly send me the courage to endure such a trial. Ah well, soon
there will be a letter from you. . . . I give you a big kiss from us all.
I believe my Henri that I love you even more than before.[7]

Even when she saw that he was happy as a monk, still all she could say
for herself was: "I wish that I could say the same. In spite of everything I
cannot get used to my Henri being a Benedictine. . . . I find it difficult
even to say the word."[8]

Is such motherly love comforting or threatening? In Henri's case it was
probably the bedrock of a certain security underpinning another layer, a
lack of confidence perceived by some of his friends; certainly his own loving nature must have owed much to her love and to the loving context in
which he grew up. At some level he can never have forgotten those first
seven years of his life, when he was the center of her universe, not needing to share him with even one sibling.

The monks left the monastery only for practical things like going to
the dentist or the doctor, and they were allowed home only if their parents were ill, for funerals or family weddings. Later on Henri was to
marry all his sisters except Anne-Louise, whose wedding took place just
after he had left for India. Agnès has a charming story of one of his rare
excursions out of the monastery, his visit to Lorient, some kilometers
away up the coast, when he was about twenty-three years old and had to
visit an optician. Henri recounted that soon, like his mother and father
and Louisette, he would be wearing glasses. But he was more interested
in the conversational exchange. The optician asked him to what he owed
the pleasure of this visit? And immediately they were discussing not the
state of his sight but the prophet Jeremiah and his marvelous relevance to
their times:

> He pointed to the prophecies of doom; I engaged him on the
> prophecies of joy, and talked about the light of hope that comes
> with the turn of the year . . . but without being too precise as to the
> reasons for my hope, since I had seen hanging in the waiting room
> a magnificent coloured portrait of the Maréchal.*[9]

Conversational gifts can emerge out of silence, and Henri was to enjoy
the gifts of conversation and company as much as those of silence and

---

*Marshal Pétain, Prime Minister of France 1940–1945. He established the Vichy gov-
ernment and was imprisoned for life for treason.

solitude. In the context of this life at Kergonan alone, he was to have more friends and a larger correspondence than most, yet always he returned to silence with a sense of relief, joy, sometimes almost of bliss.

The members of the family were allowed to visit twice a year—events that were not only eagerly awaited by Henri but were highlights for the family too. Marie-Thérèse remembers an occasion—she was about twelve at the time—when she had a nasty boil and was crying with the pain, though she refused to let anyone treat it; the air rang with her shouts until she was told that if she was not quiet she would not be allowed to accompany them to see Henri at Kergonan. The threat silenced her immediately. Even as an elderly nun she had vivid memories of those visits, recalling how when she was little more than a toddler running along behind this almost unknown elder brother (remember she was not born when he left home) and playing with his flowing black scapular. She also remembered leaning out of the guest house window when she was just three years old and looking at the neighboring convent and saying, "That's where I shall be when I am big!"

These visits became part of family tradition. There was even an element of ritual in the way that on every visit they would park the car and walk down the same little path and visit the frog pond on the way to the monastery—though Louise was so impatient to see her son that they cannot have stopped for long. With six young children, from Louisette at twelve years old to Marie-Thérèse, a baby of just three months when they made their first visit, there was always the problem of keeping them amused—in fact the nuns deputed to look after them were happy to let them go out, preferring their absence to their noisy presence. So they would pick up Henri and go to the *boulangerie*—which in those days was also a restaurant—on the edge of Plouharnel, then on to the beach. The visit would end with the Office, the children delighted by the singing of the monks.

Since 1952, when Marie-Thérèse fulfilled her childhood ambition and became a nun at Saint-Michel's, the nearby convent she had yearned for from the window of the guest house of her brother's monastery, the family has visited her too, honoring the same traditions, never missing the little path or the frog pond, even visiting the owner of the restaurant and reminding the owner, now a comfortably round Breton great-grandmother, of those visits in the 1930s. So deeply are these little rituals embedded in the family memory that Louis jokes that he's "not sure he can remember the *exact* place on the beach where his uncle sat."[10]

Henri wrote to his friend Raymond Macé of that first visit and of how he appeared to be in high spirits and very happy. But afterwards . . .

When I was alone, the tears flowed and I wished I could go home with them; but He did not will it, and so for His sake alone I remained, while the storm raged within. . . . The battle is sometimes fierce, but with Him one is always victorious. And now I am at peace, until such time as He ordains something different.[11]

So, CONTENTEDLY LOCKED INTO the regular pattern of prayer, work, and study, Henri began his slow progress through the various stages of monastic life. In those days before the Second Vatican Council candidates for the priesthood or for religious orders had to be "tonsured," that is, to have their head shaved over quite a large area. As Henri had been a seminarian, this first ritual had been carried out before he entered the monastery by the archbishop of Rennes. (Later the monks would tonsure each other, Henri being a popular target for the scissors because his thick, wavy brown hair was such a delight to cut.)

On May 12, 1930, after the first six months as a postulant, that stage during which the vocation is tested, he received the Mandatum, a ceremony in which the candidate's feet are washed by the abbot and kissed by all the monks, which is the traditional way of welcoming a new monk into the community. At Kergonan the ceremony had four sections: for the oblates (in France an oblate is a member of the community), for the novices, for brothers specially designated to do manual work,* and lastly for the monks, the priests, and the choir monks—those monks who have decided that they are eventually going to become solemnly professed. The next day Henri was clothed as a novice.

The normally predictable stages from the Mandatum to the taking of final vows was, in Henri's case, interrupted after only five months. For the next year his life was to change dramatically as he was thrown back into the world to do his military service, which had been established in France at the end of the nineteenth century in the wake of the Franco-Prussian war. Now he was moving up a very different ladder. He became a corporal, and, just before his release, a sergeant. He did not want to become an officer, as this would have meant that he would have to go back for his *périodes* (regular times of recall); in any case it is impossible to imagine him having any military ambition. This interruption of his monastic life had one great advantage for him and his family. He was stationed at St. Malo, close by Saint Briac, so every Saturday evening his father would pick him up in the car and bring him home for a few hours.

---

*This category, known as "converts," no longer exists.

His military service over, he returned to the abbey on October 16, 1932, the next three years leading to that great climax of a monk's life, the ceremony in which he makes his solemn profession, the moment when he promises himself to God and the monastery for life. During this period of preparation he continued the normal life of prayer and worship of the Benedictine, but he did not have had a specific post, his time being taken up by his studies in church history, theology and patristics. There does not seem to have been a formal system of passing exams, though before final profession the novices had to go through three "scrutinies," when the novice master, the members of the chapter, and all the monks who had taken solemn vows, gave their opinion of the novice and his suitability to be finally professed. These assessments are not written down, so there is no record of how Henri fared. In May 1935, as the day of his solemn profession approached, he wrote to his friend Raymond Macé, urging him to come to the ceremony and to bring other mutual friends with him, and above all to pray, for he had "such a need at that moment to be surrounded with prayer, that the oblation may be pleasing to the Father."[12] His ambition to serve God well had not weakened; it is seen again as Henri asks Macé to use his chosen prayer from the Missal:

> You will pray it for me, won't you? So that the total religious life which I shall soon begin may be at the level of which I have always dreamed, so that I may not be a commonplace monk—the Lord has no need of such—but a sacrifice *jugiter immolata* (continually offered).[13]

On May 9, 1935, Ascension Day, Henri made a solemn promise to observe the three vows of poverty, chastity, and obedience—or, rather, the slight variation adopted by the Benedictines (which predates the vows taken by the other religious orders), obedience, conversion of manners, and stability. Conversion of manners—an acceptance of the continual call to repentance—embraces poverty and chastity, while stability means that the novice vows to remain in a particular Benedictine community for the rest of his life. He then walked up to the sanctuary of the abbey chapel with his hands outstretched, repeating three times:

> Uphold me O Lord, that I shall live;
> And do not confound me in my expectation.

Next he was clothed in the cowl, a heavy outer garment with long sleeves, and knelt at the feet of the abbot with all the other monks who had made their profession. They exchanged the kiss of peace and, in that age-old and most moving action of humility and surrender, he lay prostrate on the floor—a black, horizontal reminder of his crucified Lord. He had consecrated his life entirely to God.

Seven months later, having passed swiftly through the orders of sub-deacon and deacon, he was ordained priest, when he honored his home-town by giving himself the additional name of Briac. A solemnly professed monk does not necessarily become a priest, but in Henri's case there never seemed any doubt that he would follow that course, and his ordi-nation took place on December 21 of the same year in the Cathedral of Vannes.

All the main events in Henri's monastic life were not only highlights in his personal life and ceremonial events in the life of the abbey but also important family occasions. Marie-Thérèse still remembers, when she was just six years old, making her first communion at her brother's first Mass, and later when she became a nun and entered Saint-Michel, the convent next door to her brother's monastery, she timed her entry so that it would take place on the feast of the Ascension, choosing the same fes-tival her brother had chosen for his final profession. The family members still remember his first Mass at Saint Briac, the least mention of it caus-ing them all to chant with the rhythm and nostalgia only seen in a fam-ily setting—"January the twelfth nineteen hundred and thirty-six."

At twenty-six years old a fully professed monk and an ordained priest, Father Le Saux (or Dom Le Saux), as we can now call him, could also be given a position in the community. He was immediately made librarian, a position suited both to his intellectual interests and to the practical side of his nature—he enjoyed organization and was good at it. He was sent to Clervaux to learn the skills of a librarian and remained the monastery's librarian for twelve years. As a novice he had not had free access to the main library; now he could roam to his heart's content, read as he willed. He was particularly drawn to the Greek fathers and the fathers of the desert. Later, when he himself gave lectures, he liked to talk particularly about Athanasius, Cyril of Alexandria, and Gregory Palamas. He also served as assistant master of ceremonies.

Was he a good monk? What did the other monks think of him? Monastic manners may be more discreet than the manners of the world, but there seems no reason to disbelieve what his contemporaries say of him. Some of them remember "a sort of weariness," which they took to be problems with his health. He would sometimes feel the need to stretch himself out on a stall in the Chapter or "retire to recover a little." He even sometimes missed the Offices altogether—always, of course, with permission. He was clearly very well liked and is still remembered with great affection and admiration. He was "*amusant, 'très gai,*" "he knew how to liven things up." He was "very sensitive, very emotional, but he didn't let it show too much."

Perhaps the comment that would have pleased him most came from Father le Boucher, who said that Henri was "an exemplary monk" who "lived the monastic life properly, searching all the time as was the nature of his spiritual temperament."[14]

3

The Second World War

1939–1945

It's nothing but rumors all the time.[1]

FOR FOUR YEARS HENRI LIVED the outwardly uneventful life of the monk. Then his monastic routine was interrupted again. The summer of 1939 was oppressive, heavy with rumors of war. In Brittany, as all over Europe, people stocked up their larders against the restrictions that war would undoubtedly bring.[2] Events moved inexorably on and in September 1939 Germany invaded Poland, and Britain and France declared war on Germany.

Those who had done their *périodes* had already been recalled, but now general mobilization was decreed. Monks were not exempt, and the younger among them, thirteen including Henri, were called up. He was not an officer—a photograph shows him without stripes and wearing the forage cap of the infantry rather than the officer's peaked cap—but he had command of some soldiers. His sister Marie-Thérèse recalls with delight how one of his superiors rebuked him because one of his officers did not do a good military salute. "Maybe, mon Adjutant," said Sergeant Le Saux, "but he's my best grenade thrower."[3]

Nothing could stop Henri from writing letters, and though the soldiers were told to avoid as far as possible giving precise details of where they were and what was happening, one can catch a glimpse of the life he was leading in his letters to his family, particularly to Marcel, Louisette's first husband, who was killed in the bombing in August 1944, with whom Henri clearly had a good relationship and to whom he could speak as one soldier to another. These letters gave him the outlet he had sought in a journal, which after ten months of war he was forced to admit was use-

26

less, "as the Germans will pinch it from me again as they did the first one."[4]

It is hard to imagine so gentle a man living the life of a foot soldier in a fierce and bloody war, but these letters give some idea of his life in the army as, presumably—for that was the rank with which he had finished his military service—a sergeant. There are not many, for the civilian post soon ceased and his unit was too much on the move to use the military post; moreover, some may have been intercepted by the censor, for Henri was not always totally discreet and in surviving letters he admits to being in Bordeaux, Poitiers, Chatellerault, and Le Mans.

For the first eight months of Henri's service the war on the western front was at the stage known as the "phoney war," with both sides entrenched behind defensive lines. He tells his father and his sisters how he is laying barbed wire, "terracing," and endlessly digging holes and trenches; to his brother-in-law he elaborates slightly, telling him that their role is "to hold back the Germans behind the Maginot line if they manage to infiltrate between the forts; and like you with your tent for 60, I took pleasure in my gun emplacements."[5]

Sometimes he wrote as he was doing a spell of night duty, sitting at a table made of an old door balanced on a trestle, a blanket around his shoulders, a balaclava on his head: "Through the wall a great pig is snoring, he keeps tricking us as we are supposed to stop all traffic and we have already been out several times thinking we hear a car when it is the animal!"[6] Ascetic though he already was, he laments the absence of bread and wine and comments on his living arrangements, pleased to be in a charming village right on the frontier, though there was no fighting there at the time, but delighted by his lodgings and by a magnificent old clock that chimed all the hours and half-hours.

He was never seriously involved in the fighting or in danger, but he learned a little about living rough. He celebrated the tenth anniversary of his arrival as a new monk of Kergonan in Thionville, where the pouring rain reminded him of the floods in Saint Briac a decade earlier and caused him to parody St. Francis, paying homage to "our sister the rain, our brother the cold, thirst and the rest."

We take cover in our holes, holding the canvas over us as best we can; so we go on, feet in the mud, backs in the mud, helmets streaming. . . . If there had been a real German attack at various points on the Sarre, this rain would have been providential, as no air attack would have been possible, nor an infantry attack in that sort of weather. But you can take comfort from the fact that when we have to sleep in the trenches, we will have a good concrete shelter which will be better than any hay barn, since at the moment I have no bed. I may get one one of these days, but the villages are small and the officers swipe all the rooms. Otherwise all goes well—I have a four-day beard and the same clothes for twelve.[7]

They were sometimes very close to the Germans, and one day, caught up in the bombardment of a village at around the time when the Germans were entering Paris and Marshal Pétain was about to sign the armistice between France and Germany, he felt he was beginning to understand what the war was all about: "I prayed for you, for us, for poor France. What a humiliation!"[8] Like his mother, and her father before her, Henri was fiercely patriotic.

Perhaps the most poignant indication of the effect of the war on Henri lies in something spotted by his niece Agnès, who looks after the family papers. She noticed in letters written after the war that her uncle spoke of feelings stirred in him by the sight of a snow-covered countryside, saying it reminded him of what he called "la nuit de Flastroff." Agnès was so struck by the intensity of his emotion that she went to see her aunt, Henri's sister Anne-Louise, to find out why, so long after the war, he should still be so upset by the memory of Flastroff. She discovered that it was in Flastroff, one snowy night, that he had had to throw his first grenade. He had never been able to accept that he had done such a thing.[9] "I have seldom lived so intensely as that night at Flastroff, with the gunfire crackling, the snow whipped up by the bullets sprayed into my face; however all the worry, all the anxiety repressed then, comes back to me when I find myself in a snowy landscape."[10]

Henri's war was to end after less than a year with his capture and immediate escape. During July of 1940 he was in the Mayenne when his unit was surrounded by German troops and they were all forced to surrender. Somehow—his sister Marie-Thérèse thinks the corn in the surrounding fields was high enough to afford some protection—he managed to escape before the names were taken:

As I had no wish to visit Germany, that evening I took the road to Fougères and the following night, thanks to a bicycle which was kindly lent to me, managed to reach St Briac dressed in a fantastic outfit. There for a month I acted dead, and when travelling became easier I returned here.[11]

So on July 24, 1940, just before the start of the Battle of Britain, he returned to the monastery, no doubt eager to discover how his fellow monks had fared.

THEY HAD HAD TO ADAPT to the departure of thirteen of the youngest monks, which meant that they were unable to have any sung Offices; they said Lauds and Matins and celebrated a low conventual Mass. The spring of 1940 saw the downfall of the Allies first in Belgium, then in France, but the Germans did not arrive in Plouharnel until June 22, the day of the signing of the armistice. A few days later a unit of lorries arrived at the abbey. Saint-Martin, which was used as a guest house and as lodgings for the novitiate, was requisitioned and an artillery battery took over the out-buildings, erecting provisional stabling for a hundred horses. In the process they showed the insensitivity of the invader by knocking down a section of the beautiful wall surrounding the monastery.

The monastery had not lost anyone in the fighting, though Henri's friend Father Joseph Lemarié had been taken prisoner and another priest had been seriously wounded. The monks reacted with the calm optimism one might expect from men of their calling: "We can hope that, by the grace of God, the coming year will be full of blessings, will return to us our prisoners and will bring France closer to God," wrote the abbot.[12]

On his return from the war, Henri soon returned to the normal life of a monk; he taught church history and patristics and continued his work as the librarian, meticulously making a catalogue with three bottles of ink of different colors—which he sometimes muddled up after switching to multicolored correspondence. His work in these fields was highly regarded, but the position with which he is most strongly associated is as Cérémonaire, master of ceremonies, one of the most important jobs in the monastery. His love of liturgy had already led to his being assistant master of ceremonies, and in 1943 he was promoted to the senior posi-tion, responsible not only for everything that happened in the liturgy but also for much of the smooth running of the place. It was his job to look after every detail of the monastic Offices, deciding who would read the lessons and, at Mass, who would perform the various functions. He was in charge of any ceremonial movement around the church. Outside the chapel it was he who decided who would read in the refectory, who would serve at table, and who would celebrate Mass for the neighboring nuns in their separate chapel.

The Benedictines pride themselves on their liturgical precision and the beauty with which every action is performed; and though he was young to be in that position, Father Le Saux pleased the monks in every way. "Spick and span we would say," said an English-speaking monk. Fur-ther, "he did it all in a very nice and kindly and friendly way." Henri may have taken his work, and indeed himself, very seriously at the time—to do the job well he must have done—and years later Murray Rogers remembers him recalling, how "Everything had to be *exactly* right, 100% correct—walk in correctly, clothes perfectly put on—I was frightfully particular."[13] But then, a very different man, he laughed at himself.

BY THE AUTUMN OF 1940 the war was raging and the occupation "*énorme*," though for a few months the monks barely suffered at all, enduring scarcely any rationing and seeing no fighting. Their perception of the war was limited by the almost total lack of information about what was going on:

> We are greatly deprived of real news—it's nothing but rumours all the time. I don't see the "Heure Bretonne" any more, but I find the other papers from the Britanny capital aren't much better. We only get a copy every now and then. It's abominable. I am going to keep them as specimens—it will be worth it for later on.[14]

At Christmas 1941 an off-limits area was created along the coast, with entry so strictly regulated that communication with other monasteries, indeed with the rest of France, was very difficult. At first this did not affect the monastery much, simply putting a stop to visitors and increasing the solitude and silence, but it became hard to buy provisions and they were more cut off from news of the war than ever. On June 1, 1942, the monastery was requisitioned and the monks were told to be gone in ten days. They could use the farm buildings to store their furniture and books—though how books would fare in such conditions it is hard to imagine—but they must find somewhere else to live.

It cannot have been too easy to find somewhere else for twenty-four monks (two stayed with the nuns, to say Mass for them and to help generally). But again they were unfazed: "the community is full of spirit and optimism," wrote the abbot, "and I think this diversion will be good for everyone. It's a good provision against becoming too stuffy." Nevertheless, they hoped to find somewhere suited to monastic life and study.

The monks found refuge a few kilometers away with the Filles de la Sagesse in the old Chartreuse d'Auray, where they stayed for almost a year, during which time two of the monks who had been captured, one of them Henri's friend Father Lemarié, were released. Then the station at Auray was bombed and they were told to move again. So in June 1943 they settled in a Renaissance manor, Les Nétumières, near Vitré. It was an idyllic site in a wood, not well suited to monastic needs, and Henri's practical gifts were in full use, as he played a key role in adapting it. It was owned by the Countess de Legge of Kerléan, who retained the use of some of the rooms. One of her grandsons, an observant twelve-year-old, remembers how he and his elder brother shared a little of the monastic life and the teaching of some of the monks, including Father Le Saux. He recalls, "The walls were running with damp, there was no running water, no electricity, no heating, and the log-stack empty."[15] An oratory was set up in the *grand salon*, though the floor was in a terrible state and the walls were crumbling. Thus the monks continued their life of prayer, more cut off from the world than ever.

They lived in this grand improvised monastery for nearly two years, but even after the liberation of Paris there were pockets of German resistance along the coast of Brittany which the FFI* of the French army did not have enough artillery to dislodge. The Presqu'Ile de Quiberon, just a few kilometers from the abbey, remained in German hands (the troops of the Third Reich somehow having plenty of rations). Kergonan was in the front line, and the little town of Plouharnel was a no-man's land. There was still frequent bombing—one bomb fell into the abbey cloister and shattered the glass of three of the great windows—and it was not considered safe for the monks to return to Kergonan until after the German surrender on May 8, 1945. When the time came to leave Les Nétumières, Henri found he was sad, realizing that he would miss the great jungly wood and the winding course of the Vilaine. On the other hand, at Kergonan "the birds will wake me and the sea, the ocean will be there again . . . and the salt air, and the wind of open spaces and the sound of the waves."[16]

HENRI ONLY RARELY SHOWED HIS FEELINGS about the war, in terms of either its universal tragedy or any personal discomfort. He does, it is true, go into considerable detail about his travels—so squashed in a cattle truck on one occasion, that "as soon as you move a toe you start the whole truck moving,"[17] and he delighted when a barrel of cognac fell on the railway track at Bordeaux and they managed to collect five liters—some of which went into his hip flask. He even showed a mild interest in personal possessions, pleased that the Government Army Offices returned things he had lost—a leather strap for his razor, a pitcher, some medals, his portable altar, and a key for a sardine tin—in those days a necessary preliminary to eating sardines. Certain that the war would soon be over, he never appeared frightened in his letters home, though he seems conscious of his position as a protective elder brother. He rejoiced to his youngest sisters in "the teutonic humiliation" and was

*The FFI—Forces Françaises de l'Intérieur—was the name given in 1944 to the French military forces engaged in the liberation.

ready to lay bets as to who is liberated first: you, Louisette or me??
I will be really glad to hear them (the British) marching on the big
main road; on that same road where some days ago we heard and
saw the sinister teutonic march-past. The sound is still ringing in
my ears. And now, tall stories at leisure! I don't see much to be worried about.[18]

Sometimes he even showed a touch of machismo, a wish to be seen as
"one of the boys." When he heard that people were being called up again,
he commented wistfully, "I have to say that one part of me wouldn't be at
all unhappy to join the 'combat' myself." So too he wrote of the resistance
workers, gathered around the farm kitchen telling stories of the *maquis*.
He loved to hear them talk and didn't miss the chance to tell of his sister
Marie-Josèphe, who had reported regularly to an agent in St. Malo, and
had handed over plans of a military base, for which she was awarded the
Medal of the Resistance. Even on his own behalf adds, "I too have fired a
shot in the snow. In this way I am slightly less ashamed to be just an ordinary chap."[19] So Flastroff, the very night that haunted him, became
something for which he could be grateful.

THE SUBJECT THAT MOVED HIM MOST, then as earlier, was his family. His
concern for their welfare and the practical tips he suggests are touching.
He does not seem to have had much faith in the practical powers of his
father—at one point writing: "Make sure that Papa is not separated from
his papers. It would be better if Papa, Annette and Rénée each had some
on them so as to avoid losing the lot perhaps."[20] So he became the elder
brother par excellence, the stay and support when all around was crumbling:

> Don't let Maman tire herself out too much with all the shopping in
> Rennes. She must put herself before the business even if you have
> to lose a bit by doing so. . . . Are you still allowed to sell milk? Salt
> down some big pigs before meat rationing is introduced.[21]

He suggests that they advertise their 1930 Renault van: "and the tyres are
good—why not sell them separately?" He sends detailed information
about the civil code when they consider some change in the legal ownership of their family house. He is constantly concerned for their safety:

> Do you have somewhere safe to go in the bombing? I suggested to
> the others at La Chapelle Biche* that they should make a little

---

*Where some of the family had taken refuge.

trench—quite narrow and whatever length necessary and not too near the house. That's what's best—and then you have only to put a sheet of metal on some planks over it to have a shelter. Sleep on the ground, it's safer. . . . Try to let me know how things are if you can. I haven't been able to get any information at all.[22]

Though his sisters, all of whom except Marie-Thérèse would eventually marry and have their own families, are quite matter-of-fact about the family and their relationships with each other, for Henri, a celibate monk, the family was of overwhelming importance. At the end of 1944 after they had visited him at Kergonan, he expressed his sadness at their departure almost with the passion of a lover:

How was your return journey on Tuesday? I can't wait to have a word from you. We ought to have several weeks living together for it to really be any good. Two days is too short. One hardly has time to get there before the agony of going off again and for me of seeing you go. Why do we all love each other so much in our family! But it's also this affection which makes life bearable.[23]

Most of all he was devoted to his mother, and his concern for her as she became seriously ill was most genuine. He worried continually about how she was, wishing that his guardian angel would bring him news every morning and every night. In December 1943 she was so ill she was given extreme unction,* and the next day a Mass for the dying was said and she received the Viaticum, when Holy Communion gives grace for the journey into eternity. She did not die but lived for another few months—something Henri found almost as hard as her dying:

I can't think that it was entirely natural what happened the other Thursday. We were all ready to make the sacrifice, however cruel it might be. If Maman had to go it was that day. A simple respite would have been to go through death. We went through those two days in a supernatural state. Maman didn't really know which side of the wall she was on, she was as much in touch with our dead as with the us, who were around her. As for us, we already had presentiments of the other side of the wall, so to speak. Do you think otherwise we could have all survived days like that so calmly, even gently—or to have felt emotions so peacefully.[24]

---

*Now known as the Sacrament of the Sick.

But after the Mass, when a visitor called, there was a "sort of awakening from the other world" and she began to improve. Once Henri had adapted to this unexpected improvement, he immediately issued instructions for her care. They must all pray at least twice a day; Hyacinthe and Marie-Thérèse could say a bit of the rosary when they got home. And they must sing the Magnificat to give thanks. And, "What are you doing to make her stronger? You could give her injections as you did for Marcel." She had lost a lot of blood. "What about replacing that blood with something new? . . . Talk to the doctor about it again. Insist on her rehabilitation from this weak state."[25]

This imperious tone is not in character, but it shows Henri's great love for his mother and also that he did not know how to react to her continuing life and increasing ill health once he had prepared for her death. When she did die, in May the following year, he was able, at least outwardly, to cope with it and to look after the family with even more loving care than before. A man of action, he could cope when he knew what he had to do; uncertainty was a different matter.

There are other instances in the surviving letters to his family when brotherly care verges on bossiness and when practical advice becomes peremptory. As neither bossiness nor peremptoriness was characteristic of the later man, these instances deserve mention. There was, for instance, the occasion in 1946 when his sisters Marie-Josèphe and Rénée wrote by the same post telling him they were both getting married and could he come to Saint Briac to celebrate both weddings, two months apart. He was furious:

> You are quite right to think that it will be impossible for me to ask to come back to St. Briac in two months. Not to mention the cost of the journey (which must be at least 500 fr. now)—a monk does not leave his monastery every two months. Why haven't you arranged the two weddings together. That would have halved the cost and would have made it possible for me to bless both at the same time. I really am very bothered . . . I hear your cries, but having been a monk now for almost 20 years, you ought to know that a monk is not free to come and go.[26]

What prompted such an outpouring from a man generally perceived to be outstandingly gentle? Was his gentleness acquired with maturity? Was there a latent streak of anger in him that had to be tamed? Was he playing an overtough version of the elder brother—the lion cuffing the cubs a bit too hard? Or, given that there is only occasional evidence of this sort of behavior, did things sometimes touch him in a way that he found hard to handle?

The most plausible explanation is that he found his role as virtual head of the family harder than he was willing to admit. His father seems to have played little role in the lives of the family, and Henri was still bleeding from the loss of his mother. In the same letter in which he upbraids Marie-Josèphe and Rénée, he admits that for the eighteen months since her death he has not dared to reread his mother's letters to him, but while clearing his room he had to tidy them, "And I let them get hold of me. . . . But how do you think I can stand these letters from Maman? They are still so lovely. I would love to put them in an album to keep them for the family, so that all the little ones now and to come would know who they come from."[27] He loved his mother with the deepest of loves. He loved his family and felt overwhelmingly responsible for them. Sometimes, perhaps, it was just too much.

At last the time came when it was considered safe for the monks to return to Kergonan, and Henri, the practical man, was sent ahead to help restore the buildings, which had been in enemy hands for four years. He found the damage, inflicted it has to be said as much by the FFI as the Germans, was even worse than he had expected. Sainte-Anne had been bombed, though it had escaped serious damage; Saint-Michel's, the neighboring convent, had received direct hits, some of which had exploded in the interior, and other buildings had been damaged. Doors, windows, and beams had been used as firewood, and furniture and books were deteriorating in attics and farm buildings. Repairs were estimated at several million francs—to be paid for by a monastery already poor. To make matters worse, morale in the community was low, recruitment had clearly been impossible during the war years, and the abbot, a withdrawn, introspective man, was less able to keep his calm front and was consumed by worry and depression.

Henri had already been sent back to Kergonan once, in January 1945, and had spent ten days sorting out the library and safeguarding the most precious books. This time the task was heavier, though the living conditions provided exquisite compensation. He and another priest were acting as chaplains to the convent, and so he was given "a delicious little room . . . peaceful as anything, in a solitude which I find enchanting." The mattress was so soft he was ashamed to sleep on it—in fact, he made conscience-driven plans to sleep on a rug on the floor—and every morning there was coffee and milk, he was given half an ounce of butter with his roll and the meals ended with tart or "pudding." "All the wiles of the devil of greed that Rénée has such pleasure in awakening in me at Saint Briac start up again . . . and then coffee to finish; it's real spoiling."[28] He may have been a monk, but he was a French monk, enjoying his comforts and not yet totally committed to an ascetic way of life.

A curious sidelight on his stay at the convent was his nervousness at the thought of meeting the mother abbess. He didn't know whether he should call on her or not and was relieved when she herself "summoned me to the parlour" and admitted to being "a little worried, naturally, and awkward about myself as always,"[29] a self-consciousness and uneasiness that were not often apparent. Admittedly, the archetype of the abbess carries an awe-inspiring message; certainly it brought out a very different side of Henri from the confident manner that he mostly conveyed. In the event the chaplain and the abbess got on famously.

Henri's task—apart of course from keeping his monastic hours, up at five in the morning, bed at ten at night, and saying the Office whenever possible—was not only to organize the library, put up shelves, and clean the rooms, but to return all the furniture and equipment that had been stored at the farm or at Auray back to the monastery. This was done largely by horse and cart, with the help of prisoners—German, Russian, and French. He was sometimes in charge of a couple of dozen at a time and admitted with some shame that the French were not the best workers.

And so he dealt with masons, plumbers, carpenters, and glaziers, with waste pipes, water ducts, doors, unexpected holes, and staircases worn out by the boots of Russians, Germans, and Frenchmen. He had to see—tactfully—on the one hand that time was not wasted and on the other that, when the heat was insufferable (it was high summer), a glass of cider or a cigarette was available. It seems he was as good a manager of men as he was a master of ceremonies. Certainly he enjoyed himself hugely, thoroughly happy that the practical side of his nature was being put to such full use as he fulfilled the task he self-mockingly called "Chief of the Works."

> I really enjoy having to manage like this, dealing with the lorry-drivers and workmen: "I've still got such and such to do, I'll go back inside to look for this, I'll let you know. . . ." The poor monk, so humble and modest, who suddenly finds himself acting a bit as if he was the master.[30]

He was in a curious stage of his life. He was a monk, set to do worldly tasks, and a celibate young man finding himself responsible for an elderly father, a younger brother, and five younger sisters—he felt different and indeed he *was* different. He sent his family a postcard from Rennes station:

> It's strange to travel. A monk feels himself to be so different from others in a crowd, I hardly dare to be the first to speak but I think that all the people round me only live on the outside, don't have a sense of true reality, waste their thought and their will on trivialities. It's easy to pray in the middle of a crowd, you know. I only have to look around and offer up to the Good Lord all these poor people around me.[31]

The element of condescension in those words is not very attractive in the spiritually tolerant climate of the twenty-first century. Perhaps these were spiritual growing pains and Henri himself, as an older man, would have been embarrassed to read them.

AT LAST THE WORK AT KERGONAN was finished, and on a wet day at the end of August the rest of his brethren arrived from Les Nétumières, happy to be back after their four-year exile.

> Our chapel has never before seemed to us so big and resonant. Our basement refectory seems magnificent and immense. . . . Without moving from my table I admire the bay and the *presqu'île de Quiberon*. In the foreground, the trees where the moonlight plays in the evening. In the distance the lighthouses at night. . . . Perhaps next Thursday I'll allow myself to go and feel the sand and plunge into the sea . . . up till now I have not had the time. If I think about it, I'm rather afraid my bathing costume is all holes.[32]

It was Henri, as a mark of respect for the work he had done, who was asked to celebrate the first Mass in the reconstituted monastery; "It was the crowning achievement of my work over the past two months."[33] He was back at Kergonan, in the heart of his community, surrounded by his beloved Brittany with Saint Briac "still more beautiful than the horizon that I have in front of me" not far away. It might have seemed that he was settled for life. He was not.

4

Another Irresistible Vocation

1946–1948

I have been completely taken over by it.[1]

Despite his voluminous correspondence, bursting with vitality and the need to communicate, Henri's inner life as a monk at Kergonan, his secret longings, for years remained largely unknown to his friends and family. There is no doubting his faith; it was as much a part of him as his heart and his lungs—an unquestioned dimension of himself as natural as breathing. It was in a way a simple faith, owing much to his upbringing, especially to his mother, and redolent of the austerity that was typical of the Catholicism of his youth—an austerity seen in the way he reminds his beloved sister Louisette of the "example that Maman gave us, that one is not on earth to enjoy oneself. We are on earth to love the Good Lord, to respond a little to the love that he has offered us."[2] Throughout his life, Henri was grateful for that deep grounding in faith that he was later to say was essential if the mind was to "launch out on its own without too great a risk."[3]

At this time his only work put on paper, apart from correspondence, was a long typescript, written at his mother's request in 1942 and called *Amour et Sagesse* (Love and Wisdom).* James Stuart notes that though its three chapters speak from a traditional viewpoint, they already display the characteristic features of his later writing.[4] Indeed, this is immediately clear in the author's stated aim—to avoid theological speculations and to rely on personal experience. "I have set down nothing here except what is my own, I have judged it unnecessary to reproduce what can be found everywhere—which explains the fragmentary nature of this essay."[5]

---

*Held in the archives of the Abhishiktananda Society in Delhi.

38

Yet despite its traditional framework, in this early manuscript lies the essence of his lifelong search, a search that was eventually to put him at the cutting edge of twentieth-century spirituality. Not only are there already traces of a reading broader than purely Christian, but on the penultimate page comes the ringing cry, "Beyond, always beyond! It is not your gifts, Lord, that I desire, but yourself."[6] This yearning was to inform the rest of his life and to be inextricably entwined with a call that had beckoned him for over a decade. For years he kept his secret from everyone, including his family, but as early as 1934, even before he was ordained, he was filled with a passionate desire to go to India. (This date can be determined with accuracy from later references in letters and in his spiritual diary.)

How had he acquired this wish? How, living inside the high walls of an enclosed order in the 1930s, had he learned anything of India or Indian thought? What did he come across that so fired his imagination that he acquired an intense wish not just to read Hindu scriptures but to live in the land of their origin? Opinions, even among those who knew him at the time, are divided. The obvious assumption is that Henri's voracious appetite for reading would have led him to Indian texts in the monastery library, and that is the view that some of his contemporaries put forward. But Father Lemarié, who came to Kergonan in 1936 and became so close a friend that Father Le Saux wrote to him regularly for the rest of his life,* is not one of them. In fact, the question of the origins of his friend's interest in India still puzzles him:

> It remains a mystery. There was absolutely nothing on the subject in the library at Kergonan (neither Upanishads, nor Bhagavad Gita) at most a few reviews of the missions to the East. It is certain that he had an inner call very soon after entering the monastery. . . . If I questioned him on this subject before he told me of his intention to go to India (in 1946) I do not remember his reply. Neither have I any memory of discussions about India before the announcement of his departure.[7]

Were these "few reviews" the sole source of his interest? Though there is a reference in Le Saux's correspondence to "all the books on India that are lying about in my room"[8] that was much later and the memory of as close a friend as Father Lemarié cannot be discounted. Could those reviews have contained something of sufficient power to make an indelible influence? Indeed recent research has indicated that these reviews

---

*Their correspondence is published by Editions du Cerf, Paris; see bibliography.

might have contained some inspiring material.* A list of books and articles believed to have been in the Kergonan library in the 1930s includes the magazine *Contemplation et Apostalat,* which was produced in Bruges and sent free to all monasteries. Some of the articles could have been about India; there were also booklets of *Xaveriana* of the 1920s and early 1930s. In these Henri would have found articles by Jesuits not only on predictable subjects such as Christian missionary work in India and Mahatma Gandhi but also on the Buddhist monks of Ceylon, on Devasagayam, the eighteenth-century martyr, and on the great nineteenth-century sage Ramakrishna.

No firm conclusion can be drawn about the origins of his passionate longing to go to India, but another dimension must be added, and that was the influence of Henri's uncle, the brother of Henri's mother. Henri Sonnefraüd was a member of the Foreign Missionary Society of Paris and was sent to China in 1923. This older "Uncle Henri" was much admired by the Le Saux family, partly for his work as a missionary and his courage in traveling so far from France, but also because when he was injured so badly that his leg was to be amputated, he insisted that it not be done, lest as a cripple he would not be accepted for the priesthood, still less would he be able to travel to China. The family memories of him were crowned after his death at Waichow in 1940, when they were told by a bishop "that Uncle Henri was put to death from hatred of his religion and that we can think of him as a martyr . . . it's a joy and glory for us to know that the Good Lord has chosen one of ours for such an honour."[9]

On a visit to Europe in the early 1930s Henri Sonnefraüd came to visit his nephew at Kergonan, and apparently the two disagreed strongly, the older man wondering how the young Henri could shut himself up in a monastery when there was a whole world to explore. Eventually, and certainly before he returned to China, the two were reconciled, but this clash with a revered relation left a profound mark on Henri. The date of this meeting was the spring of 1934, the very year from which Henri Le Saux later dated his passionate longing to go to India.†

It says much for Henri's self-control and discretion that though he was only twenty-four years old when this desire to go to India came over him, he said nothing to anyone for years. It was just a dream, and one he would not even consider pursuing while his mother was alive. He bided

---

*This research was carried out by Dr. Christian Hackbarth-Johnson; see bibliography.

† Dr. Hackbarth-Johnson was told of this date by Henri's sister Marie-Thérèse, who consulted the Archives of the Mission Etrangères in Paris.

his time, reading anything about India he could lay hands on, studying English and reading Arthur Conan Doyle and Rudyard Kipling in the evening but not saying a word to anyone.

Eventually, after a decade of silence and some six months after his mother's death in 1944, he wrote to his sister Anne-Louise, perhaps confiding first in her as she herself was, at the time, considering the religious life. Anne-Louise promptly told Louisette, who of course immediately wrote to Henri.

Henri's reply was swift, though he made no excuses for not writing first to Louisette, the sister to whom in many ways he was closest. He admitted that he had dreamed for years of going to India, though he did not explain what he wanted to do there, simply telling her to ask Anne-Louise to fill her in with details of a venture which he admitted was a daunting prospect:

> I would like to have what it takes and likewise the skill and moral strength to bring off this particular work. . . . But I'm very much afraid that it is beyond my capability, and above all I am committed to Kergonan. I know certainly that I have my place there, that I fulfil my role there, and that my departure will create real difficulties; for if the monastery still has some chance of surviving, I don't know that it would be right to leave it.[10]

So loyalty to his mother had been replaced by loyalty to his monastery. But this loyalty was complex and contradictory. On the one hand, he had taken a vow of stability, requiring him to remain in his monastery for the rest of his life; and he loved Kergonan, only weeks before his death he would admit that "Kergonan has been the background of all that I have been able to do here."[11] On the other hand, there were times when the negative side could not be contained and he admitted to a distaste for the monastery and to disenchantment with the church, conceding that life in the monastery did not fulfill him, indeed that "it was in my deep dissatisfaction that my desire to come to India was born."[12]

Soon after he had written to his sisters, Henri went to see his abbot, explaining his intention more fully than he had to Louisette; he wanted to establish the contemplative monastic life there in a completely Indian form or, failing that, to live a contemplative life in India as a hermit. The abbot gave him permission to approach various authorities, and for the next four years Henri was to endure vacillations, hesitancy, and the changing of ecclesiasical minds. The only one to stay constant in his desire was Henri himself.

He wrote first to the abbot of Bruges, Dom Nève, and matters were proceeding quite well until Henri made it clear that his aim was "an essentially contemplative life, and not half-contemplative, half-apostolic."[13] It says something for the spiritual climate of the 1940s that the abbot was immediately put off by this, replying that it would be better if they pursued their separate paths. There was then an exchange of letters with the bishop of Pondicherry and the bishop of Salem, the latter responding enthusiastically, but saying his diocese was too poor and too newly established to take on the responsibility of a new foundation. A moment's cheer came when one of his brothers at Kergonan, with whom he was in total accord, said that he would like to accompany Henri, only to be dampened as the abbot put his foot down at the thought of losing *two* of his monks.

The only encouragement he received was from some French monks in Salem, in Tamil Nadu, who responded by saying they had spoken to their vicar general, and "we very much welcome you with open arms, so come when you can. The sooner you come the better."[14] Over the moon with joy, Henri's practical side leapt into action and he started planning—how to save money on the journey; how to "set up his sacristy" and decide what to take in the way of altar cloths, albs, and altar linen; how he should tell his father. He waited for confirmation, watching the post as impatiently as a teenager waiting to hear from his girlfriend:

> Still nothing from India. Perhaps more ample reflection has made him less impatient. Perhaps too his reply is too heavy to go by air, as I asked for lots of explanations. I am often afraid, less of the tigers and snakes than of the qualities of prudence and real saintliness that I lack. However I cannot deny that I would like to be up to it. If the Good Lord really doesn't want it, he will raise obstacles. How inadequate I feel for such work.[15]

He must have begun to think the Lord did not want it, for, after the initial encouraging exchanges with the Salem community, he had to wait for nine months, and then it was only to receive "a dismal letter from Salem," from his one enthusiastic contact there,* admitting he couldn't understand why the French monks were hesitating. Henri was shattered. So shattered, so desperate, that he suggested to the abbot that he should go alone, with nowhere to go when he arrived in India and leaving the abbot or a bishop to take responsibility for the foundation, for that uncer-

---

*The name is illegible.

tainty was what was holding things up. He must have known that it was unlikely that the abbot could agree to such terms, especially as he himself admitted that the enterprise was unpredictable. Indeed he was uncertain enough to want assurance that he could return to France should the project not succeed, a suggestion that shows something of his state of mind. How he developed such an overwhelming desire to go to India may not be clear, but the strength of his longing to go there was not in doubt. It was as strong as, arguably stronger than, his initial vocation to the monastic life.

NOR WERE THE FRUSTRATIONS concerning India the only way in which he was emotionally disturbed at this time. Henri Le Saux was a passionate man, and in these early postwar years, when he was in his mid-thirties, the fires of his emotional nature were being fanned not only by the thwarting of his ambitions to go to India but also by family events, calling up a side of him with which he had not yet completely come to terms. It was only weeks after receiving the "dismal" letter from Salem that he was asked to celebrate the weddings of his two sisters—and doubtless this heightened emotional state contributed to his imperious and untypical response.* Even by the time the two weddings took place in the winter of 1946–47, the whole question of India was still unresolved and he was in turmoil.

Mothers and mothers-in-law are expected to cry at weddings, but what about the tears of the celibate priest, celebrating for others a state to which he can never aspire? A letter to Louisette, written just after the two marriages had taken place, shows the anguish that overtook him as he, such a loving family man, realized as never before what he was giving up. "How lovely the family is!" he writes, "My little Louisette, how well we understand each other without having to say so. I, of whom the Good Lord has asked that I should not seek it, and you† who the Good Lord has deprived of it."[16]

Though there is never a mention of sexuality—and indeed that would have been unlikely in a monk at that time, especially one from his particular background—he is clearly finding celibacy a hard cross to bear, and his idealism and his nature were at war as he tried to defend both: "Virginity is beautiful, but so is human love. The Good Lord wishes them both."[17] But sometimes he lost his sense of identity, unsure how to find his own place in this world of couples and families. "Really I am not a

---

*See chapter 3 above.
†Louisette's first husband had been killed in 1944, and she did not remarry until 1948.

man, still less a monk. I am only just recovering, first from sleep, and then all the emotions that took me over competely during that week. And there was so much at once, so many things."[18]

Not only was he being forced to face the deprivation, for life, of any gratification of his natural instincts, but there is a sense in which he was inhibited by the high standards of his upbringing, sometimes uncomfortable in secular situations, particularly those where Christianity was only skin deep.

> It is only really in friends' houses that the priestly and religious vocation can flower. It is too lovely and at the same time too beautiful. Maman set us an example in marriage which is the ideal and such a high standard that her children and grandchildren, priests and nuns, can only with difficulty live up to it.[19]

Slowly he absorbed the emotions that had been so violently stirred and he was forced to face all he had given up and to remember how he had felt when he had left home to become a monk. But he was still unable to detach himself from Saint Briac, it was so deep in his bones:

> Saint Briac is like Flastroff, you see, it is too charged with emotion. There is so very much there! Mutual looking after, backing each other up over so many years. When I see myself, the monk frank and sincere, as soon as I am home, I am so much in my element again, so tender. It's the result of having been raised in such a lovely nest.[20]

It was a time of great anguish, a crisis in which he had finally to let go of swaths of his instinctive nature in order to be true to the life to which he knew he was called. For instance there are rare hints of a romantic side to his character, seen in the way he fantasized about his sister Louisette—how her "big brother" sees her home through the wood:

> Rite demands that it is Henri who carries the bag on his shoulder. He must go on the right, and once out of view of the castle offer his arm. At a certain turn in the path, we must stop to pick bilberries. When at last we get to the road to the chapel, there is a tree trunk on which we have to sit, Henri on the left this time, to get away more quickly. For when it gets to twenty to nine, I just have to rush back through the wood as fast as possible to be in time for my helping of supper.[21]

If the romantic lover was never to be allowed expression, a wistful glimpse of the family man hiding behind the monk is seen in a long letter telling of his gastronomic plans for the wedding of his brother Hyacinthe. Though he admits that the negotiations have meant that he has had to "overcome my timidity and blushes"—it was just after the end of the war when food was scarce and he could only find what he wanted by trawling the farms around Nétumières—the genial host can be seen smiling through his plans. He tells of the purchase of at least two geese, three ducklings to be made into salami, several chickens and—for what dish he does not say—eight pounds of beetroot; he will bring *charcuterie* and *gâteaux*. He is arranging for the birds to be killed and plucked and inquires whether the family will want to keep the feathers? He calculates the prices and even involves himself in the preparation of the dresses. The final piece of startling efficiency is when he informs his family that he will be at St. Malo at midday, with two suitcases, each weighing ten to twelve kilimeters, so they will need the trailer.

His emotions were overworked; he was forced to be aware of what he had sacrificed as never before. Though there was never any question of doubting his vocation, his attempts to cheer his widowed sister seem almost as if he were cheering himself:

> You would not love the Good Lord so much if he had not given you so much to bear, and you are so well suited to it. . . . But the heart suffers. I see so well in my case, and certainly I don't regret anything that I have done.[22]

By THE BEGINNING OF 1947, after two years of failed negotiations, it was beginning to look as if his dream would never be realized. At Easter he was writing to his family once again, "From India, nothing, nothing, nothing. It is almost making me ill."[23] He sent an SOS to India. An abbot he met suggested that he simply go there—he could see what to do when he got there. His own Father Abbot took pity on him and wrote to the Department of Propaganda at the Vatican—which Henri explained to his family was "a sort of Ministry of Missions." That reply came quickly—permission for new foundations could be given only where there is property and means to live and all the dioceses in the East had been ruined by the war.

He took refuge in looking after the publication of a book on Gregorian chant being published by the monastery, for a while happily submerged in work and proofs. Knee-deep in paper and prospectuses he wondered whether one day he would write a book and whether he would be able to give an oriental presentation of Christianity: "I wonder from time to time if I still have a 'European' conception of the world and of God, I have thought so much from an 'oriental' angle."[24] Still he waited and watched for the post. At one point the abbot seemed to shift from unwilling encouragement to downright discouragement. He would not hear of Henri's suggestion that he take another monk with him and even seems to have changed his mind about allowing Henri himself to go, for in May 1947 Henri tells his family that the abbot had told him he must stay at the monastery. An even more depressing letter came from Solesmes, the motherhouse:

> A lovely homily telling me that I had entered the monastic life to sanctify myself and that it was no good dreaming of going far away, that by living the monastic life here I would be doing just as much for India, and so on and so forth. . . . It would need a team to go and there is neither the personnel nor the resources to make up that team and I don't have what it takes to lead it! In a word, freezing shower. It'll take me several days to recover.[25]

At that time he was under no illusion about the possibility of receiving moral support, let alone material help, from the congregation; he knew that, given the expenses needed to repair the war damage to the monastery, they could not afford anything. But he was having to face the vows he had taken in all their solemnity:

> And what is terrible is that if I go, I will be told that by doing it I am outside obedience. It could be that I am not forbidden but I will be told that I am creating my own movement, which is serious in the religious life. However I am not going to stay in Kergonan now that it has become an issue.[26]

He tried to come to terms with the possibility of his dream never being fulfilled, even though he still had as many lines out as a hungry fisherman, including one to the apostolic delegate. He was clearly having a struggle with contradictions within himself when he managed to write:

> Of course if I have to stay here I shall make the best of it and I will try to love the Good Lord as much as I can. But I feel so much that I really cannot hope to achieve my full development here—even spiritual. I am too personal not to quickly become troublesome . . . rather like a rat in the cheese. It's not to get away from Kergonan that I want to go to India, it's for India itself that I want to go.[27]

Even as he wrote these lines, one of his letters, addressed to the bishop of Tiruchirapalli, Monsignor Mendoça, was starting its long journey to India. He had written it on the feast of the Ascension and placed it on the altar by the tabernacle while he held his nightly vigil before posting it the next day. This was the letter that was, eventually, to bring him the invitation he sought.

THE BISHOP RECEIVED THE LETTER at the beginning of August and, his French not being very good, he passed it to a visiting French priest who was working in the diocese and happened to be visiting him that day. For the priest, Father Jules Monchanin, this letter was an answer to prayer. He too had been wanting to live precisely the sort of life of which Henri Le Saux wrote; he too needed a companion to fulfill his ambition.

Father Jules Monchanin was a remarkable man, born in 1895 in the midst of the vineyards of Beaujolais and ordained in Lyons in 1922. He was that rare combination, a man of exceptional intellectual gifts, able to move easily in the highest philosophical realms, yet who chose to work as a parish priest and spiritual director. One of his friends wrote of how his intellectual and spiritual radiation expressed itself in his wonderful gift for the understanding of ideas and even more for the understanding of souls:

> This gave him the opportunity to make intimate contacts at once with the most learned as well as with the humblest, to assimilate with an extraordinary rapidity the philosophical and the scientifc works of the specialists and to share the artistic emotion of painters, poets and musicians; finally to receive with full love those who wanted to make him the confidant of their personal hopes and difficulties.[28]

Father Monchanin went to India in 1939. Though recognized as a great intellectual, he preferred to do parochial work with the Tamil people in the diocese of Tiruchirapalli, under its new Indian bishop, Dr. James Mendoça. While loving and serving his people in Panneipatti and the neighboring villages, where he lived as a hermit and was revered as a saint, he learned to speak and preach in Tamil and devoted any spare time he had to the world of ideas, particularly to the study of Indian culture and philosophy. He was years ahead of his time, seeking to embody a meeting between Hinduism and Christianity while firmly rooted in the culture of India, an ideal known as "inculturation" that has now been fully accepted by the church.

This, then, was the man to whom Henri's letter was passed, a priest who dreamed of a life of solitude and contemplation and whose ambition was to establish Christian contemplative life in an Indian form. No wonder Father Monchanin responded with such enthusiasm. "Your letter came to me as an answer from God.... I am expecting you. India expects you."[29] Henri, who had by then given up hope, even giving up his studies in English and Tamil, lost little time in telling his sisters:

> There is something like an answer from heaven in this whole set of circumstances, it seems to me. I certainly could not have dreamed of anything better. Someone waiting for me, someone initiating me himself and so making it possible for me not to delay in getting going.... And now listen to this. The Father Abbot has written to the bishop immediately, before even giving me the letter. Pretty extraordinary, don't you think? No one can say that I forced his hand.[30]

His reply to Father Monchanin, the first full record of his ambitions in going to India, was a long and carefully considered letter. He had read an article by Father Monchanin in a prewar issue of *Contemplation et Apostolat* and already felt a kinship with its author; after thirteen years of nurturing his love for India on his own, it is not hard to empathize with his enthusiasm at finding someone with whom he was so much in harmony—though he admits that his own reading had necessarily only been at a very elementary level.

> I say "joy" because it really was a very great joy for me to find someone who loves India and who enters with so much Christian sympathy into the very depths of Indian thought—something which for several years has been my own dearest occupation. You can imagine what it meant to discover someone whom the thought of the *atman**
> leads to the contemplation of the divine Paraclete,[†] and who behind the superficial pantheism discerns the extraordinary intuition of the Spirit reached by the great seers of the Upanishads.[31]

He echoes Father Monchanin's warning that there could be disappointments ahead—he was by then something of an expert in disappointments. Will they find others who will respond to their unusual monastic ideal? He has heard of similar foundations in Travancore and

---

*Atman—the Self, the ultimate ground at once in the human being and in the universe.
†Today more often called the Holy Spirit.

Jaffna—is there room for another? And he must never forget his duty as a member of his monastery at Kergonan. But most importantly he sets out the lines on which he is thinking, qualifying everything with the important statement: "For me a fundamental rule is adaptation to circumstances and submission to reality."[32]

He sees an *ashram* where Hindus and Christians come together for spiritual nourishment and is sure that he and Father Monchanin will be in complete agreement that there should be "total Indianization." A little more tentatively he suggests that their starting point should be the Rule of St. Benedict. While it might seem presumptuous to impose his own monastic rule—to which he was understandably attached—on someone who was not a monk and whose work had been mostly as a parish priest, he puts forward some convincing arguments. He contends that the Benedictine Rule, with its depth and stability, its flexible and universal spirit, would protect them from the need to launch into the unknown; then, little by little, specifically Hindu customs could be grafted onto it. He emphasizes his wish to preserve the nonclerical character of the primitive Rule, throwing wide open to Hindus "the gates of a fully monastic life, to open them to all the many people in India who seem to be touched by the call of mysticism."[33] Thus, the "tree of monasticism" could flourish in its infinite variety, with hermits, solitaries, and mendicants, the spiritual climate sanctified by the contemplative force of India. They would have no ambitions to start an agricultural venture, a publishing house, or a university—"We are monks, seeking to enter even in this life into the kingdom of God."[34]

He takes for granted that their lifestyle will be austere, that they will pray in Tamil and perhaps use Hindu mystical works, that they will work hard, both intellectually and manually, and, what attracts him most, that they will work at a rethinking of Christian dogma in Hindu terms, and a Christian reinterpretation of Hindu thought. He frequently refers to "my beloved Tamils"—though he had not yet met a single one—and dreams of the day when he and Father Monchanin will be fully Tamilian, in dress, life and customs, sitting in the lotus position and taking their meals sitting on banana leaves, sitting on the ground. He loves India with a passion that leads him to write, "her call makes my heart ache."[35]

This was his dream, in 1948, after eighteen years in a Benedictine monastery and at a time when Christians were locked firmly into their own faith, indeed into their own denominations, rarely considering, let alone honoring, other faiths. It was nearly twenty years before the Second Vatican Council began to let some air into the thinking of the Catholic Church. Like Father Monchanin, Henri was years ahead of his time, and like him he was strictly and totally Christian. Much though he already loved India, so far unseen, in those early days he was thinking in terms of the conversion of Hindus to Christianity. He wanted to fashion a Christian India, as earlier Christians had fashioned a Christian Europe. His wish to use Indian prayers and writings was in line with St. Gregory the Great, who told Augustine of Canterbury to preserve for Christ the beautiful temples of idols; in like fashion "could we not preserve for him the beautiful tones inspired by Hindu poets by their deep love of God, even if this is externalized in invocations to Shiva or Kali?"[36] He even uses the French word *païen* (pagan), interchangeably with "Hindu." His aims were unquestionably idealistic, generous, and open-armed, but in 1947, in keeping with the spirit of the time, his aim was similar to the aims of all Christian missionaries.

Henri's ideas corresponded to those of Father Monchanin, who responded warmly, writing from Kulittalai, where he had been parish priest since 1941, and taking the idea of basing their foundation on the Benedictine Rule in his stride:

> Now I am waiting for you to come—because you have really decided, haven't you, to respond to the call you heard fifteen years ago, to become an Indian in India? We shall start together. I will initiate you into Indian life—and you will initiate me into Benedictine life, because like you I firmly believe that the patriarch of the West must in the purpose of God become the patriarch of the East.* His Rule, taken in its original form, is sufficiently flexible to be adapted to every kind of situation and spirituality.[37]

HENRI'S DREAM WAS VERY NEARLY REALITY. He had the permission of his abbot, a place to go, and, most important, a companion who shared his ideals with whom he could live and work. By Christmas he was still worrying whether Solesmes, the motherhouse, would give their permission and whether Rome would give him an indult of exclaustration.† He knew that the visa would take a long time to come through and he had already set the wheels in motion to obtain one. He was torn between longing and fear: "One man who does everything to get out there and sees it through to the end, without hesitating. And the other who is afraid of the sacrifices and feels totally incapable."[38] There was also the need for money. He looked into the possibility of a free ticket to Marseilles and discovered that a reduction on the liner was automatically given to missionaries. Nor

---

*St. Benedict is known as the patriarch of Western monasticism.
†Formal permission for a monk to live ouside his monastery.

was he too proud to accept gifts from friends and relatives, though he admitted that begging for alms made him sweat with humiliation. He had much to learn and many questions to ask: What about the climate of South India? When would be the best time to arrive? What was the exchange rate of the franc to the rupee? What should he take with him in the way of luggage? Until it was possible to dress as a Hindu *sannyāsi,** would it be all right if he kept to the Benedictine habit, but in white cotton rather than black wool?

It is curious that only rarely does he express sadness at parting from his beloved family and never at leaving Brittany. He would not have considered going when his mother was alive, and in the early days of his attempts to go he still worried about Louisette and his father, both without their spouses. Though Louisette remarried in April 1948, his youngest sister Marie-Thérèse had not yet become a nun and his father was alone. And Brittany was still his beloved Brittany. But so great was his desire—perhaps one should even say his need—to go to India that nothing deterred him.

There is a sense of *déjà vu* about the early months of 1948. "No other news at all. I hope there won't be any obstacles about the visa or about Rome. However, you never know. Here I am really struggling. I have the impression that the Father Abbot is less and less happy to see me go."[39] Two months later the same refrain is echoing: "India is not getting anywhere. Rome is asking for explanations . . . what an exercise in perseverance for three years now!"[40] At last, in May 1948, Henri is able to say that Rome has softened and his dream is about to be realized. He is deeply happy and almost unable to believe it; he doesn't even mind if he stays there for ever or "comes back sheepishly. . . . It is so simple. I can't get over how simple it is."[41]

THERE REMAINED THE TASK OF TELLING his brethren at the monastery that he was leaving them. He had been extraordinarily discreet—even his great friend Father Lemarié did not know he was going until he announced his departure. One young monk, however, did come to know, purely by chance. The monk, Brother Robert Williamson, was a postulant in 1947, one of his jobs being to feed the chickens twice a day and collect the eggs. The chicken house was in the wood surrounding the monastery, and one day he was surprised to see a monk wandering around talking aloud to himself in a strange language. Later, when he questioned Henri about it he learned that the wandering monk was practicing Tamil

---

Sannyāsi—one who has renounced all, a Hindu monk, a wandering ascetic.

in what he thought was the privacy of the wood. (This encounter had a fruitful outcome for Henri, as Brother Robert had an English father, who at the time was Britannic Vice Consul at La Rochelle, so was able to help Henri obtain his visa and his passport.)

Finally the day came. On Sunday, July 26, 1948, the abbot asked Henri to celebrate High Mass and after Vespers all the monks gathered to see him off, as Robert's father drove him to Auray to catch the train to Marseilles, where he would board the ship for India. He was much loved, and there was great sadness at his going, some people crying openly and Robert Williamson saying: "For me it was terrible . . . it meant that one of the most sympathetic monks of the monastery was going."[42] For Henri Le Saux it was the fulfillment of a dream that had held him in its grip for fourteen years.

5

The Promised Land

1948–1950

I had been waiting for this moment for fifteen years![1]

On the evening of August 14, 1948, the *Champollion* dropped anchor off Colombo.* Henri was only a few miles from India, and his joy and emotion were unbounded. He stood on deck, watching every flicker of light, the stars in the dark night sky and the crescent moon reflected in the black water.

> The horizon was twinkling with a myriad points of fire, a symbol of all those who are waiting and calling. . . . I was glued to the ship's rail; people tried to talk to me, but I could only answer with difficulty. I had been waiting for this moment for fifteen years![2]

The next morning Henri said his last Mass on board, enchanted that it was the Mass of the Assumption of Our Lady and that as he celebrated her entry into heaven he himself was entering his promised land, so close now that it was almost within sight.

It was a curious time in India's history to be arriving, for two dramatic events had taken place in the preceding twelve months. Exactly a year before, Indians had celebrated their independence, and for the last year the country had struggled with the terrible consequences of the Partition of India and Pakistan. Six months later their revered and beloved leader, Mahatma Gandhi, had been assassinated by a Hindu fanatic. There is no

---

*The capital and main port of the island of Ceylon, at that time part of the British Commonwealth. In 1972, on becoming a republic, the country took the name of Sri Lanka.

53

evidence in his letters that Henri was thinking of these great events—he was living moment by moment as he dealt with police formalities, tried to find his way among rupees, shillings, and pounds, and negotiated with Cook's Travel Agency. He traveled by train with three other priests to Trichy, where he was joyfully met by Father Monchanin, who took him straight to the bishopric to meet the archbishop: everything was being done with due formality—he had received official permission from his monastery to be there and that was duly and formally acknowledged. The next day he traveled by oxcart to introduce himself to the police, already won over, as most Westerners are, by the change in tempo: "We are in the East, nobody is pressed for time and moreover nobody really knows what my coming here is all about at the moment."[3] The next evening they were on a train to Kulittalai, passing pleasant and fertile countryside, rice paddies, coconut palms, and mango and banana trees, Henri catching his first glimpse of the sacred river, the Kavery, which brings fertility to the whole valley.

He was immediately enchanted by the people, feeling not that it was odd to be surrounded by glistening dark skins but that it was he who had an abnormal complexion. "Perhaps I see them with my heart but I wouldn't be able to describe how likeable I find them."[4] He was charmed by the way they thronged around strangers—curious, offering, gesticulating—amazed at the ease with which they talked, or just watched, with impenetrable concentration. On his first day he was approached by a fifteen-year-old boy with Hindu parents who wanted to talk of God, Christ, and the church. He was so bowled over by the meeting that, not knowing what to give the boy but needing to give him something, he left him with his copy of the "Salve Regina" in Tamil, which the boy immediately read with delight.

Eventually they arrived in Kulittalai and went to the Bhakti Ashram, where Father Monchanin was leading a semi-eremitic life while working as a parish priest. To complete the joy of his arrival the night was clear and moonlit. "You can't imagine the beauty of moonlight in the middle of coconut-palms. When I wake up at night, I go out to breathe in the air of the beauty."[5]

The two priests, the missionary Abbé Monchanin and the Benedictine Father Henri Le Saux, were delighted with each other. Monchanin had been longing for Le Saux's arrival, and the next day wrote to a friend that "in essentials—conception of our mission, understanding of Hinduism and the monastic life—he agrees, *more than I had ever hoped*, with what I—what we—have always desired."[6] He was amazed that though as people they were very different, there seemed an amazing convergence in their ideas and aspirations. Henri felt the same, writing that the "correspondence of view and thought between me and Father M, is extraordinary. A providential encounter. The sense of the work to be undertaken is taking shape in utter naturalness."[7] The wind seemed set fair for a fruitful relationship.

Henri took to India as if he had been born to it, and just three months after he arrived, he was able to write to his friend Canon Lemarié, "I think I have found what I have been waiting for for so long."[8] It was as if he had lived there all his life; everything that might have seemed strange was natural to him. This was all the more surprising when one remembers that he had never been out of France before and that this was 1948, long before a visit to India was as natural for a European as a visit to Paris; long before Indian music, clothes, food, and customs had become part of so many Western lives.

He was particularly charmed by the Indian greeting:

No brutal handshakes as in Europe, but the gracious gesture of folded palms raised to the level of the chin. And Christians bow or kneel before their *sami* (priest) upon extending this greeting. In return I must give them the "*asirvadam*," that is to say, I pronounce what signifies a blessing by raising my right hand, if not making the sign of the cross on their foreheads. Because I still cannot talk to them in Tamil.[9]

Instinctively he practiced normal good Tamil manners such as leaving his shoes outside when going into a house and never letting the cup touch his lips when drinking, noting curiously that these customs were not observed by missionaries or even by Indian clergy. He happily followed other local customs, sitting cross-legged on the floor, using a banana leaf for a plate, kneading the rice and spicy sauce with his right hand, the hand he soon learned to keep clean, reserved for eating. Already a vegetarian on principle, the simple meals of dahl and rice were totally acceptable to him, though it was so unusual for a European not to eat meat that he sometimes found himself with no alternative but to join in. One Christmas, dining with a bishop, courtesy demanded that he share a meal in which, "from the rich soup to the pudding made with eggs, there was literally nothing that a *sannyāsi* could eat without sinning!"[10]

He had been advised to adapt to the Indian lifestyle slowly and accepted that he could not yet sleep on a simple mat on the ground, so for the first few weeks he slept on a wooden bedstead. So too he unwillingly used a table and armchair. Within a year he was using the chair only for writing, spending most of his sedentary time on his mat—something he admitted to finding a struggle. After all, his Western bones had, for nearly forty years, accustomed themselves to rather different positions.

At first he wore a white cotton habit in the Benedictine style, but he soon felt more at home in a simple *dhoti*, a strip of cotton cloth around the waist, with another strip, the *tundu*, thrown over the shoulders in cold weather. Six months after his arrival he tentatively—and only in the ashram—started wearing the *kāvi*, the saffron robes of the *sannyāsi*. To his and Father Monchanin's surprise, this was given the full approval of his bishop, though it had no precedent among Christian monks in India. Henri quickly became accustomed to going barefoot, wearing sandals only when visiting a town; last to go was the clerical hat.

There is, of course, great significance in dress; it is outward, obvious, and symbolic. Some Christians were so surprised at the simplicity of his dress that they misunderstood completely. Henri wrote to his family of this incident:

> I do not know if I look too poverty-stricken when I go about with bare feet, wearing a large Indian shawl in place of a monastic habit, but the other Sunday they brought thirty rupees to the parish priest . . . to have some cassocks made for me! It was useless to protest, there was nothing I could do. It is always a great matter of surprise to see me walking about with bare feet and without a hat or, if in a town I am wearing sandals, to see me removing them before entering a house.[11]

Hindus, on the other hand, take the saffron robes to mean that the wearer is a holy man. So Henri was surprised to find that before they could have had any idea of the state of his soul, they took him as a *sannyāsi*, prostrating themselves before him. He wrote of this to Brother Robert Williamson, one of the monks at Kergonan:

> They have the same respect for me as they would for their own monks. The day before yesterday two men I did not know came to make great obeisance before me, prostrated themselves and touched my feet. The other day one of them asked me to help him to understand some Hindu mythology and to direct his spiritual life.[12]

There were those, including theologians assessing his work fifty years later, who were critical of him for wearing the *kāvi*, suggesting that it was a ruse to lure people into his Christian net and was dishonest. That is a harsh interpretation of something that did, at first, have a glimmering of truth, as Henri himself admitted, "we must boldly live in an Indian fashion, think and pray in an Indian fashion, otherwise we shall always be regarded as foreigners, and no one will have any wish for Christ."[13] It might have been deliberate in its intention, but it was not dishonest—he was doing it quite openly and in full realization of what he was doing. A little later, to one of the monks of Kergonan, he wrote:

> I have completely adopted the robes and way of life of the Hindu monks. You would die of laughter if you saw me as I write. We can only succeed in our work if we become Indian right through—right to the depths of our heart and soul—right to the smallest details of daily life.[14]

The inner movements of the spirit are, however, even more telling than the outer symbolism of dress, and as significant as his wearing of Indian dress was Henri's determination to share in the poverty of those around him. Throughout his life he was moved by poverty in others and had long ago lost the slight apprehension experienced in his youth at the thought of not having possessions himself. Now he embraced poverty totally in his own lifestyle and attitudes; at one time he had so little money that he could not afford milk or soya with his daily millet. After a year in India he wrote to his family. "One thing I have learnt in these Hindu surroundings is that one cannot be a real *sannyāsi* if one keeps anything in reserve for the morrow, be it only two annas or a handful of rice. A *'samiar'** should entrust himself totally to Providence."[15] Both he and Father Monchanin believed that monks should live as simply as their neighbors if they are to claim to be men of self-denial and asceticism, and they reckoned that their food at Kulittalai cost only one rupee daily for each of them. Yet Henri heard of a family who clothed and fed a family of seven on a monthly salary of seventy-five rupees, the same money that seemed a small amount for two somehow stretching to feed the whole family.

Most visitors are shocked to the point of tears by the poverty of India. Henri was never to become accustomed to it, never to cease doing what little he could to help. Up to the end of his life he continued to send help to a family in Tamil Nadu, and his letters often speak of the poverty around him.

---

*Correctly *samivar*, the Tamil word for swami.

How do you expect Communism not to prevail here? Yesterday evening I delighted one of my urchins by giving him a vest and shorts. The poor lad did not have a single extra pair to change into when he did his washing. This same boy on Sunday had to be satisfied with a handful of rice in the morning to last him the whole day, and his case is far from unique. How do you suppose that one could take one's meals with pleasure in the midst of this wretchedness, or fail to reduce one's personal expenditure to the minimum? . . . I am afraid to help anybody, because here are always ten or twenty more in the same plight.[16]

Like any foreigner in India, Henri was constantly surrounded by small boys, and he was surprised to discover how at home he could feel with "a gang of urchins." They seemed to have sensed a bond with this strange European priest, barefoot and hatless, who sat on the ground and spoke faltering Tamil, for even the most belligerent took him by the hand most charmingly and "with me become lambs—to the astonishment of the parish priest."[17] His young friends would call for him after school and "competed for the privilege of taking him off to the fields, where they would climb coconut palms and regale him with coconut milk . . . one day he set out alone and returned with a party of forty-six!"[18]

FIFTEEN YEARS OF LONGING and dreaming were now reality, and Henri plunged himself into India with passion. Though he was already calling the Indians "my people" there were some ways in which he found it acutely difficult, almost impossible, to find his place with them, the reason being that great barrier—language. Henri studied Sanskrit, English, and Tamil, "stupefied" to find that everyone, even the well-educated, spoke only colloquial Tamil, while he, needing to understand the scriptures, had also to learn the written form. But he worked so hard and so successfully that in four months he was preaching in Tamil, despite a slight speech impedimiment, which made clear enunciation difficult. He also studied, mainly Hindu scriptures; but he claimed not to have time to think theologically, still less to write. He was never, though, too busy to write letters—he was an inveterate correspondent. So before the books and articles start pouring from him, we can be grateful for the picture of these early years that can be gleaned from his letters, particularly those to his family and to his friend Father Joseph Lemarié. By the end of 1948 he had started the spiritual diary he was to keep until the end of his life, a rare and extraordinary outpouring that gives the most intimate and extraordinarily profound insight into his developing thought.*

Like any enthusiastic new arrival, Henri traveled, visiting temples such as Chidambaram, Kumbakonam, and Tanjore. He devoured details of architecture, iconography, and worship, writing to his friend Canon Lemarié with the puppyish enthusiasm of a tourist:

> How you would love all that I see. The sky, the sun, the countryside, the enchanting Kavery at sunset. . . . And the beauties of manmade things, the great temples with their splendid sculptures. The extraordinarily grand architecture such as that of Madurai and Srirangam, seven walls surrounding the holy of holies, each with its *gopuras*,[†] the rooms with a thousand columns, each pillar carved differently, plant motifs of such a pure line, figures of deities mostly, not grimacing, as is too often said (and is only sometimes true), most often breathing peace, the soul deep in contemplation.[19]

His dress, visibly indentifying him as a priest, led to some discomfiting situations on his travels. He was, after all, a Benedictine monk, in India with the full permission of the Benedictine authorities and therefore capable of embarrassing them, not to mention himself, still an *ingénu* in Indian ways. What does someone who is still essentially an old-fashioned Catholic priest do when he is presented with the sacred ash of Shiva and told to rub it on his forehead? Or offered rice and cakes that have just been presented to the images? "You can understand that all the same our devotion could not go as far as that!"[20] he protested to his family. Perhaps the most embarrassing occasion was when he managed not to see the notice prohibiting non-Hindus from entering the inner sanctuary at the temple at Srirangam and, wearing *kāvi*, he found himself pushed into a corridor in front of a priest, who began to offer a *pūjā* in his honor:

> I have never had such good treatment but, all the same, it was nothing doing, for I should have had to make the *anjali*,[‡] prostrate, spread my hands over the flame and bring them to my eyes, put the

---

*Ascent to the Depth of the Heart. This diary was not written for publication, but a group of Henri's closest friends made the difficult decision to publish it, and the English edition appeared in 1998 (see bibliography).

†Great pyramid-like towers topped with sculptures, marking the temple entrance at each cardinal point.

‡Greeting with the palms together.

ashes on my forehead, etc. . . . I protested—horror, indignation!
"But you never asked me. . . . I have often entered temples!" Finally
I excused myself as well as I could in Tamil and English, made any
number of *namaskaram*[*]—and my confession of faith did not rate a
martyr's crown.[21]

How the forty-six-year-old French priest, audacious intruder into the
inner sanctum of a Hindu temple, must have laughed as he looked back
at the meticuluous *cérémonaire* of Kergonan. Could he have imagined
how much more he was to change in the years ahead?

As he visited the temples, towns, and villages of Tamil Nadu, he came
to know their pastors and their people. He began to realize how Christians were regarded by Indians—the extent to which they were western-
ized and oriented primarily toward good works, attracting followers who,
motivated more by hunger than by spirituality, became known as "rice
Christians." He must have blushed when he heard Christians defined as
people who were white, ate meat, wore leather, and went into holy places
with their shoes on.

Very soon after his arrival in India, Henri and Monchanin went to the
great Hindu pilgrimage at Palni, where the god Murugan is worshiped.[†]
Henri, who was longing to pray in "a beautiful INDIAN church, to celebrate in INDIAN vestments [*sic*]," was allowed to go into the temple
itself, though at that time the clergy regarded any such demonstration of
piety as "satanic." Henri did not consider, even in those early days, that
reverence for Hindu gods was of the devil, in fact he was so deeply
impressed by the occasion that Monchanin, who was with him at the
time, felt it was the moment when his new colleague really touched the
religion of India.

Henri was naturally sad to find that Indian Christians were often isolated from their Hindu neighbors, but there were occasions when they
were able to share. For instance, when he was staying at Kulittalai he was
present for the curious celebrations for the feast of St. James, when a procession of cars was dragged by hand around the village to the accompaniment of drums and fireworks. This was an old Indian custom, now
shared with Christians, and it seems to have received official approval, for
the priests, awakened by the noise at midnight, simply blessed the cars
with sandal-water and went to sleep again.

Henri was at another small village, Kosavapatti, for All Saints Day,

---

[*]Reverent greeting, prostration.

[†]Murugan, the child-god astride a peacock, is, together with the elephant-headed god
Ganesh, much venerated in Tamil Nadu.

when for the first time he heard confessions in Tamil and attended Benediction in the cemetery. So again he experienced the fusion of Christianity with Indian customs, as lights and incense were placed on the graves and the prayers were peppered with the sounds of exploding crackers. Rice, maize, millet, and fruit were heaped on the graves, and later, when the ceremonies were over, it was distributed to beggars.

Such a contrast to the measured tones of Gregorian chant and the precision of liturgical movements at Kergonan. Did he miss France? In those first months—indeed at intervals throughout his life—he would admit to "melancholy recollections of the beautiful chanting of Kergonan"[22] and would wistfully think of the time differences between his native land and his adopted one by remembering that when he was saying Matins, at Kergonan they were sleeping; when he said Sext, they were celebrating Mass. He was French enough to note in his diary that a glass of red wine (which was to become a rare treat) was *Pelure d'Oignon* and initially he was drawn to the French atmosphere of Pondicherry, once a French colony and still boasting a French restaurant, library, and bookshop. To go to Pondi he became "very civilized," wearing shoes, socks, and a *topi*, a domed sun hat:

> I admit that, Indian as I am at heart, I find joy and repose in discovering here a corner of France. Children shout "Bonjour mon Père" at me in the streets, people dress in the French manner, you see the tricolour fluttering, they speak a language you know.[23]

He never lost his love for France, and especially for Brittany; it resonated deep within him. Even in his sixties, after over twenty years of living in India, he admitted that behind all the reasons he gave for not returning even for a visit lay "my fear of not being able to bear it emotionally, and the great difficulty I would have afterwards in taking up my 'role' again."[24] In this nostalgic letter, written much later to a fellow Breton living in New York, he said how close he felt to someone from "our Brittany" and reflected on the contrast between the Himalayas and the moors of Carnac.

> The Himalayas are splendid, and Arunachala is greater still; yet what can be compared to the sea of my Emerald Coast (not blue as a jay's wing, like yours)? All this belongs to the depth of my being. It is like those Tridentine Masses and the Gregorian chant of the monasteries, which I would doubtless put on again like a glove, even after having lived the marvellous experience of "spontaneous"

Masses or of those Masses in the Upanishadic tradition which I celebrate each morning and which help me to carry on.[25]

It was not long before he tired of the French Quarter of Pondicherry and found himself equally at home in the Rue Dupleix, the Indian Quarter. His true Frenchness, the Frenchness that stayed with him all his life, rested in the deep unconscious, in the sea and the sea songs, the wild moors and the stone walls of Saint Briac.

The truth was, as he himself recognized, that he had "two loves." He quickly came to feel completely at home in Indian dress, in fact to live almost entirely as an Indian. His dreams of India did not let him down, and he never lost his feeling of belonging there—indeed others have claimed for him that he came to understand India better than any other Westerner ever has. Nevertheless, he could never forget the country of his birth. After a musical evening with European friends, he wrote to his family:

It was odd. . . . It was as if there were two men in the depth of me—one a Hindu, who finds his happiness in the Rig-Veda and the Bhagavad Gita and delights in the recitation of Sanskrit and in Tamil music, and then another "being," another "self," who bears in himself a whole experience, literary and social, from a western country.[26]

HENRI WAS IMMERSING HIMSELF in impressions of India before putting into practice the idea that he and Monchanin had nurtured for so long. He traveled widely, sometimes with Monchanin, sometimes alone, always with a special interest to his travels, for he was both looking for a site for the ashram he and Monchanin intended to found and also seeking how to flesh out their vision and develop an Indian form of Christian monasticism. He knew he would not find a model, for what he and Monchanin had in mind had not yet been attempted, but he could become familiar with the context in which they would be living.

He soon found likely sites, writing, for instance, about "two spots, just on the bank, out of the way of the flood level, surrounded by trees, far from all noise, one of them two miles (3km) from any habitation, but even so with easy access . . . it is perhaps romantic but it is not Utopia here."[27] He went to Srirangam, an island near Trichy, where the Capuchins live a rule of poverty, but who, despite being Indian, "haven't had the courage to abandon European accoutrements, the '4 paws' [the Tamil word for chairs] nor those strange implements called forks and spoons that the West substitute in a disgraceful way for the natural implements given by the Creator."[28] He was becoming as Indian as any Indian, wandering and planning and dreaming. He wrote to his friend Canon Lemarié:

> If I set myself up on the Kavery, what would you say to a Paschal night, on which following the Prophecies, we would go into procession to the edge of the river, where we would pour consecrated oil into the water, and where from these waters—whence the Hindu has sought purification for two or three millennia—the dead would rise again, the whole activity lit by the mysterious *numinous* light of a Paschal moon. . . . How you would envy me that day![29]

Of the Christian ashrams he visited, perhaps the most significant was Siluvaigiri, at Salem, about fifty miles north of where he was staying at Kulittalai. It had been started by two Benedictine monks from Kerala in 1947* and was significant both because of the deep friendship Henri made with one of the Belgian fathers, Father Dominique van Rollenghen, and also because it was a purely Indian Benedictine foundation, affiliated with the Benedictine Abbey of St. Andrew's in Belgium, the very monks who had sent Henri journals and periodicals about India in his days of despair and hope as he tried to get himself to India. They were trying to live a Benedictine life in India—perhaps their example would be helpful?

Henri visited Siluvaigiri twice in his first six months, which says something for his determination and his affection for the place, for it was quite a journey. To reach it he and his guide had to cross the Kavery in a kind of coracle, then take a four-hour bus journey before walking two kilometers to a small village where they spent the night with the local priest. The next day they took another bus to the foot of a huge range of mountains and crossed the river by foot, eventually reaching the large, shabby building where two Malayali priests and some twenty young men led an austere life of prayer and mission work. Henri was happy there and eager to return, though he was not overly impressed, later referring to the community as "our ideal, a bit watered down"[30] and suggesting that their adaptation was more on the outside than at any depth. An exclaustrated monk in a foreign country can feel isolated and cut off from any roots he might have, and Henri felt supported by the presence of these "brothers in St. Benedict"; he would visit them often, particularly at Easter, which

---

*In 1956 the community moved to Bangalore and took its present name of Asirvanam Monastery.

he was not allowed to spend alone. So, too, the community took to him warmly, calling on him in a crisis and, when they were joined by two Belgian Benedictines from St. André, inviting him to meet them.

Another community that impressed him greatly were the Rosarians, who could be described as Indian Trappists and who lived a life of great simplicity, in almost total silence, under a superior whom Henri considered to be "a real saint" and who led him to appreciate the value of his own twenty monastic years before coming to India. He also visited other orders, for instance, a Jesuit community where he said Mass in a cave where one of the original members of the Society, St. Francis Xavier, had stayed. The community even persuaded him to give some talks—in Tamil —on Gregorian chant and on his plans for the ashram.

He was determined also to visit Hindu ashrams, though it is a vivid reflection of the times that these visits had to be shrouded in secrecy; there were even certain people whom Catholic clergy were not allowed to visit. Half a century later visitors come and go in Hindu ashrams so freely that it is hard to realize how careful they had to be then: "Such visits interest me enormously, but are not to be advertised either in France or in India for no-one would understand."[31] Nevertheless, he and Monchanin visited the monks of Ramakrishna, the celebrated Hindu mystic who had died fifty years before and whose most famous disciple, Vivekananda, had made a great impact at the famous World Parliament of Religions held in Chicago in 1893. Henri also attended the *darshan** of the thinker and mystic Sri Aurobindo, then well into his seventies, who had founded an ashram in Pondicherry together with the Frenchwoman known as "The Mother."

BUT DESPITE HIS EXCITEMENT and the ease with which he adapted to Indian ways, there were disturbing questions. The first murmurings of the problems that were to engulf him, eventually almost drowning him in their complexity, were whispering in his ear. He was a Christian priest who was becoming seriously involved with Hinduism, and he well knew that the two religions were, at least on the intellectual level, incompatible. Monchanin too identified with this, commenting after the visit to the Ramakrishna Ashram that "Dom Le Saux senses, quite independently of me, the human *impossibility* of the conversion of a Hindu who is truly Hindu . . . the more spiritual a Hindu becomes, the further in a sense he distances himself from Christianity."[32] How could he bridge the gulf between the two religions?

Darshan—sight, vision—coming face to face with transcendent Reality in human form.

He wrote to Canon Lemarié about this great theological problem: "I come across spendid souls far from Christ, close to God. Pointless to talk to them of Christ, they are basically incapable of understanding."[33] And to Brother Robert Williamson at Kergonan: "they do not feel the need of Christ; they do venerate him, but for him he is only one of the many routes to reach God. The true religion is beyond the difference of religions—they say."[34] He had come to bring Christian contemplation—and Christianity itself—to India, and he found a people who politely let him know that they were perfectly happy with their own religion:

> Alas, how far these people are from us; they speak of Christ with admiration and read the Bible; but for them Christ is only one of the many manifestations of God on the earth—Krishna, Buddha, Christ, Ramakrishna. . . . The nearer I come to the Hindus, the more I feel them at the same time close to me in their loyal search for God, and far from me in their psychological inability to admit that Christanity is the only authentic means of coming to God.[35]

In bringing Christ to India, so too Henri was bringing the church. He wrote to Lemarié that in India they were living in a time before Christ. "The mystery of souls to whom Christ has never been introduced, also of those who, having heard of Christ, have never felt for them that Christ was an option."[36] So the necessity of belonging to the church appeared to him in a new light: surely where Christ was not known the church was all the more necessary. But he found that the Indian people "cannot understand that it is obligatory to have a definite faith, a fixed creed, and to belong to the Church."[37]

He had no wish simply to transfer Western Christianity to India. What he wanted—everywhere, not just in India—was a specific Christian spirituality evolving out of the particular genius of individual countries, and he felt that India "cannot be alien to this process of assimilation by Christianity and transformation by it."[38] In short, he wanted to Christianize India. He and Monchanin wrote a book together soon after his arrival in India, and they were quite unequivocal that

> Indian wisdom is tainted with erroneous tendencies, and looks as if it had not yet found its own equilibrium. . . . India has to receive humbly from the Church the sound and basic principles of true contemplation, to keep them faithfully, to stamp them with her own seal, and to develop through them along with other members of the Church.[39]

This uncompromising attitude was perhaps not surprising from a former liturgist and *cérémonaire* of Kergonan, the strict, old-fashioned Catholic priest who had been overtaken by this surprising and passionate urge to live in India. That it should eventually come to suit him about as well as saffron robes would suit a right-wing cardinal was in large part due to his meeting with one of the most extraordinary sages living in India at the time.

6

Arunachala

1949–1952

Even before the sun rises, the sky is lit up.[1]

THE MAN WHOM HENRI CREDITED with his real initiation into Indian spirituality was Sri Ramana Maharshi. For more than fifty years the great sage had lived only 150 kilometers from Kulitallai, so a visit became possible soon after Henri's arrival in India. Monchanin and Henri often talked of him, and Monchanin was deeply impressed by him, even though he said there was "not an *atom* of Christianity in that serene and beautiful spirit."[2] In January 1949, Monchanin suggested that they go to see him together. The bishop, to their surprise, supported the visit and urged them to stay in the ashram itself.

Ramana Maharshi fitted the description of holiness bestowed on St. Teresa of Avila, for though his influence was far-reaching and profound, he was, in some inscrutable way, "extraordinarily ordinary." By the time Henri visited the ashram, hundreds of people of many different nationalities, religions, and occupations had flocked there to receive his *darshan*. His first Western disciple, in 1911, was a high-ranking member of the Madras police force. In the 1950s Paul Brunton spread his fame by writing of him in his book *In Search of Secret India,* and the English writer Somerset Maugham based the guru in his novel *The Razor's Edge* on Ramana Maharshi. A powerful description of the sage comes from one of his biographers, Arthur Osborne:

> Sri Bhagavan* would turn to the devotee, his eyes fixed upon him with blazing intentness. The luminosity, the power of his eyes

---

*Literally, "God." A title used for one like Sri Ramana who is recognized as having realized his identity with the Self.

pierced into one, breaking down the thought-process. Sometimes it was as though an electric current was passing through one, a vast peace, a flood of light. One devotee has described it: "Suddenly Bhagavan turned his luminous, transparent eyes on me. Before that I could not stand his gaze for long. Now I looked straight back into those terrible, wonderful eyes, how long I could not tell. They held me in a sort of vibration distinctly audible to me."[3]

Ramana Maharshi's influence on Henri was so profound that it is worth knowing something about this remarkable man. Ramana Maharshi was born at a significant time in the Hindu calendar. It was December 29, 1879, and Tiruchuzhi, a little town in Tamil Nadu, was celebrating the festival of Arudra Darshan, when the god Siva appears as Nataraja in the cosmic dance of creation. The image of Siva was garlanded with flowers, and, all day and most of the night, it was taken through the streets to the sound of drum and conch and the chanting of the people, the men clad only in the *dhoti* and the women wearing deep red and gold saris. The processions and celebrations continued far into the night, and as dawn was breaking the image was taken back to the temple. At just that moment a child was born to Alagammal, the wife of Sundaram Ayyar, an accountant's clerk. The child was named Venkataraman and was later to be revered as an embodiment of Siva and known as Sri Ramana Maharshi.

In most ways, Venkataraman was a normal enough boy, athletic, fond of football, wrestling, and swimming, and blessed with an amazingly retentive memory that enabled him to repeat a lesson after hearing it just once. The one odd thing about him was the depth of his sleep; he would sleep so deeply that his friends would shout and bang at the door to wake him—they would even beat him and carry him around and put him back to bed, and he would know nothing about it until they told him the next mornng. He saw no significance in this, though later devotees regarded it as an early sign of his ability to plunge beyond thought. Doctors of the twenty-first century would perhaps see it as some sort of seizure.

Venkataraman read little religious theory, but he had heard of the sacred mountain of Arunachala, and when he discovered that it was a real place and not all that far away, he was amazed and excited. Soon after that he discovered the life stories of the Tamil saints and he realized that the divine could be manifested in both places and in people. A throbbing awareness began to awaken in him, a state of bliss. "At first I thought it was some kind of fever," he said, "but I decided, if so it is a pleasant fever, so let it stay."[4]

Only a few months later this "current of awareness"[5] grew until Venkataraman reached a state rarely attained permanently during life on earth, a state for which it is hard to find a name. It has been called self-realization, *sahaja samadhi*, enlightenment, unity consciousness, and mystical union. Most of the spiritual texts in Sanskrit use the word "Awakening," as did Ramana himself, and as did Henri Le Saux—Awakening to the Self.

The young Venkataraman reached this state in a curious way. He was a healthy young man of seventeen when suddenly he was overcome with a violent fear of death. He dealt with this fear by lying with his limbs outstretched, stiff as though he were already dead, holding his breath and asking himself various questions:

> Now death has come; what does it mean? What is it that is dying? This body dies . . . it will be reduced to ashes. But with the death of this body am I dead? Is the body I? . . . The body dies but the Spirit that transcends it cannot be touched by death. That means I am deathless Spirit.[6]

As his senses withdrew from outer objects and his mind from thought, in a flash he realized "[t]hat all passes away and disappears; but *myself* I remain, *I am*." "A lightning-flash; the eye blinks—Ah!—the sign of Brahman" (Kena Upanishad).[7] From that moment all fear of death vanished, and his constant questions were Who am I? What is the Self?

Soon after this experience he was drawn to the sacred mountain of Arunachala, where he spent the rest of his life as Sri Ramana Maharshi, for years in silence and solitude and then, for the last years of his life, available to the devotees who were increasingly drawn to him, aware that he had reached a rare stage of enlightenment and eager to sit in his presence.

Ramana Maharshi taught the purest form of *advaita*, or nonduality. The word *advaita* comes from the Sanskrit words *a-* and *dvaita*, literally "not two"—nonduality. It is the fundamental insight of the Upanishads and one that was to dominate the rest of Henri's life. Its central teaching is the oneness of the individual soul with the Absolute, and Ramana taught it through the discipline of self-knowledge. This is as hard to communicate as any mystical experience, and language can be a barrier, particularly because the word "Self" is sometimes misunderstood in Christian cultures, where it tends to be equated with selfishness or self-centeredness. What, then, did Ramana Maharshi mean by the word? What is the Self?

In answer to questions about the nature of the Self, Ramana Maharshi would say, "The only reality is the Self," or "The Self is the center of centers." "The Pure Mind—the mind free from thoughts is the Self." Or perhaps most simply, "The Self is only Be-ing, not being this or that. It is simply Being." He was teaching his disciples that supremely simple art that most people, especially people for whom the mind is king, find so supremely difficult—simply "to be."

He taught his disciples largely by silence but also by what he called "investigation," arguing that just as water is found by boring a well, so also you realize the Self by investigation. Some of these exchanges have been recorded.

D. How to realize the Self?

M. It is already realized. One should know this simple fact. That is all.

D. But I do not know it. How shall I know it?

M. Do you deny your existence?

D. No; how can that be done?

M. Then the truth is admitted.

D. Yet, I do not see. How shall I realize the Self?

M. Find out who says "I."

D. Yes, I say "I."

M. Who is this "I"? Is it the body or some one besides the body?

D. It is not the body. It is someone beside it.

M. Find it out.

D. I am unable to do it.

M. Find out wherefrom this "I" arises. Then this "I" will disappear and the infinite Self will remain.

D. Wherefrom *does* it arise?

M. Find out.

D. I do not know. Please enlighten me.

M. It is not from without. It is from within. Where does it come from? If elsewhere you can be led there. Being within you must find out yourself.[8]

THOUGH RAMANA'S WRITINGS had not been translated into French at the time, Henri had read enough about him in articles in various periodicals to be convinced that his visit to the famous sage was going to be a high point in his life.

The *darshan* took place in a large open shelter, supported on bamboo poles and covered with coconut leaves, known as a *pandal* in India. It had by then become something of a ritual and in view of Ramana's age—he was seventy at the time and very frail after a life of asceticism—disciples and devotees were allowed to come into his presence only at certain times. Henri was convinced that something was going to take place between them, that he would receive a message, if not in words at least something communicated spiritually. But there is nothing so destructive of fulfillment as high expectation. Nothing happened, and he felt let down and filled with sadness. He did not even like the context in which he met the sage—the liturgical atmosphere, the constant reference to him as "Bhagavan," which, as it means "Lord," he considered almost blasphemous when applied to a human being. All he could see was an old man with a gentle face and beautiful eyes. So ordinary, rather like his own grandfather. All through the meal that followed the *darshan* Henri could not take his eyes off him. He watched him eat the same food as they did, use his fingers just as they did, occasionally talk as they did. But how could he accept being called "Bhagavan"? Why did he allow himself to be worshiped in this way? Where was the halo? Ironically, in view of the importance Ramana was to have in his life, this first meeting was a huge disappointment.

Later they returned to the *pandal,* where, for the first time Henri heard the Vedas chanted, as timelessly and simply as they had been chanted by the rishis in the forests for thousands of years. These archetypal sounds drew him as nothing so far had done. Something was stirring, though this was not destined to be the high experience for which he had hoped. He woke the next morning with a fever, and by evening he knew he had to leave. He could not burden the ashram with illness.

But before he left he had an important encounter with Ethel Merston, a sensitive and kindly Englishwoman who had known Gurdjieff, Ouspenski, and Krishnamurti and who always spent her holidays at Tiruvannamalai. On hearing of his disappointment, she spoke bluntly:

> "You have come here with far too much 'baggage,'" she said. "You want to know, you want to understand. You are insisting that what is intended for you should necessarily come to you by the path which you have determined. Make yourself empty; simply be receptive: make your meditation one of pure expectation."[9]

Perhaps the outer fever was an expression of some profound inner transformation. After Ethel's firm and kindly words, his consciousness mysteriously changed, even before his mind recognized it:

The invisible halo of the Sage had been perceived by something in me deeper than any words. Unknown harmonics awoke in my heart. A melody made itself felt, and especially an all-embracing ground-bass. . . . In the Sage of Arunachala of our own time I discerned the unique Sage of the eternal India, the unbroken succession of her sages, her ascetics, her seers; it was as if the very soul of India penetrated to the very depths of my own soul and held mysterious communion with it. It was a call that pierced through everything, tore it apart and opened a mighty abyss.[10]

As the fever abated, he realized the depth of himself to which the sage of Arunachala had penetrated. He would never be quite the same again.

SIX MONTHS LATER HE RETURNED to Tiruvannamalai, now released from his Western clothes and comfortable in *kāvi*, the two strips of orange cloth worn by Hindu ascetics, only to find Ramana very ill with a tumor on his arm and unable to see anyone but his medical helpers and closest friends. However, Ethel used her influence to find him somewhere to stay, and during his time there Ramana began to hold *darshan* again, Henri saying of this that he did his best to keep his rational mind in abeyance and tried "simply to attend to the hidden influence."[11]

He spent some time wandering around the caves hewed into the side of the mountain, meditating in crevices in the rock but careful not to disturb the hermits living there, motionless in their caves. He talked to Ramana's disciples and learned more about the sage he was coming to venerate so deeply. A Telegu brahmin explained Ramana's teaching to him, using the philosophical terminology which at that time Henri found very congenial, though it was not a conversation that he recounted when he later came to write about this experience. All he said was, "But now, as I look back, I cannot help smiling gently at such attempts to define in intellectual terms that which by its very nature excludes the possibility of being reduced to *ideas*.[12] Another brahmin told him of the marvelous indifference with which Ramana bore his suffering and how his central teaching was to find the heart deep within oneself, beyond mind and thought.

But once again it was Ethel Merston who opened his eyes to something that had so far eluded him—that at Arunachala there was not only a great sage but a temple and, most of all, a mountain, Arunachala itself. Grace could be bestowed through any of these three channels. One day it would be the mountain itself that would draw him.

He listened carefully, but it was to be some time before he really understood, and understanding served only to multiply the divisions inside him. He had already admitted to having "two loves"—India and France. Now more divisions were appearing. He was a French priest wearing the clothes of a Hindu ascetic and longing to penetrate the spirit of Hinduism. He was deeply Christian, and of the old-fashioned variety, never traveling without his Mass kit and unable to say Mass unless there was room to stand upright and a door that could be locked to prevent the sacred vessels being profaned—two conditions not readily found in a cave in a mountainside. Now, as he came to love the mountain, he found his heart divided between the sacred river Kavery, where he lived with Father Monchanin, and the sacred mountain of Arunachala.

It was two and a half years before he returned to Tiruvannamalai. He had intended to go in the spring of 1950, but as he prepared to leave Kulittalai he read in a Tamil paper that Sri Ramana had died and that at the moment of his death a beam of light had flashed across the sky and was seen by the sage's disciples as far away as Madras, though they were unaware of its significance. Despite the love he was beginning to feel for the mountain, if the Maharshi was not at Tiruvannamalai then Henri had no desire to be there.

However, while taking some European friends around Tamil Nadu, he found himself so near Tiruvannamalai that he suggested they visit the ashram. The Vedas were chanted at Ramana's tomb, and once again Henri fell under their spell; even more significantly, he discovered that there were hermitages scattered around the mountainside. A brahmin, who looked after the visitors, told Henri that there was an empty cave overlooking the temple and that Henri was welcome to settle there. He began to understand. "If Ramana was himself so great, how much more so must be this Arunachala which drew Ramana to himself?"[13]

The mountain had begun to cast its spell over him.

It is all up with anyone who has paused, even for a moment, to attend to the gentle whisper of Arunachala. Arunachala has already taken him captive, and will play with him without mercy to the bitter end. Darkness after light, desertion after embraces, he will never let him go until he has emptied him of everything in himself that is not the one and only Arunachala and that still persists in giving him a name, as one names *another*—until he has been finally swallowed up, having disappeared for ever in the shining of his Dawn-light, *Aruna*.[14]

The italicized *another* is the only sign he gives of the oneness, the unity, that lay ahead of him.

So AT THE END OF MARCH 1952, Dom Henri Le Saux, a European Benedictine monk in his early forties, having by then taken the name of Swami Abhishiktananda, for the first time dressed, ate, and lived as a *sādhu*, a wandering monk, in the caves of Arunachala. The fact that he also lived in silence he attributed to the "spell-binding wiles" of the mountain: he tells how this came about in his typically self-deprecating way. When he arrived he spent a few days at the ashram, making the necessary arrangements, while admitting that the real *sādhu* would simply drop everything, bow reverently toward the mountain, and sit down in the first convenient cavity he sees. "But alas, how long it takes for those who are burdened with bodily and mental baggage to become once more simply themselves and as natural as children."[15] He was taken to a large cave known as the cave of Vanatti, previously occupied by "the pickaxe monk" (so called because he was often seen carrying a pickaxe), and introduced to the watchman, Kadirvel. Kadirvel's eyes lit up at the sight of white skin, assuming that the owner would have plenty of cash and that rich visitors would call, and he set about drawing and carrying water, cleaning the cave and running small errands. And of course he talked. Exasperated by the continual chatter, Abhishiktananda decided that the only thing he could do was to let it be known that he was keeping total silence. Arunachala had won again; Abhishiktananda had no alternative but to honor his promise. That evening he wrote in his diary: "Deep joy, deep peace. Not even any reading possible, the *antaram* [*sic*] (the interior) is too 'busy.' Hunger itself hardly intrudes, even though since last evening I have eaten nothing but bananas."[16]

His day started early in the morning. While it was still dark, he would say Mass in his cave, deep in the heart of the mountain. Then he would sit in front of his *sacro speco*,* as he called his cave, and wait for the sun to rise. As the dawn broke, blazing with the warm redness that gives the mountain its name,† he would greet it in the Indian way, hands together about his head, and, making a full prostration, sing the "Lumen Christi" and the "Gloria" as they are sung at dawn in the Syrian church. He sang Lauds, saying the Lord's Prayer with his arms stretched out facing Tiruvannamalai, the town at the foot of Arunachala. (It is a measure of his involvement with the place that the town had already become another

---

*"Sacred space," as St. Benedict's cave at Subiaco was known.
†Arunachala: *aruna* is the rosy color of the dawn; *achala* means "mountain."

word that he prefaced with the personal pronoun—it was now "my" Tiruvannamalai as it was "my" Hindus and "my" people.)

Soon realism joined him in the cave. It was all very well that he was clothed in saffron robes and sitting, relatively comfortless, in a cave. But what if . . . ? What if he knew he would be there forever? What if no one knew or cared that he was there? What if no one brought him his midday meal and he had to beg for his food? Would he still feel such joy?

Then, in the depth of his soul, he heard what he called "the call to total dispossession."

> the call to total stripping,
> which is the call to total freedom;
> since he only is free who has nothing,
> absolutely nothing that he can call his own.[17]

His silence, undertaken almost accidentally in self-defense, was to be the bearer of countless graces.

On his first evening in the cave of Vanatti Abhishiktananda received three powerful intimations, which he recorded in his spiritual diary. He accepted Hindu *sannyāsa** as an end in itself, not merely as a means of proclaiming the Christian Gospel. He embraced silence. And he went even further in his acceptance of poverty, promising himself to take his bowl and, without any feeling of shame, beg for his food, for a true *sannyāsi* has *nothing* in reserve, not even a handful of rice; he entrusts himself totally to Providence. Abhishiktananda determined that he would live for ever as a genuine Christian *sannyāsi*, a Hindu-Christian monk.

Such insights are not usually immediately fulfilled, and these were not. Only two days later he was in evangelical mode, writing "My dream is to christianize my race . . . it is a question of preparing for a Christian India, of preparing for it not by using various ways and means, but by myself being among the first-fruits by opening a path."[18] The way had changed; he would not proclaim the gospel in the traditional manner of missionaries, but the goal remained the same. He still believed that only by embracing Christianity would India find spiritual fulfillment.

His determination to bury his pride and beg for his food was a matter over which, at first, he compromised. He had wanted to share in the distribution of rice at the temple, but this practice was about to cease, so he accepted a proper midday meal, in silence, from one of the temple man-

---

Sannyāsa—the life of total renunciation.

agers, who considered it an honor to give alms to the new *sādhu*. He would then go to the market and buy a few bananas for his evening meal, showing the shopkeeper a coin, though it was never accepted. He was, visibly, a *sannyāsi* and he was treated as one.

Of these three intimations, the most important was silence, the still pool where his understanding was to mature and where enlightenment was born, the aspect of his being that was to permeate the rest of his life. This first spell of silence lasted for ten days, but he returned in May, staying at the cave of Vanatti for three weeks and then, when the building of an open-air cinema at the foot of the mountain below his cave ruined his peace, moving to the cave of Arutpal Tirtham, the cave known as "the spring of the milk of grace."

As always, he did not take himself too seriously over the question of silence, often admitting to a contradictory attitude, acknowledging his great love of company and laughing at himself for preaching silence while loving to talk. Nor did he always find it easy—sometimes when visitors called he felt the sacrifice acutely. But he had made it clear that he did not want to be disturbed and was, as he put it, "caught out at my own game" when he found he was regarded as a *munivar*, an ascetic who is vowed to silence. Even when the police came to see him they allowed the exchanges to take place wordlessly, on paper; and to the embarrassment of the new *sādhu*, people came and prostrated before him, offering him all the signs of reverence that are usually offered to idols in temples. "They sat in meditation; meanwhile the Buddha remained sitting in the lotus position, motionless at the back of the cave,"[19] he wrote. Once when seriously tempted to conversation by the presence of an interesting visitor, he asked himself firmly, "What would the professor learn from the monk if he were to divert him from the One and Only?"[20] So he kept silence, allowing both himself and his visitor to be taught by silence.

Once he had accepted the silence, he learned to value it, to love it. He was "willing to remain *for ever* in my cave, keeping silence, without any concern for keeping witness. To be the first Christian for God at the Holy Mountain of Arunachala."[21] Gradually he was drawn away from reminders of ordinary life, discovering that there were different sorts of silence. The outer form, simply not speaking, and the great inner silence, "the abstinence from all thought, of the indescribable solitude of the Alone, deep within."[22] Silence was to be the vast arena in which the drama of his search was to be played out.

Just before the end of this first stay in the cave of Vanatti he wrote a poem to Arunachala, a love poem acknowledging what his beloved mountain was teaching him.

In silence you teach me silence, O Arunachala,
You who never depart from your silence,
May I not have entered Your cave in vain;
of "mine" and "me" may nothing any longer remain.[23]

He was discovering a peace he had never imagined possible, though he knew he had not yet reached the inmost depth where,

> . . . alone and without a second, *advaita*, You are.
> "You shine in the form of Self
> You are 'I.'"[24]

The poem ends with a ringing declaration of "Jesus Brahman!" Arunachala was passing on its message that the essence of Hinduism and Christianity, indeed of all religions, is the same.

It is typical of the man that his time at Arunachala, while focusing most on deep silence, like "pure water, or air which is so purified that it has no discernible odour"[25] was full of people, encounters that he records in loving detail. There were the people dedicated to look after him as well as uninvited visitors to the cave—sometimes children would come after school and sit silently gazing at him. Wordlessly he formed a friendship with his nearest neighbor, Lakshmi Devi, a highly esteemed woman with many disciples who kept a vow of silence for twelve years.

Once his period of silence was over, he would go and visit someone every afternoon—and indeed there was a rich mixture of people, "a jumble of the devout."[26] There were Hindus, Parsees, Muslims, Protestants, and Jews, all drawn to the irresistible combination of sage, mountain, and temple. He told his friend Canon Lemarié of the French woman who worshiped at Sacré Coeur and Fatima and who considered Buddha, Shiva, and Ramana Maharshi to be her gurus; of the doctor who came to India and became first a Buddhist monk, then a theosophist, then married a Hindu girl and went from ashram to ashram "making up a spiritual cocktail as undrinkable as the 'cocktails' of liqueurs that your cross-Channel neighbours are so fond of."[27] He met the esoteric Sujata, who was impressed by the brightness of his halo, and a professor who specialized in Persian poetry, who likewise exclaimed how radiant he was looking. Abhishiktananda was intrigued—"Could it be, then, that even at the physical level something passes from the mountain of Arunachala into the hearts of those who shelter in its caves?"[28] He developed a great admiration for Srimati Radhabai Ammeyar, who lived in a cave so small and low that even when he was seated there was just a hair's breadth between head and roof and whose daily and only meal, during her three years of silence, was a few handfuls of rice flour, roasted and mixed with curds. And there was a young *sādhu* called Saccidananda, whose singing delighted Abhishiktananda as much as the chattering of some of Radhabai's guests irritated him. He readily admitted that he did not have the patience of his new friend.

While he was living in the cave of Vanatti he was living almost totally as a Hindu monk, yet, like all non-Hindus at that time, he was not normally allowed into the central part of Hindu temples; he could go only as far as the outer courts. He was to become a rare exception to this rule. One day during his period of silence he was visited by Arunachala Gurukkal, one of the priests of the temple of Annamalaiyar.* The priest often came to see him and, through signs and through writing in Tamil, they managed to communicate at such a deep level that the Hindu, clearly impressed by this Christian priest, insisted that once his period of silence was over, he personally would show him everything in the temple. Although delighted, Abhishiktananda was well aware of both his monastic status and his priesthood and was always careful not to be taken for a Christian turned Hindu; he would have to "exercise all my casuist-canonist subtlety to remain outside any participation in formal worship. . . . Above all I must avoid the scandal and false interpretations of too broadminded an attitude."[29] He accepted, of course. How could he resist it?

In the event, it was his friend's elder brother, one of only two temple priests who had the right to sit beside the image during the great processions, who was his guide. First they went around the outside of the temple, past the old banyan tree where *sādhu*s, young and old, men and women, sick and healthy, said their rosaries and chanted *OM namah Shivaya*.† As they walked through the pillared halls, cloisters, and side chapels, his guide explained the symbolism, but as they approached the shrine itself, the holy of holies, it was in darkness and silence. Eventually they entered the sanctuary itself, the place beyond symbols, where the stone of the Shivalinga stands. Of this Abhishiktananda writes nothing except that it was "the sign of the Presence of the Lord Arunachala in the midst of his people, and the pledge of his grace."[30] His brevity on this subject, his unwillingness to search for words, seems appropriate.

---

*The Tamil word for the Lord of Arunachala.
†"Om Glory to Shiva."

The depth of the relationship between Abhishiktananda and Aruna-chala Gurukkal was shown when Abhishiktananda had to leave Aruna-chala on short notice and was distressed that he had no time to say goodbye to his friend. But suddenly there was Gurukkal, standing in the entrance to the cave, asking what had happened. "I was lying half-asleep in one of the mandapas of the Temple, when you came and touched me on the side. I awoke with a start, ran straight home, took my bath, and without waiting to have my meal, I came up here. . . . It is the *lila** of the Lord Arunachala."[31]

So too he learned more about the mountain of Arunachala. The name means "dawn-colored mountain" and it has been worshiped as the abode of Siva since the beginning of time. Hindu mythology crystallizes around the great figures of Brahma, Vishnu, and Siva, who form a triad of Hindu gods. They each have many attributes, but broadly Brahma is the god of creation, Vishnu is the preserver of the universe and the embodiment of goodness and mercy, Siva combines the three roles of creator, preserver, and destroyer. The legend is that there was a dispute between Brahma and Vishnu about who came first and who was the greater. As this undignified argument raged, a vast column of light appeared between them. They agreed that the first to reach the foot or the summit of the column of fire and to return to where they were as they spoke would be taken as the greatest. Hundreds of years passed, but neither Brahma nor Vishnu could find either the beginning or the end of the great column of flame. How could they? It had neither a beginning nor an end. It was Siva who had appeared in this guise and who was seen to be the greatest. Siva, as Abhishiktananda put it, "is unique and infinite with the uniqueness and infinity of Being itself."[32]

Through the ages of the world the *linga* of fire became first a mountain of diamond, then of ruby and, in our time, a mountain of rock, accessible by ordinary mortals and able to bring salvation, for, according to Hindu mythology, in Siva-Arunachala the Supreme Lord is made visible. Ramana Maharshi wrote thus:

> To its caves, age after age, there has come a succession
> of those who are hungry for wisdom and renunciation,
> whom the Mountain, the divine Magnet,
> draws to its bosom,
> to teach them in its own silence

*The creation as divine play.

the royal path of the supreme Silence,
and how to be established in the Self.[33]

THESE FIRST THREE VISITS to Arunachala changed Abhishiktananda radically. The silence of the mountain had transformed *advaita* from an inspiring subject of intellectual discussion to an experienced reality. Not yet, it is true, a permanent reality, but something frequently glimpsed and gratefully recognized that enabled him to say, "Even before the sun rises, the sky is lit up." His motivation in coming to India had to be reassessed, and he wrote to his sister Marie-Thérèse that he was not a missionary, "just a poor Christian monk in the midst of Hindu monks"[34] and that he was "not a Hindu monk in order to bring about conversions. For me the Indo-Christian monastic way of life is an end in itself, not a means."[35] Ramana's ashram had shed new light on the gospel, and now he knew that "it will not be monastic institutions, more or less perfect in both Christian and Indian terms, that will reveal Christ to India. Only Christian Ramanas will do it. All that monks can do is to prepare the way for these Ramanas."[36]

Moments of illumination such as he experienced in those weeks are beyond words and cannot be shared easily, so it is not surprising that his early attempts to express the inexpressible are mostly found in his diary. One of the striking aspects of the entries made during this third visit to Arunachala was his struggling to make distinctions between theoretical understanding and experience—indeed between opposites of any kind. He was urging himself to be free from the mind, yet he was using his mind; he had to if he was to reflect on what was happening to him. It is as if he was drawing attention to distinctions and paradox in order to show that they can be transcended.

For instance, he was finding that in India there is little distinction between God's work and human work—all is the work of the Spirit. Then the distinction between time and eternity is stressed as he is drawn into God's *līlā*, the divine play of creation. In semi-poetic style he writes:

If I act like a sulky child who says: I don't want to play, not I!—
then from eternity I fall into time
from Spirit I fall into flesh.[37]

He overrides Pauline value judgments about the opposites of flesh and spirit, content to acknowledge that the flesh is necessary to manifest love. "The human being is also spirit, but he is flesh at the same time. . . . He cannot escape from the law of the flesh, from his condition as an incarnate spirit."[38] At the heart of this polarity, again beyond the opposites, lies God becoming Man in the incarnation, the "essential sacrament following necessarily and absolutely from the material condition of the human world."[39]

As he experienced the transcending of distinctions, so his attitude to theology and the liturgy began to change. On the feast of the Trinity in June he was deeply disappointed by the liturgy of the day, presenting the Trinity as something external, "repeating, alas, not the faltering words of wondering children, but unassimilated scholastic formulas."[40] Now he could only celebrate the Trinity inwardly: "I don't know how to adore the Trinity, for I am within it, and I do not know which way to turn to make the *sashtangam.** I am at the very centre in the centre who is the son."[41] Many times he struggles to express *satori*, or enlightenment. It is attained "when I have realized that the centre is as truly everywhere as it is in 'myself.'"[42] It is "a state of being beyond, in which we sink." But, he asks, with echoes of Ramana Maharshi's constant question, "Who am I?," "What is it that sinks?" "I do not know, but there is a 'sinking,' as when we say that we sink into sleep, sink into our mother's arms. A 'surrender' of self, but a surrender to no one and to no thing, but just a surrender."[43]

Perhaps it is a lack of confidence in this new state, perhaps his typical modesty, that leads him to write in the third person about something that it is clear he has experienced himself. An entry in his diary toward the end of this 1952 visit to Arunachala has the directness and simplicity of true experience.

> Anyone who has attained satori, anyone who has been enlightened, continues to see grass as green and the sky as blue, to consider rice as something to eat and cloth as something to wear, and the train as a means of transport. What he is liberated from is the relationship to "himself" that until then he projected onto these things. Things are seen in themselves, and no longer in dependence on "himself." Dear ones are no less loved, but there is no longer the least attachment, the least turning back on "himself."[44]

HE WAS TO VISIT ARUNACHALA many more times, times that were to bring about tensions in his inner life that would nearly cause him to break. His Hindu friends expected him to stay near the mountain, and indeed he was tempted, though did not feel he had yet the inner strength to live a life of nothing but solitude, silence, and poverty. In any case there were practical matters to be attended to. Abhishiktananda had, after all, come to India to help Father Monchanin found a Christian ashram.

---

*Full prostration.

7

A Pioneering Experiment

Shantivanam 1949–1952

Oh, the anxieties of a "contemplative"![1]

IN DECEMBER 1949, soon after Abhishiktananda's second visit to Arunachala—a visit he did not know was to be his last meeting with Ramana Maharshi, Father Monchanin and he decided on a site for their ashram. His dream of coming to India had turned into reality; now they could put flesh on the bones of their vision of a dialogue between Christianity and Hinduism. This was a path untrodden since the first steps taken by their two great predecessors Robert de Nobili in the seventeenth century and Brahmabandhab Upadhyaya at the turn of the nineteenth. Abhishiktananda was to walk this path in his own, highly personal way.

The chosen site was on the banks of the sacred river Kavery, just above flood level and far from noise, though close to the little village of Tannirpalli. It had been offered by one of Father Monchanin's parishioners, and Henri had had his eye on it since the beginning of the year. It was an old mango grove with palmyra trees, tall straight ashoks, neem trees, and the pipal, or Bodhi tree, sacred to Hindus and to Buddhists, for it was under its branches that the Buddha found enlightenment. They called it Shantivanam, the wood of peace, and the ashram was named Saccidananda Ashram, from the Sanskrit words *sat*, "being," *cit*, "consciousness," *ananda*, "bliss"—in Vedanta the attributes of God. The name was carefully chosen, for there are some who find that this ancient word finds a parallel in the Christian Trinity. At the beginning of 1950 two huts were built on this idyllic site, and on March 21, 1950, the feast of St. Benedict, the parishioners of Kulittalai, sad at the departure of their beloved Father Monchanin, came to celebrate the inauguration of the ashram and, with the full and explicit backing of the bishop of Trichinopoly, the two priests began their new life.

The two hermits wore *kāvi* robes, and around their necks the Benedictine cross with the *pranava*, the sacred syllable OM, engraved in its center. The meeting of Hinduism and Christianity was to start with their very selves. This was the moment when they took their new names. Father Monchanin became *Parama Arubi Ananda* (Bliss of the Supreme Formless One), and Henri took the name *Abhishikteshvarananda* (Bliss of the Anointed One, the Lord). Father Monchanin rarely used his new name, but Henri became known by the slightly shortened form of his new name, Abhishiktananda. Later he was increasingly to be called, especially by close friends, simply Swamiji. At the time they thought that in doing this they were following Indian tradition; in fact they were not, for there was no formal initiation into the Indian tradition.

Poverty and simplicity were central to their living conditions, as both men were adamant that they did not want to live at a higher standard than their neighbors; certainly their living conditions were primitive. Each had a hut with walls of bamboo and a roof of coconut leaves. There was no furniture, and the flooring was simply a few bricks to keep the floor dry and to serve as bed, chair, and table. Even this Monchanin said was "too spacious and almost luxurious."[2] One of the huts had a verandah, where they said Mass, and a wooden structure was built for their books, just large enough to be called a library.

Their high ideals were soon shattered as the bamboo walls first turned out not to be proof against the snakes and scorpions. The walls were then eaten by white ants and had to be replaced by solid walls. Finally the rains led to an invasion of forest wildlife, so the crevices between the bricks had to be filled with what Abhishiktananda called "luxurious cement"[3] and the roof tiled against the monkeys. So realism triumphed over idealism, and Abhishiktananda wrote wistfully, "Our hovels begin to have a palatial air."[4]

Nevertheless, the dreams that had first surfaced from Abhishiktananda's deep unconscious in 1934, the hopes that had survived so many disappointments, were being realized. Now that the permitted vagueness of dreams had turned into solid reality, what form did they take? In the context of Christians living in India, this was so unusual a venture that it is worth saying first what it was not. The venture was not a monastery with fixed times for prayer, work, and study and regulated by the ringing of bells. It was not engaged in trying to make a living from the land. It was not doing charitable work such as opening a dispensary or providing education. It was not engaged in study, and it was not a missionary endeavor seeking conversions. However, the poverty of the lifestyle of the monks, their use of Indian symbolism and postures, and their sympathy with the thought and religion of the Indian people could not fail, as Abhishiktananda wrote, "to be of singular use in the Church's great work of christianising India."[5]

For anyone familiar with Abhishiktananda's later writing, the extent of his evangelism in these early days, though softened by his real love for all things Indian, is surprising. Sometimes there is an almost imperial ring which, while in accord with his Benedictine background in the days before the Second Vatican Council, sits strangely with the man he was to become:

> India has to receive humbly from the Church the sound and basic principles of true contemplation, to keep them faithfully, to stamp them with her own seal, and to develop through them along with other members of the Church. The genuine Christian contemplation is built on the unshakable foundation of revealed truths concering God and man, and their mutual relations.[6]

While one of the ashram's aims, certainly to start with, was the development of a truly Indian Christianity (a world apart, it should be said, from the Christianity that Western missionaries had until then sought to impose on Hindus), there was, as Abhishiktananda wrote, "much less and much more."[7] Less, he argued, in that this could only come about through contemplation, without which the whole venture would be meaningless; more, "because the matter involved was something reaching far beyond even the christianization of India."[8] Already he was seeing how it was a two-way process: he still longed for the christianization of India, but now he knew how much Western Christianity needed the spirituality of India. He looked forward to the time, once India became Christian, when she would urge Christianity "to an even more inward penetration of those depths, as yet unknown, of the unfathomable mystery which she carries in her breast."[9]

At this stage both men held to a "fulfillment theology," in which, without question, Christianity was the superior religion to which all others must eventually lead. But more than anything they were contemplatives, believing that the *sannyāsi* was one who was "fascinated by the mystery of God, His transcendency, His universal and life-giving Presence, and who remains simply *gazing* at it, unable to see anything else in the universe, in his brothers, in his own heart."[10] In short they wanted to honor the tradition at the heart of both Hindu *sannyasa* and Christian monasticism by simply *being* in the presence of God.

In 1949, years before the Second Vatican Council blew fresh air into the Roman Catholic Church, these two Christian priests were seeking to be Christian-Hindu priests, to live "the contemplative life of the pristine tradition of Christian monasticism and the closest possible conformity to the traditions of sannyasa."[11] How were these ideals clothed in the moment-by-moment garments of daily life? What did it involve in practice? They shared a wish that their daily life should be based on the Benedictine Rule, indeed Abhishiktananda went so far as to write, presumably with Monchanin's agreement, "It is upon the Rule itself that Indian monasticism must be built."[12] It might be thought that so long-established and venerated a Rule would not be conducive to the changes they would have to make to embrace Indian ascetic customs, manners, postures, and gestures. However most people are agreed that St. Benedict was not attempting to fashion a fixed rule for future generations, but that it was open-ended and that changes could be made according to circumstances.

At first Abhishiktananda wanted a detailed timetable, but Father Monchanin persuaded him that that would not be in keeping with their aims of adapting the Rule to Indian conditions and that, for instance, silence "should proceed not from a rule but from some inner necessity."[13] Broadminded as they were in adopting Indian customs, it was the pattern of the Benedictine day, with its age-old balance of prayer, manual work, and study, that shaped their lives, the regular hours of prayer at dawn, dusk, and midday, traditional times of worship in both Christian and Indian traditions, giving a structure to the day. Mass was celebrated every day, and there were periods of meditation in the early morning and at night. These were sometimes held in the ashram, sometimes on the banks of the Kavery. So prayer united their daily activities, work and study, the monks' task being "to live every moment in the Presence of the Almighty and keep themselves alert for the mysterious and inward promptings."[14] Prayer in the life of monks is not limited to specific times; it should be, as Abhishiktananda wrote, "the permanent state of their soul and the very breath of their holy life."[15] The deep peace that visitors often noticed in the ashram was evidence that this was indeed the case.

Gradually the customs and traditions of ashram life, handed down through the centuries, embodied in the Upanishads themselves, found their place naturally within the Benedictine framework. Many were the same: solitude, silence, poverty, abstinence, fasting, and chastity are ideals common to both traditions. Some were different: Tamil and Sanskrit texts and songs were used as they took their first tentative steps toward using readings and ceremonies from their double tradition. In the unlikely event that they were wearing shoes, they would remove them on entering the chapel; they would uncover their shoulders, Abhishiktananda noting wryly that while Westerners put more clothes on to worship, Indians take them off. Indian traditions of reverence were followed, and they would greet each other with joined hands and make a full prostration when entering or leaving the church. Sitting cross-legged did not come easily to two men who were middle-aged before they even tried to do it, but Abhishiktananda wrote home in delight, finding that the exercises he practiced so assiduously were bearing fruit and had made him so supple that he had begun "to be capable of reaching the so-called 'lotus' position. Soon I shall be able to remain in it."[16] They were not blindly imitating Indian customs—they could not be accused of syncretism. These things were done with a real longing that Indian spirituality and Christian spirituality should meet, not just at this outer level of detail but in the deep heart of the two faiths, as Bede Griffiths, who was to follow in Abhishiktananda's footsteps at Shantivanam, wrote some twenty-five years later:

We are not seeking a syncretism in which each religion will lose its own individuality, but an organic growth in which each religion has to purify itself and discover its own inmost depth and significance and then relate itself to the inner depth of the other traditions. Perhaps it will never be achieved in this world, but it is the one way in which we can advance today towards that unity in truth which is the ultimate goal of mankind.[17]

Abhishiktananda was aware that they had to proceed slowly. "Even the daring plans that have been approved in principle, I must set up in secret, because they won't understand my way of putting them into practise."[18] He admitted to much trial and error, many changes of mind, but writing early in 1952 he felt that Sanskrit should be used, with the vernacular languages like Tamil added, rather as, in those days of the Latin Mass in the West, vernacular languages were occasionally added to the basic Latin.* The Mass and most of the Offices would remain virtually the same, though he questioned whether psalms relating to the history of Israel were appropriate in India and regarded the singing of Indian hymns as essential.

---

*Later Abhishiktananda prepared a Sanskrit version of the Canon of the Mass, based on the Vedas and the Upanishads, but this was hardly ever used.

He loved the ceremony of lights known as *arati*. It is not clear when this was first used at Shantivanam, but Abhishiktananda's vivid description of seeing it take place in Hindu temples encourages the thought that he would have celebrated in this way as soon as he felt it was possible:

> You have to have seen the temples illuminated in the evening, even the smallest, the crowds hurrying there, craning forward when the celebrant lights the fire on the tray and lifts it to the Divinity making various patterns in the air as he does so. Then the celebrant comes to the people, each of whom puts his hands to the fire and touches his face with it, rubbing his forehead piously with the ash.[19]

"But," he wonders sadly, "Who of our Christians would understand that?"

MANUAL WORK AND STUDY were not equally distributed beween the two men. Father Monchanin, saintly, charming, and immensely intellectually gifted, was utterly impractical, so the running of the ashram fell entirely to Abhishiktananda, and he did not conceal his occasional irritation on that score. "Do you realize how complicated a matter it is to prepare a place where one need no longer occupy oneself with worldly matters? One tries in vain to be small, simple, poor. How complicated it is."[20] As far as study was concerned, Abhishiktananda worked hard on his Tamil and went to classes in yoga and chanting with a Hindu swami, but found he had "little time to think theologically and still less to write."[21] Between them, however, they wrote a memorandum in English about the aims of the ashram, originally just thirty pages, but which grew to a booklet entitled *An Indian Benedictine Ashram.**

So it fell to Abhishiktananda to be constantly involved in manual labor—either doing things himself or overseeing local workmen. The work that most concerned him, indeed obsessed him, was the building of the chapel. Once again he was bemoaning "the anxieties of a 'contemplative'!" and lamenting that he had to postpone his planned journey to the Himalayas as he raised money, discussed plans, and supervised the manufacture of fifty thousand bricks. He met problems with his workers, three skilled men and several women doing the fetching and carrying, not least the ever-present difficulties with caste, which made a problem of the apparently simple matter of supplying drinking water, for the upper and lower castes could not drink from the same well or share the same drink-

---

*Published in French as *Ermites du Saccidânanda* (1956). Revised edition, *A Benedictine Ashram* (1964). Also in Portuguese and German.

ing vessels. He received one thousand rupees quite quickly, but for the first time in his life was anxious about money as he realized that he had not enough for the additional building of two small cells and a kitchen. As the finished chapel became a reality he met another hazard of land ownership when the bishop of Trichinopoly, James Mendonça, refused—understandably—to dedicate the chapel until the ownership of the site was legally confirmed. By September the deeds of the land had been acquired and the bishop was invited to bless the chapel and to say the first Mass on October 11, 1951, at which time the booklet *An Indian Benedictine Ashram* would be released.

The foreword of the booklet was written by the bishop, who showed considerable courage in his support of the ashram, though he did not come to the ceremony. It is not hard to have sympathy with his ambivalence. He was delighted when they began to wear the *kāvi* dress and insisted on being photographed with them, yet when he saw the stone altar and tabernacle of hewn rough stone, he exclaimed, "It hurts my eyes to see that; that is not worthy of our Lord, that should be all decorated or at least covered." "No doubt," as Abhishiktananda gleefully added, "with plaster from Saint-Sulpice."[22] As the bishop of their diocese, Mendonça had given his approval to Abhishiktananda's visits to Hindu ashrams and had written generously that the two priests, who he admitted looked like "Hindu Sannyāsis or Buddhist Bhikshus" and who had already raised criticisms and doubts, had his full approval for "this revolutionary mode of living."[23] He had come to the inauguration of the ashram six months earlier, but now, with the dedication of the chapel, he could not quite summon up the courage to support these statements with his physical presence. Abhishiktananda wrote that he "has nothing at all against us; as far as one can see, he is more upset with himself for being so . . . cowardly."[24]

So the dedication went ahead without him, and the little chapel, just nine feet square and modeled on an ancient Chola temple in Pondicherry, became the center of their prayer and worship. It was:

dark and bare, save for an altar and tabernacle of roughly hewn granite and a few oil lamps. Despite the very limited means available, in its simplicity and bareness something had been caught of the sacredness and mystery, the "numinous" quality which characterizes the sanctuary of a Hindu temple—yet at the same time it was no slavish copy.[25]

Visitors were moved by this little Christian-Hindu chapel, saying that they had rarely been to a chapel that invited them so strongly to prayer, but its building was at quite a cost to Abhishiktananda, who was caught, as he was so often to be, between the polarities of outer and inner living and stressed by the practical work thrust upon him by setting up an ashram and by the health and temperament of his companion. Even as the last touches were being made to the chapel, he was once again having to put off his trip to the Himalayas, writing to his family:

> How complicated the contemplative life is, I think it would be much easier for me to live as a real *sannyasi*, tramping the roads, or settling near some village, and receiving my daily food as alms. One day, I think I shall come to this.[26]

It is as if the emphasis of his life was beginning to change. Even before the ashram was completed he was dreaming of greater solitude, greater poverty, of a life more totally dedicated to God—even of the greater internal and external freedom of the life of a wandering *sannyāsi*.

By THE BEGINNING OF FEBRUARY 1952 the ashram was complete:

> For a chapel, a cube of a few feet, the simplest Hindu form. The altar: an unsophisticated stone table on two unsophisticated pillars. Tabernacle: a stone. Two cells under the trees, made of bamboo lianas, but with cement floor. Two years' experience has amply proved that buildings that are too primitive need continual upkeep and therefore money and preoccupation. Also at this moment I am doing a kitchen of brick and tiles. Bathroom: the river. No table, no chairs, no beds. Clothing: a length of orange cotton round the waist, another on the shoulders—when going out, a tunic of the same colour so as not to cause alarm. Bare feet, a great rosary round the neck, as worn by Hindu monks, completed by a wooden cross at the end. Outward appearance of a Hindu monk.[27]

The word "ashram" is often used so loosely that its real meaning becomes obscured. Abhishiktananda was scornful of so-called Christian ashrams in which members ignored Indian conditions of abstinence from meat and alcohol or were simply guest houses; he had even heard of ashrams in America that were known as "weekend ashrams." According to ancient tradition, an ashram is "the place in which settles a 'holy man,' i.e. a man who has dedicated himself to the only quest of God in abstinence and poverty, solitude and silence. Any place where he *sits* is his ashrama."[28] Abhishiktananda and Monchanin were both humble men, and placing the expression "holy man" in quotation marks certainly indicates that they considered themselves holy men only insofar as they were seeking God in the true way of India.

He held to this strict definition of an ashram as essentially Indian, partly because *ashrama* is a Sanskrit word but even more because it carries with it both the idea of a life of total renunciation, *sannyāsa*, and the Indian way of spiritual accomplishment known as *sādhanā*. To call a foundation an ashram is, if one is using the word in this sense, to make a strong statement of intent. To call it a Christian ashram, more specifically a Benedictine ashram, both focuses the aim and makes it even harder— nothing less than "the assumption into the Church of the age-old Indian sannyasa itself."[29] The Jesuit theologian Jacques Dupuis spelled out their vision:

> Their intention was to embody within the framework of Christian monasticism the best of what India had to offer in the way of contemplation and renunciation. Their venture was based on a twofold conviction: that the Church would only be truly present in India, that mystical land, if its own contemplative and monastic dimension was solidly established there: and that it would only become Indian (and hence catholic) through the taking up into Christian monasticism of that ceaseless quest for the Absolute which was characteristic of the religious tradition of India.[30]

It is important to remember that at the time Catholicism was not open to the insights of other religions, and interfaith dialogue barely existed, the study of religions being called "comparative religion" and remaining at the level of concepts. The church had no idea of liturgical adaptation to the culture of the country. The idea of people from one faith seeking to *experience* the faith of another was inconceivable: this was a pioneering experiment of great significance. That today we take so much religious exchange for granted is possible only because of such ventures.

So at that time, over half a century ago, what did the world make of it all? There were, in Abhishiktananda's words, "bitter criticisms of the infant ashram." It was all very well in theory, when it was just a question of a brave vision, of unrealized ideas—then there was great sympathy. But now it was tangibly before them. Two Christian priests looking like

Hindu ascetics, living almost as poorly as the poorest Indian villagers, walking barefoot, sitting cross-legged, putting the sacred word AUM at the beginning of letters and using Sanskrit and Tamil texts in their liturgy—what could a good mid-twentieth-century Christian make of it? And what about the Hindus into whose territory they had strayed? The strangest criticisms came from the strangest quarters.

A visiting Hindu monk, a brahmin, was captivated. However, Abhishiktananda wrote, "he finds our life too austere, we are beyond the level even of holy people. The other day he told us very seriously that we shall certainly not have to be reborn. . . . In Hindu terms he could not have put it more strongly."[31] A *sannyāsi*, Swami Kaivalyananda Saraswati, shared their meals and their silence; he stayed with them several times, the three being very happy together, even though as a brahmin he had to eat food prepared by a non-brahmin in the company of non-brahmins— and that was a considerable sacrifice. But a later visit was cut short as he found the life too austere, the ashram too damp, the food too plain; in addition he caught a cold. Abhishiktananda—no doubt not wanting to worry his family with these tales—assured them that they lived in luxury compared to most people around them. Had his family known just how "people around them" lived, they would not have been greatly reassured.

Less surprisingly, various Jesuit fathers considered their standard of life too low. Shortly after their visit Abhishiktananda and Monchanin visited the Jesuit College at Trichy wearing the *kāvi* (up till that point they had worn white when visiting towns) and creating a sensation in these conformist surroundings, "like two 'pagans' as people say holding their noses."[32] They were asked to eat separately. They did so, then went on to a nearby convent to buy Mass wafers, where the Tamil sisters, seeing the *kāvi*-dressed priests, "could not have been more appalled by seeing the Devil himself walking in."[33] In keeping with his ambivalence, the bishop was pleased that they had caused a stir among pious Christians and received them kindly. As for Abhishiktananda, he seems to have been quite unmoved.

Abhishiktananda does not write exensively about Shantivanam in his spiritual diary, and some who have written about him pass quickly over the Shantivanam period, concentrating on his overwhelming experiences and the anguish he endured in trying to reconcile Hinduism and Christianity and respond to the unique vocation to which he felt summoned. But a biography has to take seriously the founding and shaping of the ashram, for it occupied a large part of Abhishiktananda's first twenty years in India. It was also his home, though admittedly a base from which he often wandered.

In his memoir about Monchanin, modestly written with occasional reference to a "companion" but no acknowledgment that he himself was that companion, Abhishiktananda wrote: "The greatness and the novelty of Shantivanam was precisely that it was not a *means* to anything like the development of the Church or the conversion of India. It stood by itself and was an end in itself."[34] In other words, according to Anthony Kalliath, it would create "an Indian atmosphere and context where one can confidently hold Indian perspectives and horizons; there, *sādhanā*s and Hindu customs become congenial and natural."[35] Kalliath goes on to suggest that the ashram offered Abhishiktananda "the needed credibility in the eyes of his friends and the hierarchy . . . friends and well-wishers could associate with him without prejudice and fear because Shantivanam had ecclesiastical approval and recognition."[36] This may indeed have been the case, but if so was merely an unexpected offshoot. Abhishiktananda made no such calculation—it was not in his nature—nor does he make any such reference in his letters or books. Shantivanam may, with hindsight, have been a launching pad, but it was much more than a sophisticated laboratory where experiments could be made in the blending of Indian and Christian liturgical practice.

But it was not well understood.

> Even the most sympathetic (apart from some Europeans) don't understand a quarter of our thinking. And if the half of it were revealed to them, they would expose us to public contempt. . . . Once the first wave of astonishment has passed, lay people like our poverty and the simplicity of our life. Priests are generally charming (to us). More than one, let me say, would love to see Shantivanam fall, for basically this example, this lesson given, and what is more by Whites, is a thorn in their flesh.[37]

What is so curious is the absence of passion in Abhishiktananda's writing about the ashram. After six months at Shantivanam he writes, "We are really living a hermit's life here. I would never have thought that my dreams of 1934 would be so completely realized."[38] But that is a rare spark of enthusiasm amid the practical problems and financial worries that beset him. Generally the subject seems to bring out little more than a weary affection and mild disappointment. "The future of Shantivanam? . . . for the moment it is the cave of Subiaco.* Will it ever be anything else?"[39]

---

*The cave where St. Benedict spent many solitary years.

Raimon Panikkar, in a wise and loving "Letter to Abhishiktananda" written on the second anniversary of the latter's death, wrote: "You wanted to found a monastery; you did not. You wanted to begin an Ashram; you could not."[40] But at least Abhishiktananda put the pioneering ashram on the geographical and spiritual map; together with Monchanin he established something entirely new. If they failed to make this extraordinary venture the success for which they might have hoped, it was owing to three things.

In the first place, the climate was not ripe for it—the fact that it attracted no vocations was at least partly because it was so far ahead of its time. Second, Abhishiktananda had been so shaken by the Damascus Road experience of Ramana Maharshi and Arunachala, which had lifted his gaze from running an ashram to wanting to live the purest *sannyāsa*, that it was almost impossible for him to give himself wholeheartedly to anything else. From the time of his second visit to Tiruvannamalai in August 1949 there is a sense of lethargy in his references to Shantivanam. He was so drawn to the holy mountain of Arunachala that his life at the ashram was more duty than joy. Returning to Shantivanam after a visit to Tiruvannamalai in April 1952 he admitted, "Shantivanam seems very dull to me now."[41] By the next year he confessed in his diary that "Shantivanam, the work of the hermits of Saccidananda, henceforth interests me so little. Arunachala has caught me."[42]

Third, there was the problem of the uneasy relationship between the two founders, for Father Monchanin and Abhishiktananda were not getting on as they had hoped they would; they respected and liked each other, but increasingly they questioned whether they could work well together. It has even been suggested[43] that they deliberately found opportunities not to be at the ashram together. Certainly they traveled much—Monchanin to the north and to meet his theological friends in Pondicherry; Abhishiktananda spending long periods at Arunachala.

The Anglican writer Donald Allchin has an interesting musical metaphor for why people who in broad outline think alike do not always have an easy relationship. If two people are an octave apart, he suggests, the sound resonates pleasingly; even at a fifth, a fourth, a third. But as you get closer, discord creeps in, and a semitone, struck simultaneously, is harshly dissonant, yearning for resolution.

So it was with Monchanin and Abhishiktananda. They had so much in common; they were so close and yet so far. Both longed to bring Christian monasticism to India and for Indian culture and philosophy to enrich Christianity, but the differences were vast. Monchanin, the child of upper-middle-class parents who owned rich vineyards in the southeast of

France; Abhishiktananda, a Breton from seafaring stock whose family ran a small provisions shop. Monchanin the saintly intellectual, essentially a thinker; Abhishiktananda, determined to put experience before intellect and urging himself in his diary to "Get free from your mind and its need to know, to read, to learn, to understand."[44] Monchanin admitting freely, "never have I felt—intellectually—more Christian and I must say more *Greek*."[45] Abhishiktananda constantly needing to redefine his Christianity and reprimanding himself whenever he found himself still being "Greek." (Both men used the word "Greek" to indicate a preoccupation with speculative thought.) Monchanin liking to think and to talk with his theological friends; Abhishiktananda in love with Arunachala and happier talking to a hermit than a theologian. Perhaps their most basic difference was that Abhishiktananda was increasingly drawn to a place beyond the opposites, where "One simply IS. And this fundamental experience is at the same time that of the unique and single EXISTENCE."[46] Monchanin, on the other hand, felt "a growing horror at the forms of muddled thinking in this 'beyond' thought which most often proves to be only a falling short of thought, in which everything gets drowned."[47]

The immediate problem, however, lay in Monchanin's impractical nature. Though his poor health—he had a chronic tendency to asthma—understandably excused him from manual work, he could have helped with the plans, with financial arrangements, but he did not. He simply was not temperamentally suited to such work, and it did not take the intensely practical Abhishiktananda long to realize this. Within weeks of arriving he was worrying about the suitability of his companion for such a venture: "he is a man of intuition, not of getting things done, you can draw your own conclusions as to how this affects my work on the future foundation."[48] His fears were borne out. Two years after the founding of the ashram, wondering if it had a future, he admitted,

> There would be one, if my companion were not a pure thinker. The hermitage will only develop into an institution if the Lord sends another companion. Without Father Monchanin I can do nothing, with him alone I can do nothing. . . . The example of my companion who could do anything and does nothing does little to encourage me.[49]

And later, "I am so weary of having to struggle constantly for the last three months with Fr M, or more precisely to drag him along. . . . He will never come out of his dream."[50] For his part, Monchanin makes an interesting and rather melancholy distinction between them, writing that

Abhishiktananda "lives in eternity," while he himself is "a man who lives in time, and time for me, at almost sixty years of age, is the past rather than the future."[51]

Nevertheless, there was deep mutual appreciation, and they were never less than polite to each other, never less than loyal in public or in written works. In private letters both sides of the coin could, as we have seen, be given: "He is certainly much too intellectual and idealistic to do his bit, from which all who know him suffer. But that in no way diminishes his very great intellectual and spiritual value. He has a humility, a gentleness, a calm, a spirit of poverty which is rare."[52] Perhaps Abhishiktananda's most complimentary assessment of the companion who caused him so much heartache is found in the memoir he wrote soon after Monchanin's death:

> The life of Fr. Monchanin will always remain for Saccidananda monks a remarkable example and type of their vocation. Without trying altogether to emulate his practical and external unconcern—everybody receives his own gift from God, and Providence needs at times "concerned" and "practical" instruments too—they shall share by all means in his complete indifference to whatever is not the essential and be always ready to be carried away by the current of the Spirit at any time and whenever He likes, unattached to any plan or to any preconceived ideas.[53]

CERTAINLY ABHISHIKTANANDA HAD PROBLEMS in the running of the ashram, but they were nothing to the problems within. He had come to India to found an ashram, but instead he had discovered Ramana Maharshi and Arunachala. The storm clouds were gathering as he realized just what he was embarked on in trying to live fully as both a Christian monk and a Hindu *sannyāsi* and to be completely faithful to both. The one thing he knew for certain was that to pursue it at the level of theological discussion and liturgical experiment was not enough; Christianity and Hinduism had to meet *in him*. He had to pursue his strange calling at the level of experience.

8

Christianity and *Advaita*

1953–1954

It was as if there were two men in the depths of me.[1]

THE WAY OF EXPERIENCE IS HARD. One has only to compare the challenge of climbing a high mountain with the challenge of writing a thesis on the dangers of mountain climbing. To actually *do* the thing needs a particular kind of courage—and that is what Abhishiktananda had. He longed to reach the state of union, of oneness beyond the opposites. Many words and phrases have been used to describe this state—it is often called the search for God, but it has also been called realization, enlightenment, awakening, satori, the advaitic experience, *nirvāna*, a state of Being, *kensho*, living in the present moment, the search for the Holy Grail, even the search for "That which cannot be named." Abhishiktananda mostly used the word "awakening," sometimes "the other shore," or his "spiritual adventure," even "the call of the higher abyss." The words themselves are less important than the idea that those who seek to follow his journey should have a glimmering of the object of his search. For him it was not enough to know *about* enlightenment; theory was always secondary to experience, to making the journey himself. He felt compelled to answer the question Who am I? and to learn to live in a state of pure Being, every moment a present moment. Following the twists and turns of this search for the Holy Grail is as enthralling a journey as a human being can make, and, like any journey with such a prize, it is dangerous. Abhishiktananda was well aware of the dangers, and he was probably not too surprised by the anguish through which his chosen path led him.

These years—from March 1953, when he made his fourth visit to Arunachala, to the end of 1956, when he went on a thirty-day retreat in complete silence and solitude—saw Abhishiktananda go through a terrifying spiritual crisis as he tried to reconcile the Christianity that had been rooted in him for forty-odd years with the advaitic experience of Hinduism, an experience he could not gainsay and yet could not reconcile with his Christianity. It was, as he said more than once, as if two men were fighting inside one body.

The origins of this crisis were in 1949, when he first met Ramana Maharshi, and it marks what Bettina Bäumer calls a change

> from the convinced missionary with a certain fulfilment theology to the stage of one who was shaken by a real encounter with Hindu spirituality and torn apart by two experiences, two "ultimates," two identities, two worlds of religious expression, and, in his own words, "two loves."[2]

The end of the long period of holding to this "fulfillment theology," which claims that all religions find their true resolution in Christianity and only in Christianity, was painful and slow. Perhaps the beginning of the end was when, flushed with the excitement of his discovery of *advaita*, he had to accept that there were good spiritual souls who not only were not Christians, but who had no interest whatever in Christ.

He missed his Christian brethren and longed for his Hindu friends to share his faith: one Christmas he spent alone at Shantivanam, agonizing that his Hindu brothers in the village were not sharing the joy of the birth of Christ with him. On the one hand he admitted to being "terribly nostalgic" for the choir, the Gregorian plainchant, the readings from the early fathers and the "long habit of liturgy"; on the other, he realized that this long habit was now being rivaled by another:

> *Advaita* is so overpowering—disappearance in the One! And so is Hindu worship, at least in its purest manifestation—the offering of flowers and milk to the bare stone—phallic-shaped, but nothing obscene in the idea—placed in the holy of holies, the cave, that small dark chamber deep in the heart of the temple, which one only reaches after passing through numerous courtyards and halls. . . . I am torn, rent in two, between Christ and my brothers; my brothers more even than my blood. . . . When I pray per Christum, they cannot follow me. And I can no longer rejoice in our feasts as formerly, because my people are not with me. And I cannot unite myself to my people in their symbolic religion, *because I am a priest of the true religion*, and thus I fail to have communion with my people in what is the highest and most divine in them.[3] (emphasis added)

". . . because I am a priest of the true religion"—there was the core of it. Not only was Christianity deep in his bones, instilled by his parents, nourished by his family and his time in the monastery at Kergonan, but he had, as he later said, a "visceral attachment to the Christian myth."[4] He was not just a Christian by conviction and by intellect; he was a Christian instinctively and intuitively. For him, at this deep level, Christianity was the true religion; further, he had taken solemn vows as a priest of that religion. How could he taste the waters of another faith without feeling disloyal?

There was to be little peace for Abhishiktananda as he lived through this drama of conflicting spiritual loyalties, but there were people he met who, in their own ways, tried to help him. The first of these he met at Arunachala and usually referred to by his first name, Harilal.* His full name was H. W. L. Poonja; he was a brahmin from Punjab, a disciple of Ramana Maharshi and a strict advaitin with some disciples in the area of Lucknow. In his working life he was the manager of iron and manganese mines in the jungles of Mysore and was a married man with a family. While from Abhishiktananda's point of view it was a providential meeting, Harilal himself had set about finding the Frenchman quite deliberately. He had passed him one morning in the bazaar and, seeing into the Frenchman's eyes, he was immediately convinced that this was someone he had to meet, so he persuaded a local Tamil to take him to Abhishiktananda's cave on the side of the Holy Mountain.

Abhishiktananda could not understand how anyone had found him— he had thought he was hidden from the world. "You called me," said Harilal, "and here I am . . . the Self attracts the Self. What else do you expect?"[5] This unusual introduction set the tone for a relationship, not the relationship of a disciple to his guru but more the friendship of two souls, with one, at the moment, more advanced. It was precisely what Abhishiktananda needed at this moment in his life, and the relationship was to resonate through the next years.

Abhishiktananda has written at length about his encounter with Harilal in *The Secret of Arunachala*, so we have a detailed record of their exchanges. Harilal never minced his words, and he started as he had every intention of going on, with a severe reprimand. It was caused by Abhishiktananda, with his usual ability to laugh at himself, admitting that he liked to quote from the Bhagavad Gita and the Upanishads, as he found it impressed people. He was about to quote a text, adding—might

---

*Harilal's story is told by Abhishiktananda in *The Secret of Arunachala* (Delhi: ISPCK, 1979), 81-97.

one guess with a self-conscious casualness?—that he had learned a little Sanskrit, when Harilal interrupted: "And what is the use of all that? All your books, all the time lost in learning different languages! Which language do you use to converse with the *ātman*. The *ātman* has nothing to do either with books, or with languages, or with any Scripture whatever. *It is*—and that's all."[6]

He softened for a moment, admitting that he was once a keen reader and the words of the Gita "were all the time ringing like music in my heart," but soon he was off again, saying he no longer repeated the divine names, he did not say litanies or sing *bhajans*, he did not even meditate. He believed that it is only in the ultimate silence that the *ātman* is revealed. He was convinced that Abhishiktananda was very close to the true awakening experience, but the demands were huge. It was not only books that had to go, even harder sacrifices were needed:

> There is only one thing you need, and that is to break the last bonds that are holding you back. You are quite ready for it. Leave off your prayers, your worship. Your contemplation of this or that. Realize that *you are, Tat tvam asi*—you are That![7]

It was as if Abhishiktananda was being stripped of everything. He had given up his country, his family, marriage, any sort of financial income or physical comfort. He spent days in solitude and silence, away from his friends. Now he was being asked to give up both his beloved books and his Christian identity and worship. He was impressed by Harilal, realizing immediately that "he lives his advaita. . . . He spoke as one who knew."[8] Yet this was too much. How could he give up his liturgical practice and the obligations of his Christian faith? In any case he argued—neither man was refusing the use of his mind on this occasion—surely until the moment of awakening actually arrives, religious observances should be practiced? Surely one should not act as if one had realized the Self until one actually had? Harilal replied that this was simply an excuse to try to escape from the Real and that a life of prayers, devotions, and asceticism was stunted, satisfying only to the ego. He already had great respect for this surprising Frenchman, saying that he had rarely met anyone like him, even among his own people, and he readily accepted that his continuous observance of religious practice, whatever else it was, was not laziness or dishonesty. Though Harilal had no wish to threaten Abhishiktananda's Christianity, he pressed on, insisting that at the stage he had reached it was meaningless to say that he was a Christian; for one who had seen the Real, there is neither Christian, Hindu, Buddhist, or

Muslim. "There is only the atman, and nothing can bind or limit the atman."[9]

Then the encounter switched to another dimension as he asked Abhishiktananda to tell him, with or without words, about his spiritual experience. They were both sitting cross-legged, facing each other. Abhishiktananda said nothing, he simply closed his eyes. The silence deepened and after a while they both looked up at the same time and gazed at each other; the second time Abhishiktananda opened his eyes, he noticed that Harilal's eyes were wide open but "as if unseeing." "You are a lover of silence," said Harilal eventually. This silent exchange confirmed Harilal's instinct that Abhishiktananda had reached a high spiritual stage. "Now I understand everything," he said. "You are quite ready. What are you waiting for?" Abhishiktananda's response, in the mode of his Christian upbringing, that he felt himself so feeble before God when he realized his inadequacy, released Harilal's feisty side once more:

> Enough of this nonsense! Stop talking about differences. There are no differences anywhere. There is only the atman. God is the atman, the Self of all that is. I am the atman. You are the atman. Only the Self exists in itself and in all. . . . When a woman is ready to give birth, can she be unaware of it? And every woman who has already been a mother knows the signs without a shadow of doubt. It is the same with those who are near to the awakening, or rather whose *I* is on the point of disappearing in the light of the essential and unique I. I saw it in your eyes this morning when we passed each other in the bazaar without you noticing; that is when you called me.[10]

AFTER THESE FIRST MEETINGS, Abhishiktananda continued as normal for a while, reading and doing some Sanskrit. He had much to reflect on. Then he found there was no attraction in reading and thinking; in fact, it wasn't possible any longer, since everything said or written or read *about* God is a long way from God himself. He began to see theology, indeed any sort of theorizing, in a new light:

> The satires of Isaiah against the makers of idols of wood and gold apply just as much to the makers of conceptual idols. The simple man sculpts a bit of wood and prostrates himself: "You are my God." . . . The intelligent man sculpts a concept and does likewise. And he thinks he got there because he has made a god of his own size![11]

He easily accepted the difference between theological speculation and experience and began to look at theology in a different way, but *advaita* presented him with problems, endless problems. A look at some of the things he wrote about *advaita* during this period shows how his thinking changed and developed.

As early as 1952, before his encounter with Harilal, a diary entry admits that so far *advaita* has only been an inspiring idea, one much discussed with Father Monchanin. But he was beginning to catch glimpses of the transcending of the ego:

> Dive down into myself, to the greatest depth of myself. Forget my own "*aham*,"* lose myself in the "*aham*" of the divine *Atman* which is at the source of my being, of my consciousness of being. And in this unique—or primordial—*Aham* feel all beings to be oneself.[12]

While that reads more like an instruction to himself than an experience, in only a few months he was writing to Lemarié that when he meditated on the Office the visualization of heaven "means little to the *advaitin* that I have become."[13] He was wandering far enough away from his traditional Christianity to wonder how people could accept what he was thinking and writing. Yet March 1953 found him less confident, for he wrote in his diary that Harilal was daring him to make "the final leap into pure *advaita*" but that he was timorous, recalling his days on the beaches of Saint Briac, the cold Atlantic pounding the shore:

> For the time being I am playing with *advaita*. I am like someone on the point of taking a swim in the sea, who reassures himself, dips a toe in the water, and indefinitely postpones the dive which alone will give peace. I try to understand my *advaita* as a Christian and a Westerner, and once at the other end of my experiments, of my tortuous reasonings . . . how complex and *an-advaita* [non-*advaita*] "my" *advaita* is![14]

Then, in apparent contradiction, he marks this same period—Lent 1953—as the time when "in the cave of Arutpal Tirtham I understood advaita"[15] and tells how he spent the morning of Palm Sunday in the temple, where he claimed to be "the Christian monk of the place,"[16] sitting beside the *linga* and remembering the depth in which Ramana

---

*Aham—I, myself.

Maharshi was held, "that depth which is mine!"[17] Barely was the ink dry on that diary entry before he wrote to Lemarié, confirming the impression that something in him had changed radically: "Last year I thought I had *UNDERSTOOD*, but it was for me an intellectualized concept."[18] Then a few months later he was, with characteristic honesty, doubting his own motivation:

> Am I not more or less attached in a human way to *advaita*, to my experience of *advaita?* Attached because it is exotic, rare, etc. With a human fear that this *advaita* must finally yield to a higher truth which would in fact only be that which I have quite simply believed until now. . . . But how can we ever suppress the human element in "our reason," our attachments?[19]

So Abhishiktananda, a man of both intellect and imagination, constantly seemed to think he was there, yet Harilal, experienced in assessing the advaitic state, while he had been impressed by the stage Abhishiktananda had reached in 1953, was disappointed that by March 1957 he had not yet "arrived"—a conclusion with which Abhishiktananda did not appear to disagree.

This pattern of apparent arrival at the goal, followed by acceptance that he was still on the journey, certainly shows the inadequacy of words to describe such an experience, but it also highlights the distinction between the words "understand" and "experience," or "encounter," in Abhishiktananda's case probably carefully chosen for he knew very well that the understanding of the head is not the same as the experience of the total person. But even more acutely it shows that not only is it impossible to find words for the state of realization, but it is not always easy to know when one has reached it. Today's blinding flash of light is thrown across yesterday's darkness; it is not necessarily total illumination.

Sometimes a person's conviction that they have found a truth is so profound that the impulse to accept what they say is overwhelming, for instance C. G. Jung's famous remark "I don't believe, I know." Or the words of Thomas Aquinas: "All this [theology] is but as straw compared to what I now know." Sometimes people are clearly deluding themselves, their behavior quite incompatible with the state they claim to have reached. From the position of the observer, there are subjective signs, like a radiance perceived in a person that it is hard to ignore. More objectively, there are teachers, gurus, and Zen roshis, who are specifically trained to *know* when the moment of illumination, what Zen practitioners call the *kensho* experience, has come. At this stage of Abhishiktananda's life, the only recorded reaction to the stage he had reached is Harilal's, and in the light of what Abhishiktananda was to write in later years and the extraordinary mystical heights he was to reach, it is clear that Harilal was right—he had not yet arrived. Why, then, did Abhishiktananda seem, at least intermittently, to think that he had? Could he not distinguish his imaginings from the reality? It is not hard for the vast majority of us, far from such a state, to believe that it exists, but how do we recognize it, either in ourselves or in others?

Perhaps it can be compared to climbing a mountain. There can be many occasions when it seems as if the peak has been reached, only to find, when you have scaled it, that there is yet higher to climb. And Abhishiktananda, despite the level he had reached when Harilal spotted him in the bazaar, had a few years to wait before full enlightenment came to him.

ABHISHIKTANANDA ADMITTED that his understanding of Harilal was limited. He was not only a mystic but an eccentric, impulsive man, known to have fathered a child by one of his disciples and given to indulging whims to take off for some distant location at short notice. Yet he held down a very responsible job, and clearly his ordinariness was important to Abhishiktananda, who, writing of the tendency to assume that the life of an enlightened, realized person is quite different from normal life, made the point that outwardly nothing changes. "Jesus eats, drinks, weeps, gets tired. Poonja [Harilal] manages his mines. Janaka* rules his kingdom."[20] Even after several years of friendship he wrote that though they were very close "advaitically speaking," there was a whole part of Harilal's mentality that bewildered him. "His psyche often disconcerts me. Even his experience, high as it may be, is based on an Indian psyche in which there are so many points that I am unable to understand."[21]

It turned out that Abhishiktananda's instinctive reservations were well founded. For instance, it turned out that Harilal would give "certificates of enlightenment," and one only has to think of the impossibility of Ramana Maharshi even considering such a thing to realize that no respected Indian sage would behave like that. Harilal's behavior with women was, to say the least, uninhibited, and increasingly his disciples became disillusioned. Bettina Bäumer knew Harilal well many years later and witnessed the strange, ecstatic states into which people fell when under his influence, and how they sometimes became so unbalanced they

---

*A king at the time of the Upanishad, who was venerated as a realized person who continued to fulfill his duties in the world.

needed hospital care. Even Abhishiktananda himself was not immune. On one occasion Bettina and Meera, a young woman who was very close to Harilal, were cooking, and "Abhishiktananda was sitting in the corner talking to us and we were in such a high state. Then I started to sing and he went into a trance and fell into a tin of flour. He became completely red in the face—he was completely gone, and we didn't know how to bring him back."[22] Others have criticized Harilal's lack of moral and ethical behavior; for instance, the writer and public speaker Andrew Cohen, one of his pupils in the 1980s, later denounced his former teacher.

Harilal was enlightened—there is no doubting that—but having been given the experience, he did not always handle it well; spiritual power is not necessarily the same as wisdom. To be disillusioned by someone who influenced you so much is a hard lesson, and it is a measure of Abhishiktananda's basic sanity that he was able to go through an experience like that and take from it the good, without being overwhelmed by it.

Nevertheless, at the time, in the early 1950s, Harilal's influence was immense. Abhishiktananda was in no doubt that he had been sent to help him hear the voice that was continually singing in the depth of his heart, to "dare to make the final leap into pure advaita."[23] Nor is it surprising that at one point Abhishiktananda put such trust in him that he wondered why, if he was so near to awakening, did Harilal simply not go ahead and awaken him? Harilal's answer is quoted at length in *The Secret of Arunachala* and, ringing of Ramana Maharshi as it does, it clearly impressed him —and it certainly robbed him of words, for no answer is recorded:

> How could one awaken that which does not sleep and has never fallen asleep? . . . When you are in deep sleep, do you still have any thought or awareness that you are? But still, even when you exist, you are.
>
> It is through YOU that it is seen and heard, through you that it is thought and willed. You are what remains when nothing is any more seen or thought, willed or heard. That is the atman, the Self; it is what YOU ARE yourself in reality and beyond all outward appearances which change and pass away. *Tat tvam asi*—You are That! What prevents you from realizing this?[24]

What indeed held him back? Why, if he was already so close when the two men met, did it take him so long to reach his goal? It is fairly clear that, apart from the fact that mystical illumination takes its own time and has its own reasons, he was held back by his inability to reconcile *advaita* with Christianity. Indeed, not long before he met Harilal he admitted, with scarcely a whisper of irony, that it was his long acquaintance with the liturgy and the early fathers that "saves me from Shankara's* advaita."[25] (It should be said that Abhishiktananda's *advaita* was based directly on the Upanishads, not on Shankara or on any of the schools of Vedanta that have grown up. As Bettina Bäumer said, "He was not concerned with differences."[26])

It was perhaps some reassurance to Abhishiktananda when Harilal had a vision of the "immeasurable Christ, higher than the heavens and also infinitely close,"[27] especially that in this "shattering vision," feet on earth, arms and head above the heavens, Christ's arms were held out to welcome Harilal, a brahmin and a strict *advaitin*. But there was little comfort for Abhishiktananda as he struggled with the two men fighting inside him.

The outer differences between East and West did not present him with a serious problem. Though there were obviously difficulties inherent in being a European living in India, they did not tear him apart or even bother him too much. In the early days he was rather taken aback to be expected to make prostrations, to offer rice and sweets to images, or to apply the sacred ash of Shiva to his forehead, but his objections were couched in a gently self-mocking humor: "But I am not a Hindu—look at my outrageously white skin!"[28] He missed the Office; indeed, he often admitted to a "terrible longing" for it, but quite soon after his arrival in India he was delighting in being able to live like an Indian and took to inscribing OM at the beginning of his letters, explaining to his no doubt rather bemused family in France that it was pronounced AUM and is for Hindus and Buddhists the symbol for God as the Absolute. "As it is one of the points where Christianity and Hinduism can profitably meet, we have adapted it, and I have had it carved on the cross of St. Benedict which hangs at my neck."[29]

But the tension of trying to reconcile *advaita* and Christianity, to live out his deep-seated Christianity in the context of this new peace, caused him the greatest anguish for most of his life. He never used a human analogy, but it must have been like being in love with two people, deeply and simultaneously and forever.

He wrote endlessly and poignantly of this dilemma, using different images to communicate the extent of his suffering. "I am like someone who has one foot on one side of the gulf, and the other on the other side. I would like to throw a bridge across, but do not know where to fasten it, the walls are so smooth."[30] Again, "How agonizing it is," he wrote, "to be perched on the knife-edge between the opposite slopes of Hinduism and Christianity."[31] During one of the periods when he felt that the advaitic

---

*Shankara was a great philosopher of *advaita* in the eighth century.

experience was within his reach, he was overcome with the fear that as a Christian he had no right to the peace of Hindu *advaita.*

> What gnaws away at my body as well as my mind is this: after hav-ing found in *advaita* a peace and a bliss never experienced before, to live with the dread that perhaps, most probably, all that my latent Christianity suggests to me is none the less true, and that therefore *advaita* must be sacrificed to it. . . . In committing myself totally to *advaita*, if Christianity is true, I risk committing myself to a false path for eternity.[32]

The problems were incessant and unrelenting. Abhishiktananda's diary is full of outbursts, sometimes measured, sometimes in pure anguish. In a moderately detached mood he wrote that the gulf between Christianity and Hinduism was that Christanity, born in a climate of Judeo-Greek thought, is basically realistic, taking man and the earth he lives in seri-ously and placing great importance on our present lives. But for Hindus —and so great is his involvement that here he writes "us Hindus"—"such a view of reality has no meaning. We feel too deeply the abyss between the permanent and the impermanent."[33] More often the anguish pours out of him that he should have found peace so far from the place and form of his original commitment:

> What does it mean, to feel that the only obstacle to final peace and *ananda** is one's attachment to that place, that form; to that *mythos?* Who is there on either side of the frontier to whom I can cry out my anguish—who, if he belongs to this side, will not take fright and anathematize me, and if he is on the other side, will not take an all too human delight because I am joining him?[34]

He summed up his own dilemma in a few words:

> From now on I have tasted too much of *advaita* to be able to recover the "Gregorian" peace of a Christian monk. Long ago I tasted too much of that "Gregorian" peace not to be anguished in the midst of my *advaita.*[35]

And of course he had to face that great stumbling block to anyone strug-gling with Christianty in relation to the other faiths: "I am the way, the truth, and the life: no one comes to the Father, but by me" (John 14:6).

---

*Bliss.

And he gave the controversial line a twist: "The Church claims to be the Only way of salvation. The advaitin claims that he has understood the message of Jesus better than the Church."[36] How does someone who has been, who still is, so close to the church cope with that understanding? His intellect told him to find Christianity at the core of *advaita*, but his heart could not follow. Years later he wrote to his friend Raimon Panikkar:

> You cannot be torn apart in the depth of your soul, as we are by this double summons (from advaitin India on one side, and from Revelation on the other), and by this double opposition (from India and the Church, in their ritualism, their formalism and their intellectualism), without being lacerated even physically.[37]

THEN THERE WAS THE PROBLEM of the liturgy. Here his agonizing tension lay in the fact that the church treated itself, the sacraments, and liturgy "as absolute in itself." With a rare reference to the ashram he had come to India to found, he continued; "It is precisely the role of Shantivanam within the Church to live this tension and there discover the further mystery. . . . But the Church, snugly protected at its centre from draughts, like 19th century episcopal palaces, . . . DOES NOT UNDERSTAND" [Abhishiktananda's capitals].[38] Later, when his views had begun to settle, he was to express views that were both on the face of it shocking to some devout Christians yet unquestionably true to Christ and the deepest meaning of Christianity, but for the moment his writings reveal mostly confusion. For instance, he wrote to Canon Lemarié:

> from long habit I am extremely attached to the Liturgy; on Easter morning, I insisted on reciting Matins and Lauds in spite of the non-obligation, etc., however the Liturgy meant nothing to me any more. . . . The Psalms are so exterior, so *maya** as they say in India. I would have liked my Holy Week better in solitude. . . . In the Eternal, what is a celebration of the Time? How artifical, it seems, to give life to a particular day in time, which is "consumed" in the eternity through which we pass.[39]

This question of time, one of the central problems in the encounter of India and the West, haunted him for years. The deeper he went within,

---

*Māyā is the indefinable condition of the world of manifestation, which cannot be called either real or unreal.

the more he experienced worship and ritual, whether Christian or Hindu, as external.

All the time he was changing, moving, thinking, exploring, risking, being—"Each time one thinks one has touched the bottom; and as one goes into the depths, one discovers circles ever deeper in that depth."[40] The experience was everything; the conceptualizing did not, for the moment anyway, concern him too much, though he was beginning to make notes toward the controversial essays that would eventually take shape as *Guhantara*. But this uncompromising spirit of exploration led him to change in ways that must have been very painful for one trained as a priest to care for the souls of others. He began to wonder if he was any longer fit for the work:

> Last year I liked to feel at Arunachala priest of my People, to sing *Gloria, Pater*. . . . This year, one single attraction: the "Within," beyond time and place, beyond concept and number, beyond full and empty. . . . I spoke to you before of projects of Christian integration of certain Hindu liturgical acts . . . now, I no longer feel capable, for I no longer have any personal interest in it (while feeling interest for others); all that I would achieve would be artificial.[41]

He made many comparisons between 1952 and 1953: last year he liked going to Hindu temples, taking part in the rituals and then resolving any apparent incompleteness in a Christian act. This year he felt he had gone beyond outer expressions:

> It is not because I am Christian that I have lost interest in the exterior things of Hinduism . . . it is as a guest of the within, having penetrated the within. But here again the passing beyond is only healthy if the savouring, the nostalgia, the agony, have gone before.[42]

Two or three times Abhishiktananda climbed Arunachala, something he found grueling but where he could find some reconciliation of the opposites fighting within him. On one occasion he was at the top of the mountain on the night when the sun sets at the same time as the moon rises, the sacred fire is lit and Shiva is honored. He felt the need to witness to Christ, so he sang the Lord's Prayer and the Gloria, then picked up an ochre stone and wrote on the platform of rough stone the first century profession of faith, *Kyrios Christos*, then in Sanskrit, *"You alone are the Lord, and there is no other, oh Master of the World."* The thought came to him that he should make a prostration—but, he wondered, how could he prostrate himself, how could he greet and adore the Holy Mountain when he was standing there? "You are YOURSELF the summit of Arunachala! There is no room left for gesture either of body or of spirit when you have arrived at the Supreme."[43]

Abhishiktananda had many such moments; he called them *éblouisse-ments* (literally, dazzling moments, illuminations). They flash through the pages of his spiritual diary, as, for instance, when he wrote of *satori* as "the true Baptism, that new vision of oneself and of the world, a not-knowing intellectually, but a deep, abysmal, cataclysmic transformation of being."[44] But the pain of his strange journey was never very far away. At the end of 1953 he managed another visit to Arunachala, from where he wrote most poignantly:

> Pray for me, profane or else Hindu, I who no longer know how to pray, except for the ritual prayer of the office, since to pray, to praise, or to worship, one has to say "Thou" to God, and Arunachala does not permit that.[45]

He had suffered much, but he had not yet reached the limit of his suffering.

9

Spiritual Crisis

1955–1956

Free and naked at the heart of the abyss.[1]

IN JULY 1955, Abhishiktananda went to Bombay to meet Father Francis Mahieu, a Belgian Trappist who was considering becoming a postulant at Shantivanam. The relationship between Abhishiktananda and Mahieu was not as happy as they might have expected after their long correspondence and all the work they had put into obtaining a visa for Father Mahieu. Perhaps Abhishiktananda was affected by the difficulties he had been having with Monchanin before he left Shantivanam, but probably even more by the spiritual crisis that was overwhelming him.

The two traveled together for a couple of weeks, and then Father Mahieu continued on his travels alone and Abhishiktananda came back to Bombay, where he met someone else who became involved with his spiritual life. Dr. Dinshaw Mehta was a Parsi doctor who had served as Mahatma Gandhi's doctor. He was committed neither to the advaitic path nor to Christianity—a position that might have seemed ideal to Abhishiktananda. Mehta did, however, have a personal and highly idiosyncratic devotion to Christ, from whom he claimed to receive mystical, esoteric communications. He had also founded a society for nature cures, something that in those days would have been considered unusual, certainly by traditional Christians. He was much admired and had a following of people who came to see him every evening, prostrated themselves before him, and listened to "talks which give good advice, but stuffed with clichés, no order. . . . But it comes from above and they listen open-mouthed. Inextricable mixture of order and fantasy."[2]

However, the doctor, an eccentric figure with a beard tied with a rubber band, was someone to be reckoned with. His circle of friends was drawn from the highest society in India, and his relationship with Gandhi was demonstrated in a letter written to a government department in January 1944,[3] in which the Mahatma asked for Dr. Dinshaw Mehta to treat his wife, Kasturba. Though he had initial reservations, Abhishiktananda liked the doctor and considered himself fortunate to have met him, appreciating particularly his ability to listen, which must have been a great blessing to someone suffering such long-drawn-out, deep, and lonely anguish.

That Abhishiktananda was open to Dr. Mehta's influence was in a sense surprising—Henri Le Saux, the strict liturgist of Kergonan, would most certainly not have taken him seriously. The explanation can be found partly in his constant hunger for experience, but now, poised on the edge of an abyss as he struggled to reconcile Christianity and *advaita*, he was in desperate need of help, his critical faculty perhaps less alert than usual. He agreed to spend two weeks with the doctor in Bombay in July 1955, followed by a further two weeks in Poona the following month. During this time his anguish grew more and more intense; indeed, he wrote in his diary that this time seemed to be "the culminating point of a crisis which has gone on for the past two years and more."[4] With hindsight he must have been been grateful to Dr. Mehta, for in his strange way the doctor was to help Abhishiktananda at this critical time.

Dr. Mehta advised on such matters as the control of sleep, food, and sexuality, but, according to Abhishiktananda, the essence of his method was very like a method of psychoanalytical treatment, involving a transformation of consciousness itself. He advised concentration on a single point, something that would hold the attention—for instance, "the Beloved." But something in this word, perhaps its devotional, dualistic implication, did not appeal to Abhishiktananda: "I think that I am already too Hindu and too advaitic for that. Even the symbol of the Cross no longer speaks to me. So I concentrate on the Heart of Christ, *hrid*,* as the Hindu understanding of the Sacred Heart."[5] What must have seemed very alien to Abhishiktananda was that Dr. Mehta would pass on guidance he received during his meditations every night and which he believed came from Christ himself. But his desperate disciple received them with great humility, simply saying that he did not believe the messages were dictated from outside so much as "the translation, often painful, of a 'revelation' received from a higher plane and incapable of reaching the level of normal consciousness."[6] Nor would he condemn the inadequate expression of the guidance or the magnitude of the claims; rather he

---

*Heart, the spiritual center.

compared them to "the first babblings of Christian theology, a revelation received from on high and seeking to express itself."[7] So Abhishiktananda found himself in the curious position of being encouraged, by someone not formally a Christian, to put more emphasis on Christ than at the time he found helpful. It did not seem to occur to him that perhaps his own understanding of Christ was more mature than his teacher's. In the same diary entry in which he humbly strives to understand this teaching and follow the revelations, he writes:

> Christ is the essential intermediary between the Father and myself. But an intermediary who does not cause any separation. For he is at once identical with me and identical with the Father. I say "I" only in him, and he says "I" only in the Father. And the mystery of the Spirit is all-pervasive. . . . In my return to my origin, there is a stage at which my consciousness, in its movement toward definitive advaita, passes through the condition of Christ's consciousness, having in truth become Christ, as St Paul said.[8]

He could not accept the teaching totally, for Dr. Mehta stressed that although we are destined for "*oneness*," we have not yet attained it, a position Abhishiktananda found incompatible both with the church and with *advaita*. Again his understanding, if not his experience, seemed to be ahead of his teacher's: "There is no opposition between Christ and *advaita*, but the identity is something so deep and essential that it cannot but escape those who have not plunged into the mystery of the within."[9]

If he found it hard to accept Dr. Mehta's very personal idea of Christ, even harder to accept was the advice, in keeping with that given by Harilal, that he should abandon the church:

> If Dr M. were leading me on the path of *advaita*, I think I would abandon everything to go along with him. But what frightens me is that he wants to lead me back to Christ, and to a Christ who is not the Christ of the Church. He himself is torturing me, despite the wonderful peace into which my stay with him has plunged me.[10]

If on these levels he did not find Mehta's teaching helpful, he was, however, learning something else that was to prove of the utmost importance. His willingness to submit to his new teacher, whether or not he always agreed with him, was to teach him the value of "surrender"—a word Abhishiktananda always used in quotation marks, probably because it was the English word Dr. Mehta used to express this basic requirement of the spiritual life.

It is hard to express the importance of surrender in Abhishiktananda's spirituality. Most of us think we have surrendered if we grant a point in argument, give in graciously to demands we did not want to be made, accept that we are not well, accept even that we are dying. We may acknowledge that Christ "demands my soul, my life, my all," but do we understand what this involves? For the hermit, however, for one seeking enlightenment, *everything* has to be surrendered, it is the sacrifice that has to be made on the way to freedom; the hermit or the mystic may be asked to surrender ideas, beliefs, identity, even to surrender God himself. Most people are shocked when they first hear the injunction: "If you meet the Buddha on the path, kill him." The mystic understands. Surrender is the last toll gate to the void, that place of oneness and ultimate truth which he seeks.

Abhishiktananda's first reference to surrender came in 1953, when he was living in a small hut at Arunachala, the roof so low that his head touched the ceiling if he stood upright. One day he went to the temple to say goodbye to some visting *sādhus* and returned to the cave to find that thieves had been there in his absence. They had, he wrote, been "very decent," leaving his millet flour and a piece of cotton he had bought for two rupees; they had taken only three ten-rupee notes they had found with his identity papers. Abhishiktananda accepted this small crime gratefully; it was for him a lesson in detachment.

> The hermit in his cave has not yet made the total "surrender." He has settled down there, under cover. I was too comfortably "settled" in the little house of Vadalur Ammal. That is why the "Self" took the form of a thief to unsettle me and invite me to a more complete stripping. I would have completely missed the point, if I had been content to have a "*money-order*" sent so as to recover my position of two days ago.
>
> Some day I will have to accept being in the temple, only retaining a "room" simply for the Mass, and for the rest living here and there, looking for a corner for recollection, going out every midday as a genuine mendicant monk . . . not even possessing my own "my" solitude and "my" cave.[11]

Now Dr. Mehta was urging him toward *total* surrender, and, rather as he felt he had experienced *advaita*, then realized he had not, so now he felt that he had surrendered all that was asked of him, only to find some-thing more that needed to be given up. Dr. Mehta made him think about surrender in a new way; it is significant that most of the entries on the subject in his diary date from the time he spent with the doctor in Bom-bay and Poona.

By the time they met, Abhishiktananda had already surrendered much of what most people take for granted; he also knew a great deal about sur-render theoretically and appreciated the importance of the "total surren-der" that Dr. Mehta was advocating. At the beginning of their time together he was able to write:

> Only to the extent that you are not attached to any thought, to any point of view, to anything at all, that you do not desire or fear any-thing, that you do not feel delight or sorrow in anything—only so can the void be created in your intellect. If I am worried about what will happen tomorrow, about what I will have to decide tomorrow, I will not be able to reach this void. I must have absolute faith in this mystery of the beyond into which I throw myself. Whether I call it Christ, Shiva, Paramatman does not matter. Total acceptance that someone is there to receive me, to take complete charge of me, or rather that in the end I will find myself set free from all my present limitations.[12]

He found that for the surrender to be complete all stability had to be "blown up," and he constantly refered to nakedness, "a nakedness which could perhaps be more accurately called a flaying." Here is not only sur-render but an impressive humility:

> I have been "*stripped stark naked*" in my soul these days in Bombay-Poona. And my "pride" in having realized something has been swept away, and I have been made to understand that everything that I had, not only through my intelligence and through my previous study and meditation, but also everything that I thought I had learned when hidden in the heart of Arunachala, was nothing, noth-ing at all, simply the babbling of a child. . . .
>
> Here I have to be simply a disciple, and even to receive through this other person the message from him with whom I thought I was one. Great pride in the conviction that one has passed beyond *advaita*, when one has scarcely set foot on the road, entered the stream.[13]

For a few weeks during the summer of 1955 he thought he had made the surrender demanded of him: it was, he felt, only the clarification of the moment he remembered so precisely, on January 9, 1928, when he accepted that his life was to be dedicated to the pursuit of holiness. Now he had surrendered his priesthood, his monastic life, even his belonging to the church. So too he recognized that outward obedience is merely a substitute for the true guidance of the Spirit within; personal choice too must be surrendered. Always there was more to surrender: "One thinks one is naked and discovers that one is decked out in a veritable parody of evening dress."[14] By the time he had returned to Shantivanam he was able to write that the surrender of things that had been his pride and joy had been made: "I keep it and cultivate it like a piece of land that no longer belongs to me." Yet he knew that he would never be at peace until he had yielded even more, until he had "*let go all my moorings*" [Abhishiktananda's emphasis].[15]

A journey such as he was making has few easy patches, little respite. As if he had not drunk deeply enough of the bitter waters of humility, he had to taste them again as he urged himself to surrender both his desire to remain a Christian and his desire to live as an *advaitin* Hindu, "in total surrender to the mystery. Free and naked at the heart of the abyss, hanging there."[16] It is impossible to tell whether at this point he is saying that he *is* in a state of total surrender or whether that is what he is striving for. But it is clear that six weeks later the struggle is on again:

> I must "surrender" not only my eagerness "to plan" but even more, my anxiety to know "intellectually" what all that means, and the solution to the mystery of the Church and the mystery of Christ, and also to know what is going to happen to me. . . . Things in fact will only happen "in accordance with" my deepening in the within.[17]

And there is no ambiguity in his painfully honest statement that

> I have not managed to achieve it—the "surrender" of my "ego" as a Christian, a monk, a priest. And yet I must do so. Perhaps it will then be given back to me, renewed. But meanwhile I must leave it behind—totally—without any hope of its return.[18]

Paradoxically, to let go, to surrender is the hardest of struggles. Despite having sought the state of surrender for so long, it was no easier for Abhishiktananda than for anyone else.

ON JULY 30, TOWARD THE END of his first week with Dr. Mehta, Abhishiktananda discovered that his portable altar stone lay broken at the bottom of the case in which he kept the things he needed for celebrating Mass. This may sound insignificant to the Roman Catholic of the twenty-first century, but for a pre–Vatican II priest, especially for one with a background of such liturgical strictness as Abhishiktananda, it was disastrous, for the old Canon Law forbade a priest to celebrate the Eucharist without a consecrated altar stone, and if the stone was broken the consecration was lost. Already he was having grave misgivings about saying Mass; in fact he was relieved that under Dr. Mehta's guidance he did not have to do so, but this enforced abstention was a cause of guilt and worry to him for, as he often said, "the Mass crystallizes my inner struggle."[19] The matter disturbed him deeply, especially as the only money he received came from Mass stipends and it was abhorrent to him to say Mass in order to eat. He was beginning to question his right, thinking as he did, to say Mass at all and wondered whether he should not renounce the church "with all the psychological and material stability that carries with it."[20]

Then to find his altar stone broken and therefore to be forbidden, under the church's law, from saying Mass was so full of symbolism for him that it shook him to his roots. Was it a punishment, an invitation, a liberation? What did this ominous sign symbolize? He took it as a way of "giving me a rather rough shake, so that I might understand the language of events."[21] At the very least, he wondered, "Is it a warning to make me halt at last on a path that is so dangerous from the Christian ecclesiastical viewpoint?"[22]

Once again he was split in two. After years of being dependent on the Mass, he found that part of him was so intoxicated to be free of the obligation that he wanted "to don white vestments and sing of blessed liberation";[23] but another part wept with grief, the grief of a child torn apart from its parent. Yet the child grows up and leaves home—even Jesus left his mother: "The Church cannot prevent her child from going all alone to God."[24] And yet, and yet . . . he had spent his whole life in the arms of the church and he could not bear to be without it: "If now I had to die, I would want to receive absolution and especially the Host for my final departure."[25]

He could find no consolation in the church, no help, no comfort; he only kept up his liturgical obligations out of a sense of duty. It was not that he wanted to become a Hindu; it was harder even than that. He had hit bedrock; he was confronting in all its fearful uncertainty the chasm over which he was poised. It was not simply a question of reconciling Hinduism and Christianity, though that would be hard enough; he was being taken even further, to the point where he had to say, "The Hindu myth, just like the Christian myth, must be left behind." He was not to be allowed the comfort of church or temple, of liturgy or ritual; he was to seek God alone.

His dilemma also had another dimension. He could not celebrate Mass if he did not belong to the church, yet if he belonged to the church he was obliged, whether he wanted to or not, to celebrate Mass. He loved the Mass, though it brought him into unspeakable realms of anguish; a not untypical diary entry reads:

> All was agony in my Mass. The Mass an entreaty. I need to be freed from the Mass, the Office, etc., for a long time. Homeopathy. Afterwards would perhaps come back to it? Who knows? If I did not come back it would be because the summons to the beyond is true for me.[26]

But he was becoming more and more critical of the church, more and more disillusioned by it; in fact sometimes—with a surprising equanimity—he contemplated leaving it:

> If some day I have to leave the Church, it must be done independently of every kind of consolation, congratulation, etc. from the other side; I must be ready to be completely neglected, left on the side, even by my Hindu friends, for the sake of pure and naked obedience to the voice of my conscience.[27]

And only a week later he was asking, "How can one honestly remain in the Church?" and suggesting that "God's word to Abraham, 'Depart from your country,' holds at every stage in the advance towards the supreme Goal."[28]

It is a measure of how even-handed he was in his approach to the teachings of both Christianity and Hinduism that he found help in his problems with the Mass in the Bhagavad Gita. There he read that if it was his *karma* to celebrate Mass and say the Office, then why try to escape from them before he was ready? The secret lay in non-attachment: "Let me not be attached to my Mass and let me not desire to be freed from it."[29] He might have found some comfort in the idea of being free to say Mass or not, without attachment, but he felt compelled to add, "If some day a Christian reads these pages, how could he fail to conclude that the one who wrote them had completely lost his faith."[30] He minded very much how people saw him in relation to his Christianity, and he was to continue to mind for many years.

So the Mass too was affected by his desire for complete surrender. He was being asked to surrender something that for forty years he had been told was of central importance to his faith. Was there anything left he did not have to surrender? "I must surrender, not only to my impatience 'to plan,' but still more my anxiety 'to know,' to know 'intellectually what all this means. . . .'"[31] But now he knew there was no solution on the rational level; only "total abandonment to the Lord, in total nakedness."[32]

He had to admit that, since he had tasted *advaita*, with its "diamond-hard purity"[33] the things of the church, from a long day of confirmations at Shantivanam to the most beautiful singing of the Mass, no longer satisfied him. But he still believed that the church's teaching was true at the level of symbol, and over the next few years he began to discern two layers, both in the teaching of the church and in its liturgy. He distinguished between the "fable" and the truth Christ's teachings proclaim, just as with the liturgy he perceived two planes:

> Liturgy is on one particular plane, and on this plane it is marvellous.
> . . . Advaita places you on another plane, and says that all the other
> planes are a game, *lila, maya.** And the advantage of Shivaism is that
> it very readily accepts that it is a game which has to be left behind
> ("When I was a child, I thought as a child. . ."); while in the Church
> the plane of sacraments, liturgy, Church, is treated as absolute in
> itself. And therein lies the agonizing tension.[34]

His criticisms of the church were no pleasure to him. In his way he still loved it and he certainly needed it; it had been central to his whole life. Yet having tasted the pure fresh water of *advaita*, he now found it immature, over-institutionalized and over-protected from the truth it sought to proclaim. He longed for the institutional church to be "freed from its strait-jacket, purified, baptized in water and fire."[35] His tragedy was that he had found a peace and joy in Hinduism that he had never known before, yet there was this great obstacle, his attachment to the church, an institution with, he felt, a super-ego so imperious that he feared that if he rejected it his very being would be destroyed. He loved it with the love of long ago, and now he did not know how to escape its clutches. This

---

*Līlā is the creation as divine play. *Māyā* is "divine magic," which veils reality and projects the universe.

dilemma, this crucifixion between his need for the church and his dissatisfaction with it, exploded in a poignant cry: "If only the Church was *spiritually radiant*, if it was not so firmly attached to the formulations of transient philosophies, if it did not obstruct the freedom of the Spirit . . . with such niggling regulations, it would not be long before we reached an understanding."[36]

ABHISHIKTANANDA'S INSTINCT WAS ALWAYS to find an outlet for his thoughts and emotions in the written word—he was a natural writer and a very talented one. The appalling anguish he endured in the 1950s is, not surprisingly, most fully recorded in the privacy of his spiritual diary, but he had also, since he stayed in the caves of Arunachala in 1952, been making notes of his attempts to integrate the Christian and the advaitic experience for a book he called *Guhantara*, literally a pseudonym for himself, "one who dwells within the cave." As an overflowing river breaks its banks if it is confined, so did Abhishiktananda need an outlet, and *Guhantara* was the first detailed articulation of the confrontation between Christianity and *advaita*. It was also an attempt to highlight something he was convinced was the special grace of India, the grace of interiority; he could see no future for the church in India unless it recovered the mystical dimension that was, for the most part, so sadly neglected.

Guhantara was written at intervals through 1952 and 1953—James Stuart thinks that Abhishiktananda probably started making notes for it as early as March 1952. Stuart also thinks that the first essay, "The Special Grace of India," "virtually sets out a programme which he was to elaborate in much of his later writing."[37] A good description of the book comes from Father Monchanin, who was supportive, despite his reservations about the path his friend was taking; Abhishiktananda felt he understood the book better than most but was "too Greek" to give it unstinting approval. Monchanin asks whether it is a metaphysical poem, a theological meditation, or the scattered notes for a diary of the soul? Or is it:

A dialogue partly real, partly fictional (but in the sense that the fiction is more true than any shorthand), between a Christian and a Hindu committed, both of them, to explore the implications of their respective faiths to the very end? Simply, perhaps, a spiritual essay, which, born of silence, yearns to return to that silence. *Guhantara*, the interior of the cavern, does it not evoke the descent on the end of a poorly tethered potholer's rope? In these dark places where there is no longer a guide, the words explode, logic wavers, and paradox alone can pull together this desperate effort to tell that which is beyond words.[38]

Monchanin is, however, convinced, that the book should not been seen as syncretic or wishing to go beyond Christianity or indeed any religion. It is not, he ends wistfully, a theology, a philosophy, or a theses; it is "a call: *vox in deserto.*"

Abhishiktananda himself thought that nothing like it had ever been written before, but he admitted that the essays were repetitive and lacked logic. He also realized they would arouse opposition. Like most authors Abhishiktananda wanted his book published, but he had both an added motivation and an added problem. The book was not only an outlet for the moments of blinding illumination that he experienced, but a way of drawing the attention of the church to a problem on which, he felt, its future depended. This amounted, in effect, to a criticism of the church, and so he had to face the censor appointed by a bishop in order to get the necessary *imprimatur** before it could be published. The author never had the pleasure of holding the completed book in his hand, and it still cannot be read in book form, though substantial sections can be read in two volumes published much later by Editions Présence.

The failure of *Guhantara* to be published is a sad story. At the end of 1953 Abhishiktananda sent the manuscript off to his friend Canon Lemarié to be typed and sent to the Paris censor, Father J. Guennou. He knew very well that much of it was likely to meet with the censor's disapproval and considered submitting it as a supplement to *Ermites du Saccidânanda*, an expanded version, in French, of the earlier booklet he and Monchanin had written together, *An Indian Benedictine Ashram*. This was a much less contentious book based on the experience of Shantivanam, an invitation to Christian monks to take their place in the great tradition of Hindu *sannyāsa*; by presenting the two as a single manuscript he hoped *Guhantara* might slip through the censor's net unnoticed. This, however, was not allowed, and *Guhantara* went naked and alone before the eyes of the Paris censor. Let us have a taste of what he read.

The first essay encapsulates many of the themes that were to preoccupy Abhishiktananda. For instance, he distinguishes between learned understanding and experience; he explains the way India can live simultaneously "without" and "within," her worship clothed in outward forms that are often crude, even vulgar, but are seen as part of the divine play, *līlā*, and are known to be gateways to the transcendent. He compares the

---

*"Let it be printed." The certification that a book has been passed for publication by the appropriate authority.

Indian to an actor, playing his various roles against the backdrop of the unshakable Absolute: the idol may be stone or metal, but its presence is a necessary stage on the way to the beyond. So too he tries to explain concepts like the *ātman*, using well-chosen and accessible passages from Indian scriptures:

> This *atman* is only defined by negatives: *neti neti*
> impossible to grasp, for it cannot be apprehended;
> indestructible, for it cannot be destroyed;
> unattached, for it is attached to nothing;
> without ties, inaccessible to all disquiet and all suffering.[39]

But this essay is not extolling Hinduism at the expense of Christianity; he writes gratefully that the values of the within can be found in Christianity. They live in the souls of mystics like Ruysbroek, Tauler, and Meister Eckhart; they have been expounded by some theologians. But he suggests that perhaps these experiences and formulations are not given their rightful place in Christianity, for "Western rationalism has always been in defiance—and in fear—of the mystery of the beyond, the interior beyond above all."[40] What richness Christianity could bring to mankind, he writes, if the Upanishadic texts were illuminated by the light of Christ.

As Abhishiktananda nervously awaited the censor's verdict, he was also worried about the renewal of his indult of exclaustration. In fact, he was so worried that he might not be allowed to stay in India that, aware that the degree of his concern was not in the spirit of *advaita*, he even wondered if he, who had written *Guhantara*, had understood it himself. The distractions of practical life at Shantivanam were welcome, and his practical side reasserted itself as he attended to hedges, keeping the banana plantation watered and protecting the library books from forest insects.

When the censor's report finally arrived, in November 1954, his worst fears were realized. The report was "totally damning, attacking the book on every conceivable ground, and finding 'heresies' on every page. It was so negative as to be ludicrous."[41] Abhishiktananda and Monchanin's reaction was surprising—after a moment of sheer astonishment, they laughed, with a great roar of laughter. Criticism they could have accepted, but from a censor, reading for the Vatican, surely it would be *intelligent* criticism, something useful to the author? It is a measure of the value Abhishiktananda still put on his monastic status that if it had not been for his vows of obedience and poverty, he would have considered making several hundred photocopies so that at least it could be read by those with open minds, willing to consider the problems the book posed.

He realized that rewriting was not an answer—in any case there were bad reports from other theologians to whom he had sent the book. It was heavily criticized by a Dominican, slaughtered by the reader for Editions du Cerf, who had been interested in publishing it, and while the Jesuit Father Bayart received it with courtesy, his criticism cut Abhishiktananda to the quick. "I shall give up writing. . . . Father Bayart rips me to shreds. By considering me as a non-Christian, they will finally make me one. Agony, agony, and in the depth, advaita—pure, total, complete. How it calls! Fascinating!"[42] It was too Christian for Hindus, too Hindu for Christians. Even his friend and great admirer Odette Baumer-Despeigne did not like it. Later, with the wisdom of distance, Abhishiktananda was able to write, "What is the use of going on writing? It can all be said in a few lines."[43]

He had to accept that the church was not ready for what he was trying to communicate, though he must have been confused in this judgment when he read Panikkar's *Unknown Christ of Hinduism*, which was published a few years later in 1964, as Abhishiktananda considered that "its boldness far exceeds my *Guhantara*."[44] He also realized that the adverse opinions he had received would probably be shared by most theologians and missionaries. Even had it passed the censor, it would have been attacked in reviews and might have led to his being sent back to his monastery, for there was an Internuncio in Rome who was deeply resentful of this French Benedictine living outside his monastery and would have leapt at an excuse to return him to France.

There were oases of approval, notably from the professor of dogmatic theology at the Institut Catholique de Paris, Father Paul Henry. His response delighted the anxious author, whose confidence was slightly restored by "such cordial and encouraging approval," and its importance was recognized by no less a theological luminary than Father Henri de Lubac, who very much wanted the work to be published and said that many people were reading the manuscript and thinking about it. "What am I to conclude?" asks Abhishiktananda of Canon Lemarié, "That only contemplatives will understand!"[45]

So 1955 ended. Abhishiktananda's spiritual life had reached a crisis point, and he was feeling more and more that he could not live any longer at Shantivanam. He had been deeply influenced by two men, Harilal and Dr. Mehta. He had put his soul on paper and been rejected. But there was another important meeting ahead, which he felt was foretold in a veiled way in Dr. Mehta's messages. He met an old Hindu *sannyāsi* to whom he felt he could give himself completely.

10

Total Immersion in Hinduism

1956

I have become a real Hindu monk![1]

To BE TRUE TO HIS DESIRE to live everything at the level of experience, it would be entirely natural for Abhishiktananda, Benedictine monk though he was, to seek God in the way of the Hindu—through a guru. He knew that sometimes divine grace simply descends, without explanation, nor did he discount the value of intelligent and careful reading of scripture, but he was already so deeply immersed in India that the way to realization for him meant to follow the Indian tradition and learn from the lips of those who have trodden the path and know its joys and dangers for themselves.

The relationship of the guru and the disciple is much misunderstood in the West and so is rejected, even sometimes mocked. At its best and purest this is a truly wonderful relationship whose aim is to impart the highest knowledge and understanding. Most importantly, the guru knows, as is said in the Katha Upanishad, that the disciple "cannot be taught by one who has not reached him; and he cannot be reached by much thinking. The way to him is through Teacher who has seen him."[2] The one who becomes a guru is one who speaks only from experience, then, if the disciple comes, an extraordinary bond can develop between them:

> To his guru the disciple must give complete faith, that total surrender which includes both faith and obedience in the fullest sense of the words. For the disciple the guru is the manifestation of God himself, and his "devotion" to the guru is for him the final stage— beyond all external worship. . . . To such a disciple the guru will

123

impart the ultimate knowledge, mouth to ear, and finally, for the
most part silently, heart to heart. He will guide him step by step in
the control of the senses and of the mind. He will foster in him
renunciation and discrimination. He will sometimes be very hard on
him, allowing him neither ease nor respite. But he will temper his
firmness with gentleness, leading him in the path of true understanding.[3]

The task of the guru includes, traditionally, the recitation of the Vedas
and the writings of the Masters—reading for oneself is not considered
enough; they should also be *heard*. But the true guru does much more; he
reaches the heart of the disciple:

> The whispering of the sacred *mantra* into the ear of the disciple on
> the day of his initiation is the symbol of a mysterious and effective
> whispering from heart to heart. The disciple is connected to God by
> his guru, not in the sense that the guru would be an intermediary
> between disciple and God. It is in the person of the guru that God
> appears to the disciple.[4]

The word guru is hard to define and is often misused. A guru is not a
master or professor, he or she is not a preacher or spiritual guide; he is
not a director of souls or anyone who has learned from books and is passing on what he has learned. The guru is someone who has truly awakened, found his own fullness; for a person to meet his or her guru is a
mystery, deep in the heart, for it is to meet oneself, with all pretense gone.

> The guru is one who has himself first attained the Real and who
> knows from personal experience the way that leads there; he is capa-
> ble of initiating the disciple and of making well up, from within the
> heart of his disciple, the immediate ineffable experience which is his
> own—the utterly transparent knowledge, so limpid and pure, that
> quite simply "he is."[5]

Where then, would Abhishiktananda find his guru? He knew, of
course, that Christ was his *sad-guru*,* historically revealed in Jesus and
mysteriously present in the Sacrament: that conviction was strong in his
very bones and would never leave him. His encounter with Ramana
Maharshi, blinding as it was in its significance, was so short—just two virtually silent meetings, cut short by death. His friendships with Harilal

---

*The true guru, master.

and Dr. Mehta, though of great value and significance, had not completely answered his need. At some level, barely conscious, he sought a living guru, teaching in the traditional way of India.

There is a well-known proverb, "When the disciple is ready, the guru appears," and so it happened. One day Abhishiktananda's friend Harold Rose,* an Englishman who had originally been a Trappist novice but was at the time a disciple of a Muslim sufi, asked him if he had heard of Sri Gnanananda, the holy man of Tirukoyilur? He had not, even though Tirukoyilur was less than thirty kilometers from Arunachala, and he was intrigued to hear of this swami, believed to be 120 years old, of whom incredible stories were told. Two days later, on December 12, 1955, despite Father Monchanin's efforts to dissuade him, he set off with Harold Rose to see the holy man. Just as six years earlier, when he went to see Ramana Maharshi, he was convinced that this was to be a turning point in his life.

Later Abhishiktananda wrote a vivid account of this encounter in *Guru and Disciple*, some modesty or discretion causing him to refer to himself in the third person as "Vanya." (Writing to Marie-Thérèse ten years later he said this book would not be published during his lifetime, as it would not be understood. In fact it was published in French in 1970, three years before his death.) The two men left Arunachala early to avoid traveling in the heat of the day, and they saw evidence of the veneration in which the holy man was held as soon as they got off the bus, which stopped outside Tapovanam, the guru's ashram; they learned that the bus driver was a disciple of Gnanananda and that every evening, on his way home, he would stop at the ashram, run in and prostrate himself before his guru, touch his holy feet, and receive his blessing. Then he would stop again in the jungle nearby and break a coconut under a sacred banyan tree to offer a libation.

It was still early in the morning when Abhishiktananda and his friend arrived. There was no temple, no pomp and ceremony, just a modest little house and a young man returning from his morning wash. They were told that Swamiji was always available, day or night—in fact he rarely slept. They found the guru sitting in a corner on a rickety old couch, unshaven, deeply peaceful and giving out an immense tenderness. He wore the saffron *dhoti*, with one shoulder bare and the end draped over his head, and on his forehead—so smooth it was hard to believe his reputed age, though there are records of him as an adult in 1860—were the three lines of ash and the vermilion mark worn by devotees of Shiva.

---

*His real name was Ronald Fullwood Rose.

The two Westerners could not bring themselves to prostrate or touch the feet of the master—such gestures did not sit easily with Europeans in the middle of the twentieth century. They simply greeted him with folded hands and began to ask questions about the spiritual life. The young man who had greeted them translated into English, but it soon became clear that the subtleties of the Guru's thought were too much for him, and Abhishiktananda tried his own Tamil, though he admitted it was elementary and the pronunciation lamentable. But somehow there was an immediate understanding, beyond the words being spoken, between guru and disciple.

Abhishiktananda's first questions received answers that must have reminded him of Ramana Maharshi: "What is the use of such questions? The answer is within you. Seek it in the depths of your being. Devote yourself to *dhyāna*, meditation, beyond all forms and the solution will be given to you."[6] A further similarity appeared when Abhishiktananda asked if Swamiji performed rites of initiation, which have the value of a sacrament? This he admitted was posed as a test question, though he does not indicate what sort of answer he wanted or expected. What he was told was quite unambiguous: "What is the use of initiation? Either the disciple is not ready, in which case the so-called initiation is no more than empty words, or else the disciple is ready and then neither words nor signs are necessary. The initiation then happens spontaneously."[7]

Abhishiktananda quickly established himself as a favorite of Sri Gnanananda's—if gurus are allowed to have favorites—sitting beside him and sometimes even being passed questions put to the guru. He found that this first encounter with Gnanananda pierced to his heart, revealing unknown depths, "living water of incomparable sweetness."[8] Two hours sped by—even sitting cross-legged had not caused the discomfort he usually experienced. He knew he had come face to face with the actual experience of realization; that the man he had approached almost as a tourist had taken possession of his very being. In his third-person account he writes:

> He realized that the allegiance which he had never freely yielded to anyone in his life was now given automatically to Gnanananda. He had often heard tell of gurus, of the irrational devotion shown to them by their disciples and their total self-abandonment to the guru. All these things had seemed utterly senseless to him, a European with a classical education. Yet now at this very moment it had happened to him, a true living experience tearing him out of himself. This little man with his short legs and bushy beard, scantily

clad in a dhoti, who had so suddenly burst in upon his life, could now ask of him anything in the world . . . and he, Vanya, would not even think of asking him for any sort of explanation. Without even considering the matter Vanya and Harold found themselves on the ground pressing the master's feet with fervent hands.[9]

Abhishiktananda knew that it is as rare to meet a real disciple as it is to meet a real guru. Now he understood how guru and disciple form a couple, two poles existing in relation to one another. They were "a pair on the road to unity."[10] It is not a meeting of two people in the ordinary sense, but a meeting beyond the level of the senses and the intellect, a meeting that happens in the most subtle part of the soul. Abhishiktananda made a distinction between even the deepest of human encounters, when two become one in love and desire, and the meeting of guru and disciple, where "there is no longer even fusion, for we are on the plane of the original non-duality."[11] It is not even one person talking to another; it hardly matters what words the guru uses, somehow they come from the heart of the disciple himself, who "comes face to face with his true self in the very depth of his being, an experience every man longs for, even if unconsciously."[12] The guru, with such wisdom and love, is leading the true disciple to hear the *Tat tvam asi*—the "Thou art that" of the Vedic *rishi*s.

So the first visit ended with Sri Gnanananda asking Abhishiktananda to return:

Come back and be near me. We shall talk again. Above all you will have time for silent meditation. No one will disturb you. You will not have to worry about food or anything like that. Apart from our conversations, you will remain in silence. So come in a few months time after the celebration of Pongal.* I shall be expecting you.[13]

ABHISHIKTANANDA WROTE TO HIS FRIENDS and his family about the experience, sometimes with high seriousness, sometimes in the humorous, self-deprecating way that was so much a part of his approach to himself. "I met a man unlike any other that I have ever come across. Outwardly there is nothing extraordinary about him. He does not read your thoughts, does no miracles; but when he speaks to you, it is as if what he says was coming out of your own heart."[14] The irony of the situation was not lost on him as he continued, "it was mighty strange to see this Benedictine monk seated on a tiger skin beside the master, with bare

---

*A Tamil festival in mid-January to mark the end of the harvest season.

shoulders, saluted with prostrations."[15] He seemed quite taken aback by the fact that prostration, hitherto something quite alien to him, was now something he was happy, even impelled, to do. He wrote to his sister Marie-Thérèse, herself living the conventional life of an enclosed Benedictine nun, of her brother's dramatic change:

> You see that I have become a real Hindu monk! My guru is the first man before whom I have been willing to prostrate. I now do it in fine style; a controlled fall to the ground, with arms extended, touching the ground first with the ears, then with the forehead; then half rising, you do it again, then you stand up and touch the master's feet with your hands, which are then brought up to the eyes. . . . You see the drill you will have to perform, if one day your brother presents himself at the grill of Saint-Michel![16]

He wrote of his guru in his diary, referring to the period between Monday December 12 and Thursday December 15 with loving precision as "my overwhelming encounter with Sri Gnanananda"[17] and described himself to his friend Canon Lemarié as being totally "caught," admitting, "If that man were to ask me tomorrow to set out on the roads naked and silent like Sadashiva Brahman, I would be unable to refuse."[18] This, however, was not demanded of him. What Gnanananda actually wanted was for him to devote his whole time to meditation without thoughts, foregoing conversation, even reading—if he did this, the full experience of *advaita*, of awakening, of realization, would surely come to him. Abhishiktananda was less optimistic, writing, "I should need months, perhaps years, of deep silence to find my bearings at this point which transcends the intellect."[19]

It is no surprise that the new disciple, so deeply impressed, could not wait to visit his guru again, but again Monchanin resisted, Abhishiktananda recording that he "pounces on every excuse for advising me to put it off."[20] He did not want to cross his friend and partner at Shantivanam, but he knew that this resistance would fuel his doubts about the ashram and was likely to make him want to leave it for good. He delayed for a while, but his good intentions did not last long and by the end of February 1956 he was at Tirukoyilur again, this time alone, to spend three weeks with Sri Gnanananda.

Abhishiktananda arrived on the agreed date, but there was no sign of the guru—he learned later that the Swami's movements were consistent only in their unpredictability—and after several hours, beginning to feel hungry, he decided to live like a real *sādhu* and beg for his food, something he had only tried to do once, on that occasion finding he was so overcome with embarrassment that he had to give up. This time, however, he was determined. He took staff and begging bowl, twisted a cloth round his head against the heat and resolutely set out for the village. *Bhikshā*, begging, is only done when the door is open, and arriving there and seeing so many closed doors he began to realize that the people of that village had already eaten. At this he lost his nerve again and decided there was no alternative but to fast, though he could not stop hmself looking longingly ahead to the evening meal.

But the honor habitually paid to his robes saved him from this involuntary hunger, for just as others, seeing him wearing the clothes of the *sannyāsi*, had prostrated before him, so now a man approached, telling him to follow, as the priest of the temple was asking for him. His guide, intoning softly as he walked, led him to the Shiva Temple, where the priest greeted him and silently performed the ritual, customary on entering a temple, of pouring water over the visitor's feet. The priest asked neither his name, his caste nor his religion, but simply showed him a seat, sprinkled the earth in front of him with water, and placed a banana leaf and a silver goblet before him. Then the priest and his wife brought some rice and condiments.

After the meal, the priest, whose name, he discovered, was Kailasanadar, invited him to sit on a carpet; holy ash and incense sticks were brought, and soon he was surrounded by men, women, and children wanting to offer their homage and receive the *darshan* of this fair-skinned holy man. He was then taken around the temple, proudly shown the religious articles brought by pilgrims, and, as the sun set, they went to the river, where the priest mixed water and ash and traced the three symbolic white lines of Shiva on his forehead and chest. The priest did not know that this *sādhu* was also a Christian monk, but it does not seem likely that the knowledge would have worried him.

Abhishiktananda rejoiced that it was not only in Christian monasteries that the monks are bidden to receive a guest as the Lord in person, that there are strange similarities across time and space in those "who have discovered the mystery of the presence in the depth of their souls."[21] He thanked them, saying, "Is it not Ishwara* who offers the *bhikshā* and just as truly Ishwara who receives it? Did not Shiva appear many times disguised as a beggar to test the sincerity of the faithful?"[22]

The manner in which he voiced his thanks to the priest and an entry in his diary a few days later when he revisited the temple and stood before

---

*Lord; cf. *Paramesvara*, the supreme Lord; *Mahesvara*, the Great God.

the *Shiva-linga*,* show how deeply the influence of Sri Gnanananda and Ramana Maharshi had entered his soul. He was beginning not just to understand, but to experience, the essential unity of everything:

> How can I fail to prostrate myself before it when I return to that temple, this time with other people, and no longer secretly, with my forehead also marked with the mysteriously threefold sign of the sacred *linga!*
>
> But is not the Shiva-*linga* myself just as much as this stone? Who is prostrating, and before whom? And this body sinks to the ground and this intellect collapses, just so that finally there may emerge, from the deep womb of the heart, which has at last been discovered, at last attained, that sign, that pure sign, which is the sacred stone in the centre of the place of rebirth in Being.[23]

ABHISHIKTANANDA SPENT THREE DAYS as the guest of the village and its temple, living among Hindus as one of them, experiencing Hinduism in practice at a depth rarely possible for Westerners; it was part of the process he both wanted and needed—total immersion in Hinduism. Eventually news came that the guru had returned, and Abhishiktananda left the temple and went back to Tapovanam.

This break occasioned by Sri Gnanananda's absence had given Abhishiktananda the opportunity to witness and share Hindu rituals and customs in the temple and by the time he returned to the ashram he felt more at home with what had, on his first visit, seemed strange. Now happy to prostrate himself, he was fascinated by noting how the fervor of devotion is measured by the number of prostrations and how it was bad manners to prostrate only once, how the women simply knelt demurely down and touched the floor with their foreheads. When the farewell prostrations were made, each person was given a piece of fruit or a flower, known as *prasāda*, grace. The children, noting this, would manage to make their ritual departure with a frequency that did not escape the indulgent guru.

The most sacred hours of the day in Hinduism, as in Christianity, are dawn and dusk, the mysterious meeting of night and day, the moments of ending and of beginning. So before sunrise the brahmin will stand by the river, or if he is not near a river then he will have a jar of water at his side,

---

**Linga is the phallic symbol of Shiva, a simple conical stone, venerated in temples and in the open air.

for water, the life-giving womb of creation, is intrinsic to every Hindu ceremony. So the devout Hindu will take his bath, recite mantras and ritually sprinkle his body. He will then honor the four points of the compass, throwing water north, south, east, and west, then close the orifices of his face with his fingers to control his breathing. Finally, as at last the sun appears over the horizon, he raises his hands above his head and prostrates himself in adoration.

The evening ceremony, bidding farewell to the day, also stretches back into Vedic times and is considered the best time to pray, when for most people the tempo of life eases and the cares of the day can be put aside. Abhishiktananda described the ritual he had experienced at the temple. Each image of a deity would be honored according to what it stood for— so a few dance steps would be made before Ganapati,* hands would be clapped in front of another, who was always lost in contemplation and had to be awakened, while before Dakshinamurti, the embodiment of wisdom and a name given to Lord Shiva as the silent teacher, the worshiper would remain in quiet contemplation. Then all approach the dark central sanctuary and prostrate themselves, as the priests chant litanies and throw flowers onto the sacred stone of the *Shiva-linga*. Finally *arati* and sacred ash are offered; the celebrant holds out the ash and the light so that each person can mark the forehead with ash and take the light to the eyes. The light is made by burning camphor, which leaves no residue and is the symbol of the soul that has passed completely into the fire of divine love.

Abhishiktananda was not too sympathetic with anyone who found these rites idolatrous—and in the middle of the twentieth century there were plenty of them. For him they were a mystery both inner and cosmic, a "marvellous epiphany of God in his creation." After several years in India he was coming to understand the place of ritual in his life and to understand that liturgy and *advaita*, the nonduality that was the true goal of his search, were on two different planes, not contradicting each other.

This attitude to liturgy was influenced, if not determined, by his understanding of the difference between the manifest and the unmanifest, or what Zen practitioners call the phenomenal and the essential. Liturgy, however beautiful, belongs to the manifest, the phenomenal; *advaita*, nonduality, concerns the unmanifest, the essential. So, increasingly at home in the world beyond duality, Abhishiktananda had no diffi-

---

*One of the names for Ganesha, the elephant-headed god of wisdom and good fortune and one of the most popular Hindu gods.

culty in bringing Hindu and Christian worship together at Shantivanam, writing from there soon after his second visit to Gnanananda:

> We sing Lauds, Terce, Sext, None, Vespers and Compline, with each Mass each morning after Lauds (Matins in private). We add hymns in Sanskrit and Tamil before and after the Office. We prostrate, give greetings in Indian style, offer the light just as I have seen it done in Hindu temples and ashrams [i.e., *arati*].[24]

He was completely at home living in the ashram with his Hindu brethren, where the day ended gently, the guru's disciples revealing as they drifted into sleep that the unconcious does not have to distinguish between one religion and another.

> When they were tired of singing and conversing, they quietly stretched out under the pandal and dropped off to sleep. Murugan Das continued his songs and litanies long after the others, and, as if echoing his invocations to Murugan,* other ejaculations soon broke the silence. The rhythm and intonation strangely resembled those of Tamil Christian worship. Surprised, Vanya listened more carefully. There was no doubt that "Our Fathers" and "Ave Marias" were endlessly following one another, punctuated by ejaculations to Murugan uttered by a neighbour. This continued for a long time. Gradually however the rhythm slowed down, the voices became weaker and finally all that could be heard were single invocations at increasing intervals. "YESUVI (Jesus)! ANDAVARE [Lord]! MURUGA! TAYARE [Mother]! MARIYAYE (Mary)!" . . . then at last all were enveloped in the deep silence of sleep.[25]

ABHISHIKTANANDA DESCRIBED HIS TWO WEEKS at the ashram as a time of "utter peace and fulness; some of the rare moments of life that one longs to relive again and again; very special times when one knows one exists in the depths of oneself where all appearances are left behind and one is on the level of the True."[26]

The timetable was simple, long periods of quiet interrupted only by meals and by ritual. Sometimes there would be just a few people eating together, sometimes as many as sixty, for Sri Gnanananda would invite all the visitors to the ashram to stay for the meal and would not eat his own rice until everyone had eaten. Occasionally a disciple donated a meal, and

---

*Murugan is a Tamil deity, worshiped in a frenzied sacred dance.

on these occasions the usual ritual of ablutions became a ceremony. The Swami was asked to stand on a stone and a disciple washed his feet, pressing them and adorning them with sandalwood paste. He then walked around with folded hands, prostrating deeply.

The brahmins in Tamil Nadu are strict over matters of etiquette and Abhishiktananda, coming from a Breton family with no such pretensions, was often nervous that he would breach the code of good manners. For instance, it was important to drink without one's lips touching the cup. If an ill-mannered guest drank in the European way, repugnant in these parts, no person of caste could even take the cup to be washed. Some of these customs might sound absurd; indeed, one day Sri Gnanananda asked if people knew their meaning—and if they did not, what was the point of performing rites and reciting mantras? Many of them did not, so as everyone was preparing to eat their meal, served as usual on banana leaves, the Swami showed them that the sprinkling of the earth and the leaf with water and the tracing of a circle round the food symbolized the setting apart of this food for the needs of the body. As soon as the food is placed on the leaf another circle is traced to sanctify its use as nourishment and a drop of water is swallowed symbolically purifying the stomach, which is to receive the food. Touching the earth acknowledges that it is through the earth that all material blessings come from God. Only then does one actually take the food into one's mouth.

One incident at the ashram shows a side of Abhishiktananda not often in evidence—irritability. This was brought about by a visiting *sādhu* who continually interrupted the Guru, speaking at the top of his voice, until Abhishiktananda reminded him that it was Sri Gnanananda they had come to hear, not him. The *sādhu* continued, asking the two Westerners questions about themselves, where they were born and when, until Abhishiktananda, beside himself with irritation, took the man to task openly and publicly. These were not questions that should be asked between *sādhu*s, he said, from the moment a man puts on his saffron robes he has renounced everything and has not the right to call a single thing on earth his own. "What I was or where I was yesterday or ten years ago is utterly irrelevant. What does it matter where this body was born, or what name was given by those who received the child at birth? The real sadhu possesses neither name nor country and should in fact possess no 'I.'"[27] The Swami was visibly pleased with this reply, adding that such questions did not even deserve to be remembered.

Abhishiktananda reacted in similar fashion to a discussion about Sri Gnanananda's age. Someone produced a piece of paper in Tamil saying he was born in 1814; another claimed that he was two hundred years old;

these were swiftly capped by a claim that he knew a famous poetess who lived twenty centuries ago who . . . Abhishiktananda could bear it no longer and spoke up.

> What does it matter if we know whether Swami-ji is fifty or two hundred or even four hundred years old? Will knowing that give us moksha, salvation, the vision of the One who is? . . . This very mystery which he allows to shroud all that is other than the present moment seems to me to be his way of impressing upon us his most important lesson, that the only moment that really matters is the one when a man becomes "aware of the self."[28]

These interpolations, in an almost entirely Hindu audience and in the presence of the guru he so admired, show a confidence that must have had its origins in his own ever deepening awareness and understanding.

SRI GNANANANDA'S TEACHING, primarily through silence, sometimes through talking, always through his very being, occasionally took the form of stories—not surprising in a culture that has produced epic stories as powerful as the Mahabharata and the Bhagavad Gita. Abhishiktananda retells them, sometimes in detail, and if ever his memory fails and imagination steps in, they remain convincing. One story illustrates how Gnanananda said that there is no reality except the *atman*, that it belongs to everybody, and that the way to its realization is through *dhyana*, meditation, or silent concentration within. At this Abhishiktananda exclaimed, "If the cure is so simple, how is that so few people make use of it?" This is Sri Gnanananda's response:

> Just think of children. When they are ill, their mothers prepare a suitable brew for them and give it to them to drink. But the trouble is that the children do not like it. They wave their arms, kick their legs in the air, wriggle this way and that and shut their mouths tight. If the mother does succeed in inserting the spoon into their mouths, they promptly spit out everything. Ignorant people who refuse wisdom are exactly the same.
>
> Wisdom and true knowledge, will never enter a soul against her will. They must be continuously and single-heartedly sought. Supposing one day you come to know that there is a swami on the opposite bank of the river, about whom everyone tells wonderful tales. You want to have his darshana at all costs. You set off and come

to the river. It cannot be forded and it is too dangerous to swim across. By the bank you see a ferryman with his boat and you ask him to take you across to the other side.

"Very well," he says, "but first of all throw away your bundle. I only take men not their luggage."

"But I cannot leave my bundle behind. How can I do without it? I have food for the journey, blankets for the night, and fruit and flowers to offer to the Swami. I have my holy books which I read each day. After all, my bundle isn't very heavy. Look here, ferryman, be reasonable! Take me over as I am, with what I am carrying. I will pay you for your services."

"Do as you like," replies the ferryman. "Take it or leave it. I take you across without a bundle or I leave you here with your bundle. Which of the two do you want—the darshana of the Swami or your old junk?"[29]

If this reminded Abhishiktananda of Christ telling his disciples how hard it is for the rich man to enter the kingdom of God, he does not mention it here.

Gnanananda told good stories, and Abhishiktananda enjoyed them and appreciated their message, but his main teaching was to encourage his disciple to abandon conversation and even reading, and to concentrate on meditation without thoughts—"the royal way, the only effective means of achieving realization of the Presence in the inmost depths of onself."[30]

Abhishiktananda does not indicate any method or technique that the guru taught, but he tells how, when asked about meditation, Gnanananda would repeat, time after time, short Tamil verses on which he would then enlarge:

> Return within
> to the place where there is nothing
> and take care that nothing comes in.
> Penetrate to the depths of yourself,
> to the place where thought no longer exists
> and take care that no thought raises its head!
>
> There where nothing exists
> is Fulness!
> There where nothing is seen
> is the Vision of Being!

There where nothing appears any longer
is the sudden appearing of the Self!
Dhyana, it is this![31]

In one of the last conversations Abhishiktananda had with Sri Gnana-nanda, the Guru stressed to him that "to be ignorant of the Real is a more dangerous fever for the spirit than a severe ague is for the body." And the cure for his fever is *dhyāna,* silent concentration within. A diary entry at about this time gives a rare insight into how Abhishiktananda meditated:

The important thing is to fix the mind on something that leads to transcendence and frees from wandering thoughts. For me, it is the thought of the within (*ullam,* Tamil) , the *aham* (I) for example. To make my abode within, to sit there, plunge in, vanish. If thoughts still come, they should be like birds flying in the open space (*akasa*) of the heart, over my head without disturbing me. What is impor-tant is to make my abode stable . . .

To go within through the idea of the within is a good way. How-ever the idea of the within is in itself distinction (*bheda*). As long as I distinguish the *within* from myself who seeks the within, I am not within. He who seeks and that which is sought vanish in the last stage, and here is nothing left but pure light, undivided, self-luminous (*jyoti akhanda svaprakasa*). The last work to be done is to cut through the final distinction between he who seeks and that which is sought.[32]

A month after this retreat Abhishiktananda wrote an essay called "Esseulement" (Total Solitude), in which he nails this in all its complex simplicity. "At the very moment that anyone becomes aware that he *is,* he realizes that the precise awareness he has of being is not equal to being."[33]

WHAT HAD HE LEARNED FROM HIS GURU? He was at peace, full of joy and inner freedom. He writes of "Days of fullness—a peak"[34] and insists, "There is no place for anguish in one who is totally "surrendered." Indeed, the sign of full surrender is precisely the radiant peace, the equa-bility, equanimity, *samatva,* that is so evident in my guru."[35] Yet he also writes, "But I have to leave behind my joy! But I have to leave behind my peace!"[36] He is talking once more about surrender, about renunciation—renunciation on a scale that few people have contemplated. *Everything* must be given up, even "the thought and the feeling of my joy, the thought and the feeling of my peace."[37] The last work to be done is to "cut through the final distinction between *he who seeks* and *that which is sought*."[38] He felt he could no longer see the truth, no longer knew what he had to do, how he had to live—he just knew he had to renounce everything:

> Renounce my God, which does not mean renouncing God.
> Renounce my joy, which does not mean renouncing joy.
> Renounce my peace, which does not mean renouncing peace.
> Renounce my renunciation.[39]

If there is any distinction between the seeker and the goal, the one within and the within itself, the within has not been found. Eventually nothing will remain but light itself, the self, pure undivided Being. The final task is to overcome the distinction between the goal and the way:

> The man in search of the *self* is seized by a real onset of dizziness when he reaches what seems to him, from his point of view, to be the last bend in the road. He then realizes that he must henceforth renounce for ever, without any possibility of turning back, everything which up till then has seemed to be the ground of existence, which gave him being, his idea of self and his own consciousness bound to this idea of himself. In the abysses of the heart to which he feels himself inexorably drawn, there is absolutely nothing he can grasp hold of or hang on to, nothing solid on which he can, so to speak, put down his foot, no air from outside in which to draw breath.[40]

These meetings with his guru had led Abhishiktananda closer to the heart of *advaita*, but far from being radiant with peace and optimism, he was still torn apart by conflict; he still could not reconcile the advaitic path with the Christianity that was so deep in his heart.

He had been shaken by his encounter with Harilal; he had learned from Dr. Mehta; most of all he had been enriched by his days at the temple and by finding a guru. The next step had to be taken by himself, alone. He had to follow his destiny in silence and solitude.

11

A Month in Solitude

1956

A milestone in my life.[1]

ABHISHIKTANANDA FOUND A PLACE where he could make a silent retreat at Kumbakonam, a typical south Indian town in Tamil Nadu, forty kilometers from Thanjavur, the ancient capital of the Chola kings. Kumbakonam itself has an enormous Chola temple, but, more important for Abhishiktananda's purposes, it had a Temple of Silence, a Mauna Mandir, which offered free accommodation and food to sincere spiritual practitioners. He had learned of the place from one of his Hindu friends who spent 108 days there every year, and he decided to spend some time there himself.

He was given a large dark room in a separate building in the garden. There was a bathroom attached and, like an enclosed nun, he received his food through a revolving hatch. Apart from that silent human contact, he was in a solitude even greater than the solitude he had experienced in the caves of Arunachala. Even the outside air could barely penetrate, as the doors and windows were shut, and the door let in neither fresh air nor friend, for he saw no one, not even the hands of the silent messenger who delivered his food.

There he lived for over a month. He had no books apart from the New Testament and the Upanishads; he neither wrote nor received letters. Thankfully, he kept his diary, and through these pages we are privileged to glimpse his anguish and his serenity, his experiences of solitude and silence, of fear and of nakedness before God. Most profoundly of all, we can see his growing understanding of the awakening to being, of the experience of "I AM" becoming more and more a reality.

In doing this he was following the advice of both Dr. Mehta and Sri Gnanananda, deliberately placing himself in conditions likely to lead to the experience of *advaita*. He was convinced that there, beyond concepts, in "that mystery of the depth,"[2] lay the only real answer, the only solution to his agony. For the *advaitic* experience still eluded him, dancing, tempting, tantalizing—showing its face only to disappear again. He longed for the complete experience, while finding "even its dawning is a blessing, and gives one a zest for life, whatever the turmoil on the surface."[3] Would this retreat lead him to it?

It is hard to tell of his experiences at Mauna Mandir without imposing a false structure on his time there. His experiences were not like the structure of the first movement of a classical symphony—exposition, development, recapitulation, and perhaps a coda. They did not go tidily from anguish to ecstasy, from uncertainty to certainty, or from hope to despair. All these elements were there, but as we learn of them directly from his pen, innocent of the structure he, so elegant a writer, would have imposed had it been for others to read, they simply move from day to day and from week to week.

ABHISHIKTANANDA EMBARKED on this austere retreat with great expectations that he would arrive at the full experience of *advaita*, and to this end he had committed himself to fixing his attention on the present moment. He did not, however, anticipate fear, though fear was to stalk him, often coupled with a sensation of nakedness, something he had also experienced during his time with Dr. Mehta. On the fourth day of the retreat he wrote:*

Yesterday morning I was scared. In the depth, in the lowest depth of this waking sleep, my breathing much diminished, the scarcely felt rhythm of *Om tat sat, Om*—and then a glow on my right. It was as if in front of a bend in the road, like a tunnel, where like a train the rhythm of *Om tat sat* was as if entering. And this glow became more and more intense, threatening, aggressive. Anguish in my whole being. As if that glow was going to make the whole psyche explode. And this fear made the brightness vanish and the train was derailed. ... That glow—the Presence, the Present, the *sakshin* (witness). ...
Twice the cross appeared and immediately disappeared. ...[4]

*This was a diary, not intended for publication, so Abhishiktananda's layout of lines and occasional grammatical slips have been retained.

In his fear the train with which he identified came off its tracks; then in total openness to the divine, he leaves the ego behind—he is naked:

> As I hasten towards you, I leave behind all my skins, all my shells, everything I had, everything I thought I was, everything I identified with—all this falls away, for the hole I must pass through gets narrower and narrower. And as I run in pursuit of You who are slipping away, I slip away from myself.[5]

His longing to break through duality to an experience of *advaita*, of oneness, was growing even greater, the unresolved tension was becoming unbearable. Yet if it were resolved—and his increasing difficulty in distinguishing between himself and God suggests that resolution was not far off—then he had to accept completely not only his own loss of identity, his fear that he had slipped away from himself, but that there is "a gaze, without anyone gazing or being gazed at."[6] Even God is in a sense "not there":

> No longer a You to embrace, no longer a You to kneel before, no longer a You at whose feet to sit. No longer an I to embrace You, no longer an I who kneel before You, no longer an I to sit at your feet. For if there could still be an I for other people, how could there still be one for myself, since I have slipped away from myself in pursuing You?[7]

Is it a wonder that he was full of fear? He knew that "the moment is coming at last when it will be necessary to face him in the Self. The true religious terror. The feeling of 'awe,' of the 'numinous.' Nothing to help in this meeting."[8] Fear is an appropriate emotion when approaching the divine, when contemplating being alone with God, alone with the Self; perhaps seeking company in his fear he draws on the wisdom of the Old Testament, as he quoted Exodus ("And the people were afraid of being in contact with the living God"), Deuteronomy ("God is a consuming fire"), and Hebrews ("It is a dread thing to fall into the hands of the living God").

Fear of the living God was hard enough, but Abhishiktananda's great anguish was still caused, as it had been ever since his first meeting with Ramana Maharshi, by the tension that tore him between Christianity and advaitic Hinduism—the anguish that knew the mystery within could not be two, that it was "sometimes called Jesus and sometimes called Arunachala,"[9] that saw the Christian Trinity as another formulation of the experience of the *rishis*. He was so poised between Christianity and Hinduism that he felt that to wipe off the ashes on his brow, symbol of Hindu affiliation, was to wipe off the cross of Christ also.

This was his crucifixion. He loved Christ to the depth of his being, yet increasingly he found it a struggle to remain a Christian, fearing that if he remained tied down by the church he would have to renounce the inner mystery, the revelation of Ramana Maharshi and Arunachala. The anguish caused him to cry out: "And if to become Christian I had to give you up, O Arunachala, to abandon you, O Ramana, then I would never be able to become Christian again."[10] Yet there was the nagging fear—"if only I could be completely sure that there is no eternal risk to be run in following Ramana to the end!"[11]

He was living in a maelstrom of emotions. There were times of serenity, times of something approaching ecstasy, times when he burst into a poetic style reminiscent of the Song of Songs itself . . .

> I will sing a song for my Beloved
>   my Lord Arunachala
> with the words that he himself drew from my heart
>   in his own heart.

> I will plait a garland of flowers
>   for my Beloved Shiva Arunachala
> with flowers that he Himself plucked in the garden of my heart
>   in his own heart.[12]

Poetry and prose are not far apart in Abhishiktananda's writing at this time; in fact it is often hard to know where prose ends and poetry begins.* Sometimes the prose becomes more poetic, less structured, less grammatical, until its exuberance bursts the banks and overflows in an ecstatic torrent of words. It is not easy to find the catalyst that brings this about. The extract quoted above, nine verses in all, was preceded by a day of comparative serenity. Four days later his mood has changed. He pours out his anguish that the mystery he experienced under the name of Jesus was followed by an experience under the name of Arunachala, the "light was so great that it dazzled me" and again erupts into verse, or at least lines that are laid out in verse form, berating his Beloved for playing tricks on him, for wounding him, leaving him limping and reeling on his feet, for holding him, while taking everything from him:

*The American scholar Judson Trapnell, who was working in this area before his death in 2003, identified some seventy passages as being poems.

And you have not even given me a kiss!
Your face brushed against mine, your arms were extended,
and I offered my lips and held out my arms,
and You, You laughed at me,
and withdrew into your mystery,
beyond my reach.[13]

At the heart of these overflowing emotions is the theme to which he returns again and again—the struggle to remain a Christian in the light of the joy experienced at Arunachala. He knew the mystery is one, that the divine appears in every form and that "You want us to seek You beyond all forms!"[14] Yet he fears that to worship the divine in all forms is to be unfaithful to Christ, a Christ who, in some way at which he only hints, but which is clearly the result of years of conditioning in the Catholic tradition, is different from the God that, at this period, he experiences under the symbol of Arunachala: "For forty years I have so much loved Christ, in his infancy, in his passion, in his glory, in his Church extended by his spirit through space and time even to the ends of the world."[15] He cannot give up Arunachala, Ramana, the divine he has experienced, yet "all my agony lies in the fact that I still want to remain Christian."[16] But how can he call himself a Christian priest, when,

I can no longer call You You. How then can I live as a Christian? How then give you as a priest? It is as if You had driven me from the very place, at the very depth of myself, in the innermost centre of myself, in the most wonderful mystery of my consciousness, where I used to adore You.[17]

He would only be at peace, he felt, if he could let go of Christianity and accept *advaita* with all its possible consequences. But how could he let go of the Christ he had loved so long? Once again his agonizing led back to the church. He found the church's viewpoint sectarian, far from universal and, with a light touch rare during these weeks, he admits, "The Church boasts of possessing the Spirit. No doubt, but in a cage. Or else in its coats of arms."[18] He had come to India to proclaim Christ, but he had found Christ in another form. "It was You who made yourself known to me by means of them in the overwhelming features of Arunachala!"[19] Yet the conflict reared up again when he found his communion hosts stuck together and had to write to Shantivanam for more; he was surprised how upset he was in case they did not arrive quickly and he could not celebrate the Mass which he thought he had learned to love without attachment.

STRUGGLING AS HE WAS WITH MATTERS so profound that the over-worked word "spiritual" does not do them justice, Abhishiktananda had also to cope with physical problems. Poverty was, as always, central to his life, and he was used to an ascetic life, but such emotional assaults affect the body as well as the mind and the spirit and are worse for someone living in damp, cold, and airless conditions. On the tenth day he admitted that not only was he tired, but he had been tired for much of the time. He wondered if this tiredness was partly disappointment, for he had counted on this retreat to experience fully what he had glimpsed with Ramana Maharshi and again with Sri Gnanananda.

By the twenty-fifth day he was exhausted, feverish, dizzy, shivering nervously. A period of deep meditation brought him a little calm, only to be interrupted by the arrival of his breviary and the need to sign two receipts. In the profound state in which he was living, this mundane action was a seismic shock—he felt it "finished" him. It was only toward the end of the retreat that he briefly regained some sort of composure, even a deep joy and calm, though he remained tired and the damp gave him a backache. But again the fever rose and he had to ask for a blanket and for hot water for his bath, a request that must have shocked his ascetic soul.

It was meditation that had given him a moment's calm—yet he rarely mentions meditation in his diary or in his letters and is believed never to have taught any method or technique. Indeed, in 1961 he wrote strongly on the subject to a Carmelite nun: "Once again we are getting lost in techniques, and the spiritual world is no exception. . . . Methods will never take us far, it's to its own source that the soul should be brought back, turned back."[20]

Bettina Bäumer, who knew him well and was almost a disciple to him, is among those who have wondered about this. Though he helped her and inspired her greatly, and though she thinks he practiced the repetition of a mantra himself, he never gave her a method: "He was of the opinion that method could be an obstacle—you might get attached to the method. There are two dangers, and I think he was aware of both: the danger of being too much attached to a method and then not being completely free, and the other danger of believing that you are above it and not practicing, and not in fact being above it."[21]

In his little book entitled *Prayer*, Abhishiktananda did, however, write profoundly and beautifully about one method of meditation, *nāmajapa*, the Prayer of the Name, the continual repetition of the name of the Lord in any of its traditional forms. He found that this kind of prayer, which includes the Jesus Prayer, was a great help in concentrating the attention and avoiding distractions, thus allowing the mind to move toward its center.

> Of all mantras and prayers the invocation of God's holy Name is the highest and most powerful. At the psychological level it concentrates and deepens the mind. At the truly spiritual level, in virtue of the divine power with which it is filled, it leads the soul to the very centre of itself and of all things, to the Source, to the Father.[22]

HE NEVER LOST TOUCH with his essential reason for spending this time in such strict silence and solitude. It was to learn to BE, to live in the present moment, and thus to experience *advaita*. In his mid-forties, after over a quarter of a century as a monk, what were his views on solitude and silence, those central elements of the eremitic life, part of the life of anyone responding to a monastic vocation?

In 1952, writing from Arunachala, he summed up the life of a *sannyāsi* as Solitude-Silence-Poverty. The *sannyāsi*, the one who renounces, is essentially a solitary, for he has renounced relationships, whether of family or of friendship, and he does not look to others for moral support. Even the food he might be given is received without expectation. Poverty was not a problem for Abhishiktananda; he was used to it and embraced it willingly, learning in his first year in India that it was not possible to be a real *sannyāsi* if he kept anything, even a handful of rice, in reserve for the next day. From the early days he agreed with Monchanin that monks should never live at a higher standard than their neighbors.

By this time, confronted as never before with the reality living this life of Solitude-Silence-Poverty, Abhishiktananda, who throughout his life had many friends, had already faced his limitations unflinchingly:

> I will not be a genuine sannyasi until the day when I am able, without the least distress or fear, to see the loss, in a strange if not downright hostile environment, of all help, all affection, all respect. And that too, on the supposition that I could no longer return to my other life (with its friendships, the priesthood and financial and moral support).
>
> I will be a genuine sannyasi on the day when there is no longer anyone to be concerned about me, when I shall be obliged to beg for my handful of rice, given with kindness here, with coldness there, choosing by preference those doors where I shall not find the

welcome of a smiling face—when I do not have an *anna** in my pocket.

Solitude, total stripping.[23]

Though he talks in terms of the *sannyāsi*, he is equating the lifestyle with the life of a monk; in fact, he wrote to his sister Marie-Thérèse, herself a religious, of "the great solitude within the soul, to which India constantly calls us back; for, as I have already said, it is here that I have at last learnt to be a monk."[24] And the monk, as he later wrote and as indeed the word itself implies, "is made to be alone."[25]

Just months before this retreat Abhishiktananda had written an extraordinary essay on solitude, called simply "Esseulement," solitude. In it he faces the fact that those who are committed to the higher stages of spiritual concentration are going to find themselves in a state of unbearable solitude. The increasing attraction of the inner light results, he writes, in a more and more complete disenchantment with all that is not the Absolute and the Absolute in itself.

> Even the doctrines of the Trinity and the Incarnation can no longer speak to the soul. The soul is absolutely compelled to lose the Triune God and the God-Man as it has conceived them, and to allow itself to be swallowed up in the abyss of Being, of the Godhead beyond all conceiving, which attracts it irresistibly.[26]

The call is always to go beyond—beyond faith, beyond human formulations, however beautiful, seeking the Absolute, the one, the nondual, and, inevitably, the alone. There only is comfort; there only can the unquenchable thirst be quenched.

The seeker called by this mystery cannot seek help, for his friend cannot attain the Absolute for him any more than he can eat for him:

> I alone can attain my end. In this situation all help is a useless burden, every attempt to help me only has the result of thrusting me deeper into the abyss of my solitude by making me realize that I depend entirely on myself. And this I myself. What is it? I cannot even find myself any longer. Nothing to lean on, beside me, behind me, before me, above or below me.[27]

---

*Anna = one-sixteenth of a rupee.

Knowing this, it must have taken immense courage to put himself in the very situation that would deepen his solitude. There he found himself alone in the hands of the living God—"Alone, without anything to fall back on. Alone in myself with Yourself . . . this duality, unbearable so long as it is not resolved."[28]

If he met fear in solitude, the fear that he was losing his very self in his pursuit of God, so also did he meet peace. His love of solitude was to grow greater—he would write often of the beauty of being alone after being in company—and that did not reflect on the warmth of his feelings for his friends. In another of those poetic outbursts here, at Mauna Mandir, he sings a song to solitude, a song of gratitude for his life:

> In serene solitude, in sovereign solitude.
> In serene fullness, in sovereign fullness.
> In blessedness,
> in the solitude of my fullness,
> in the fullness of my solitude,
> in the solitude of my blessedness,
> in the blessedness of my fullness.[29]

SILENCE AND SOLITUDE SWIM in the same water, as close as sisters. Though silence can be maintained in company, they do not mix well, while, for the solitary, silence is an inevitable companion. But the need to communicate dies hard. There are charming stories of Abhishiktananda, at a time when he was vowed to silence, meeting another *sādhu* as they passed each other. They would smile radiantly, making expansive gestures sharing the beauty of the world and their love of God; neither would speak, but they simply could not pass without in some way acknowledging each other and their joy. Sometimes when Abhishiktananda was staying in the caves of Arunachala he let it be known that he did not want to speak unnecessarily, so people assumed that he was a *munivar*, an ascetic who is vowed to silence. In India this is not unusual, and when people came to see him they simply prostrated before him and sat in silent meditation with him.

Abhishiktananda did not always find silence easy, and found it hard to forgo the chance to talk to somebody like-minded and interesting. His constant need to write, whether letters, books, or his journal, amply testifies to his need for expression, but he often maintained silence for long periods, holding that if a *sannyāsi* is not completely silent, at least he should speak as little as possible. Once he made a rather barbed comment that though St. Benedict knew the point of silence, his sons seemed to have lost it.[30]

He knew that, in the last analysis, silence was spiritual solitude, "Alone with the Alone, or rather alone in the Alone."[31] The *sannyāsi* no longer needs to speak; he only wants to hear about the highest wisdom, and that is not communicated by audible sounds. He maintained that the communication of thought by words is necessary only when there is a sense of duality, for if one is living in unity, what need is there for speech? Does one need to speak to oneself?

> In silence, you taught me silence,
> O Arunachala!
> You who never leave your silence.[32]

SOLITUDE AND SILENCE WERE THE CONTEXT of his retreat, fear and a terrifying feeling of nakedness among the experiences he encountered. The apparently insoluble problem was the tension between Christianity and *advaita*, for he was unwilling, indeed unable, to forsake either. But woven through all this, the golden thread to which he clung, however frail it might sometimes have felt, was the longing simply to "be"; to experience the awakening to the present moment, that eternal truth, that basic fact of life, apparently so simple yet more elusive than the subtlest perfume.

This was not a new longing. When he and Father Monchanin founded Shantivanam, it was simply *to be* in the presence of God, without any further object at all. He had long been exasperated by the need of Westerners always to be *doing*, and he had found in India a place where he could learn simply to be. A few years earlier he had written, "Being is inexpressible. At the very centre, there is nothing but Being. . . . There is not BEING and being."[33] Was he saying that Being and God are two words pointing to one reality? Much that he said about both God and about Being indicate that he was. Abhishiktananda was capable of expressing these great truths simply. He once told a religious sister who was trying to find God in holy words that "God is as much in the making of a good soup or the careful handling of a railway train as he is in our most beautiful meditations."[34] On another occasion he pleaded in his diary, "Let me find fulfilment in each of my actions, eating my rice, washing my feet, listening to boring stories."[35] For at one level the discovery of the mystery is simple: "It is right beside you, in the opening of a flower, the song of a bird, the smile of a child."[36]

Nevertheless, for many years he found the state of "being" elusive. Did he find himself closer to his goal on this intense thirty-two day retreat? On his second day he declared, "The work of this 'retreat' is to fix my attention on the present moment and on what 'is' within me. . . . Become what you are. Direct my attention to the fact that I am."[37] He distinguished meticulously between being attentive to being *now*, rather than straining toward what the future might hold—which of course by definition is NOT "being." He was in the dilemma of anyone who longs for being, for the very desire for it put him outside its still center and into the land of regret, concept, and desire, drew him into the future rather than anchoring him to the present moment. Yet despite these all-too-human inconsistencies, it was the true awakening to being that he sought, the experience of Jesus, of Buddha, of the *rishis*.

He was, however, still in the clutches of the intellect, and the way he wrangled with his problem must have distanced him ever further from his goal. Sometimes he tussled with words with a logic as wordy as the most Western philosopher:

> The paradox of creaturehood: to attain to being! As if being could be attained! Who then attains it, if not being? And if being is, how could it attain to being?
>
> There is then nothing more than the Presence. But then Presence to whom, to what? The Presence is the name of being as long as the veil has not yet been torn apart.
>
> Who is present to whom? I try to place myself in the presence of the Presence. And in the Presence, I am finally present to myself. Who is present? The Present. The awakening to the Presence.
>
> Christ, present to Himself in the bosom of the Father, in the essential Presence of the Father.
>
> To live in the present is to live in the Presence, in being. Become all that I am—it is in this becoming insofar as it is being, that I am.[38]

When, eventually, he attained enlightenment, when it all seemed so simple and natural—how he must have laughed at the wordplay in that passage.

He well knew that these passionate intellectual efforts to solve the problem were no help and took him no closer to "presence," the word he was using as an alternative to "being." In fact the reverse was true, for intellectual endeavor of that sort is submission to the demands of the ego and an obstacle to awakening. Further, it is not a question of the ego giving up its place at center stage. That place is already taken; it is the ego who is the usurper, as he well knew, even as he took up swords with the ego. "For Being is only attained in actually being. Because being cannot really be reached, it simply is, there is only being. Every movement toward Being is a flight from being. Being is in 'embracing' the present moment."[39] What a tantalizing situation, and how familiar: to know with the head that the experience of being is reached only by living in the present moment, while finding that present moment is more elusive than the summit of Mount Arunachala, the goal seeming more distant with each struggling step.

So too he agonized with the knowledge that the experience of being is inseparable from the experience of the Self.

> No one can shackle it. They can bind my hands, my feet, my tongue. But no one can bind the Self within me, no one can bind ME. All that they do with me, all that they say about me is not done with Me, is not said about Me. Beyond all that, I (simply) am. . . . Eternally *I* issue forth within Being. . . . The God who is other is for most people nothing but the impossibility of being *oneself.* Fearing to be. The vertigo of *being.*[40]

He was caught in expectation and desire. He knew that "as long as there is desire for being there is no being."[41] He could not stop himself from anticipating the experience he longed for, yet he knew that expectation was the very opposite of being, even defining expectation as a sin, a word he rarely used.

It was a grueling thirty-two days. There were moments of serenity, times when his emotional and spiritual strings were tuned to a pitch almost beyond his bearing. Yet when the end approached, he dreaded the thought of leaving. He felt "profound joy, almost unfelt. A feeling of completeness."[42] When, on the last day, he said Mass and opened the door that had remained shut for so long, he burst into tears. He had only one wish, to return to the solitude and the silence.

12

The Other Side of Silence

1957

In all my life I have never been such a celebrity![1]

THE LOVE OF SOLITUDE AND SILENCE was at the heart of Abhishiktananda's life, the context from which everything sprang, but there was
another side, the sociable man with countless friends, who loved to travel,
to talk, and to laugh. This is reflected in a remark from an Indian
Carmelite friend who said affectionately, "There was a man who could
talk about silence twenty-four hours a day!" Abhishiktananda would ruefully refer to himself in a similar vein.

Though Abhishiktananda was never to leave India from the moment
of his arrival in 1948, inside the subcontinent he was a compulsive traveler. In his early years this was primarily a desire to experience all aspects
of his adopted country, and such curiosity, especially in so rich and fascinating a place as India, is natural enough. In any case, Abhishiktananda's
attitude to his travels was more that of a pilgrim than that of an ordinary
traveler. Nevertheless the extent of his traveling does raise a few questions. Was there a degree of restlessness in his continual moving around?
Is there not an incompatibility that the same man should so passionately
seek inner awakening and fulfillment and yet appear to find it hard to stay
physically in one place? As a monk, dedicated to poverty, how did he
afford the fares?

This last question is the easiest to answer, for when Abhishiktananda
was first in India travel was extremely cheap. It had to be, for Indians,
even the poorest, travel in great numbers. They might be going on pilgrimage; they might be visiting relatives for a family wedding. So popular is train travel that there are rarely enough third-class compartments
to accommodate those wanting seats, and to see crowds of laughing

150

Indians—usually young and male—sitting on the roof of a train was as common as seeing people queuing for a bus in central London.

But the trains were not comfortable and the distances are huge. In the 1950s and '60s, when Abhishiktananda was covering the length and breadth of India, foreign priests and missionaries usually traveled second class, but this was something Abhishiktananda refused to do—he would not travel in conditions any better than those endured by the poorest of the poor. How, he seemed to be saying, could he, a Catholic monk who had taken a vow of poverty, travel in greater comfort than his neighbor and retain any integrity? It did not matter if friends offered to pay his fare, or even if he had the chance to go by air; he insisted on traveling third class.

Imagine, then, Abhishiktananda, some fifty years ago, taking a rickshaw to the nearest station, buying his third-class ticket and joining the heaving mass of humanity waiting for the train. As soon as it chugged into the station there would be people trying to disembark, already hanging half out of the carriage, while those wishing to board pressed forward, some clutching door handles, others scrambling over each other's luggage, struggling through windows. Humanity was at its least attractive, as some would use their tin trunks, the customary piece of luggage, as a battering ram to force their way onto the train. If Abhishiktananda, older, weaker, and far more polite than most of his fellow travelers, managed to board, the search for a space to park himself began. If he was lucky he might find a whole seat, but more likely he would have to be content with a few square inches, probably on the floor. Unless a seat became vacant, there he would sit, sometimes for a journey that could take two days.

An interesting sidelight on Abhishiktananda's travels by train was that he was so familiar with the timetable that he claimed to know the times of trains all over India—his young friends used to say he must have been a station master in his previous life. Even more surprisingly, this brought out a side of him not often in evidence—the competitive. On this matter it was important to him to be right and to be seen to be right. On one occasion there was an argument about some detail of the train timetable and he had to admit he was wrong: to say he was put out would be an understatement.

Once he had reached the railway station, the same pattern would be repeated on the crowded buses, the overflow of passengers taking their chances on the roof, sometimes with roads without parapets affording them terrifying views down a mountainside. As we follow his travels, enduring such conditions literally hundreds of times, it is impossible not to wonder whether the rigor of these journeys might have played a part in his early death. Yet some inner daimon impelled him to travel, and his determination to live like his fellow Indians demanded that he share their lives in this as in living conditions and in diet. It is reminiscent of Gandhi's famous remark to an enquiring journalist, "My life is my message."

SOMETIMES HIS TRAVELS WERE TO VISIT FRIENDS, sometimes he made new friends as he traveled. A hermit may be a solitary, but, certainly in the case of someone as many-faceted as Abhishiktananda, this did not exclude friendship and conversation. One friend with whom he was staying once asked him if he would prefer to be left in peace and silence, "Oh no!" he replied, "I've come here to talk!"[2] This ambivalence was seen on another occasion when someone he did not know wanted to see him. The solitary side of him led him to say no, he could not possibly see anyone. Eventually he was persuaded at least to give the visitor ten minutes and three hours later they were still there, deep in conversation.

He was a man capable of being a close and loyal friend, and with many friends he kept up a lively and frequent correspondence. This is particularly true of the early friendships he made in France, like Raymond Macé, his close friend at the seminary who became canon of Rennes, and Father Joseph Lemarié, his younger contemporary at Kergonan, a friendship given a lifetime's lease by correspondence. Once in India he made friends with hermits and wandering *sādhus* in the temples, with Indians and Europeans, Hindus and Christians, with priests and nuns, theologians and followers of Gandhi, with artists, even with two militant members of a right-wing revolutionary party, Shri Ram Swarup and Shri Sita Ram Goel.

One distinction becomes clear: on the one hand, he had friends with whom he had to be careful how he expressed himself—there were occasions when people doubted his Christianity, and this distressed him deeply; on the other hand, he had friends with whom he could speak freely. One case in the former group was the Jesuit J. Bayart; despite their friendship, Father Bayart was unable to sympathize with Abhishiktananda's views expressed in *Guhantara*. The other group included many religious sisters; in fact, he formed friendships with entire communities, such as the French Sisters at the Roberts Nursing Home at Indore and the young men at the Indian Foundation of Siluvaigiri.* Up to this time,

---

*A Christian ashram near Salem affiliated with the Benedictine Abbey of St. Andrew's in Belgium. In 1957 it moved to Kengeri and became known as Asirvanam Monastery.

around 1957, Abhishiktananda's closest friendship in India was with Father Dominique van Rollenghem, a Benedictine from the Abbey of St. André at Bruges, who had been living with the community at Siluvaigiri for some time. Abhishiktananda wrote most touchingly of him as he eagerly waited to spend two days with him in 1955. He described him as

> The true dweller in the depth, "*guhantara*," does not foresee anything, does not worry about anything, does not desire anything, does not rejoice in anything, is not hurt by anything. He lives in the essential joy . . . inviolable by all that is "without." How far I am from all that![3]

They were both similar and opposite. Both were devout, both drawn by the life of silence and solitude, but where Abhishiktananda became expansive, laughing and joking when in the right company, Dominique was deep and silent; where Abhishiktananda strained at the leash of his monastic calling, Dominique was a committed Benedictine who would never have been even momentarily out of line with his abbot.

There were of course two sides to Abhishiktananda, and while his eremitic, contemplative side found friendship with Dominique van Rollenghem, his intellectual side, wanting to digest his experience in terms of theology, found few matches. The one person with whom he could fully share his ideas, who was an intellectual match for him as well as being something of a mystic himself, was Professor Raimon Panikkar. The two met at the Pontifical Seminary at Poona when Abhishiktananda was giving classes in Gregorian chant and Panikkar was taking part in a summer school for students. The two became firm friends, discussing theology "on the road, in the sun, squeezed together in buses, in the restaurant, as well as sitting in a room."[4]

In later years Bettina Bäumer was often a witness to these discussions, which she found fascinating and lively: "It was wonderful to see them both discussing, Panikkar representing more the intellectual side and Abhishiktananda more the experiential but both struggling to . . . really it was like seeing the birthpangs of a new theology in their dialogues."[5]

There were to be many more friendships, deep and lasting, and these, most importantly for posterity, were to include those who keep his memory alive and who ensure that he is remembered by his life and by his personality as well as by his writings.

SADLY, ABHISHIKTANANDA had problems with those most closely involved with Shantivanam, first with Father Monchanin, later with Father Bede

Griffiths, and more immediately with Father Francis Mahieu, a Belgian Cistercian monk who had been a Trappist for eighteen years and who expressed a strong interest in coming to Shantivanam. Why did Abhishiktananda not form good relationships with Monchanin, Bede Griffiths, and Francis Mahieu, the three other European men most dedicated to finding a bridge between Christianity and Hinduism? The Jesuit theologian Michael Barnes, writing about the men known as "the three founders of Shantivanam," saw fundamental differences between them: "If Monchanin was remarkable for an austere theological wisdom and Bede famous for the warmth of his hospitality, Abhishiktananda was an energetic explorer who committed himself to an ever-deeper engagement with the riches of classical Hinduism."[6] Perhaps it was these basic differences that stood in the way of complete understanding, for it is a sad fact that among the four of them— Francis Mahieu was to spend most of his life in Kerala, so had less contact with the other three—there was no deep and lasting friendship. Just as it has been seen that Monchanin and Abhishiktananda started with high expectations yet never really worked well together, so the relationship between Abhishiktananda and Bede Griffiths, despite the fact that they were both Benedictine monks passionately drawn to India, was never good.

Various explanations have been given for this situation. For instance, that Abhishiktananda, son of a Breton grocer, shy and not very imposing physically, felt intimidated by the middle-class, Oxford-educated Bede, who was to become a popular and well-known figure around the world. It was he who, when he took over the ashram in 1968, transformed Shantivanam into a vibrant place of pilgrimage, and while it should be said that not everyone welcomed this change—probably Abhishiktananda himself would not have—there is no doubt that it was Bede Griffiths who put Shantivanam on the map and who came to have great significance, particularly among Westerners. It is more likely, however, that behind the similarities lay subtle and elusive differences, particularly in their differing attitudes to their common task of bridging Hinduism and Christianity. For instance, though both men valued experience over theology, Bede felt that Abhishiktananda "went too far" in his exploration of *advaita* and Abhishiktananda is known to have referred to Bede as "the fog of the Thames."[7] Though what he meant by that is not entirely clear, it was clearly not meant as a compliment.

Abhishiktananda's attitude to the arrival of Father Mahieu showed, from the start, a strange ambivalence. Rather than the excitement he might have felt at someone so obviously suitable wanting to share their lives, he feared the arrival of a monk with a focused ambition—"for if he comes we shall have to make a foundation and 'to found' is something external."[8] One day he would feel "a very vague hope for F. Mahieu . . ."[9]; the next he returned to the brink, writing, "To invite someone to share one's life, isn't that a real gamble?"[10] (He seems to have forgotten that in his eagerness to get to India he took just such a gamble with Father Monchanin, as Monchanin did with him.) In July 1955, when the two monks eventually met, he was nervous, tired by what he felt amounted to seven years of disappointments and doubtful that they would get on, writing rather surprisingly to his family, "I sometimes find him a little too sensible—we have to be slightly mad here, don't we?"[11]

Nevertheless, Abhishiktananda welcomed Father Mahieu, took him to some ancient sites, including a visit to the caves of Elephanta, on an island near Bombay. Here are Hindu temples, hollowed into the rock, which Abhishiktananda had not seen himself. Entering the dark cave and finding himself facing the huge, impressive image of Siva, he was so overwhelmed that he wrote: "I was *thunderstruck!* . . . I simply had to hold onto the pillar for support."[12]

In September, when Father Francis and Abhishiktananda spent some time at the ashram together, Abhishiktananda's apprehensions began to fall away and he was impressed at the courage with which the Belgian Trappist applied himself to the demanding life of the ashram. But his doubts far outweighed any flashes of hope that the two men might work happily together; he felt they were simply too different in character.

So, ON THE OTHER SIDE OF SILENCE there was travel and there was friendship; there was also Shantivanam. It is easy to become so involved with Abhishiktananda's extraordinary inner life that the reason he came to India, the grounds on which he was given permission to leave his monastery while remaining a Benedictine monk—to found and run an ashram—are forgotten. What had been happening there? A chart of Abhishiktananda's varying feelings about the ashram would run from the high peaks of his enthusiasm when he set out for India to fulfill his thirteen-year-old dream of establishing monastic life in India, to a variety of lows, varying from disinterest to disillusion—sometimes almost to despair.

As early as August 1952 he admitted his disappointment in his diary, "Once the non-future of Shantivanam is recognized, what right do we have to continue our lives here as dilettantes, that is, to live here at our ease without any parochial or other concern?"[13] The following year, by which time Arunachala had claimed him, he went further: "So you see how little the founding of an Order interests me from now on? All that is on the outside; I no longer have any taste for it."[14] He was to express these doubts with increasing frequency, yet he was to live at Shantivanam, regarding it as his base and his responsibility, for another fifteen years.

He was oddly indifferent to the fate of the ashram, recognizing that the situation was becoming critical, yet adding "What does it matter to me personally? Provided I find a corner here in India, where I should be free to be a poor hermit, I shall gladly leave others to run Shantivanam."[15] Then—as can happen when difficult decisions have to be made—events took over. The subject of his indecision, the ashram, suddenly took on a new lease of life, and for a few months in the middle of 1956 there were so many people staying there that they had to build new cells and extend the refectory. The liturgical pattern of the day took on a new energy as they sang Lauds, Terce, Sext, None, Vespers, and Compline together, and they developed the practice that Abhishiktananda and Father Monchanin had started and which, in some similar form, is still practiced today, of singing hymns in Sanskrit and Tamil. Other practices, previously rather tentative, now became a natural part of their lives—for instance, greeting each other in the Indian style, making prostrations and offering *arati*—the ceremony of the lights that so moved Abhishiktananda in Hindu temples. But despite his interest in these new developments he found that "Arunachala has dug depths in me which the Opus Dei (the Office) cannot touch."[16]

So neither this real attempt to bring Christianity and Hinduism together in the liturgy or the evidence of some success could engage Abhishiktananda. Apart from his failing interest in the ashram, there were the differences between himself and Father Mahieu; in particular, they had a serious disagreement about the training of novices. Abhishiktananda longed for others to take over Shantivanam so he could return to Arunachala, and by the end of 1955 he was determined to leave, saying that he preferred the solitary life of a hermit and that Father Mahieu would be the ideal person to take his place. He did not want to be part of an expanding venture, such as Shantivanam would almost certainly become; his deepest wish, despite the convivial side of his nature and despite a natural fear, was for solitude. He also felt "very violently"—and had done for some time—that Shantivanam should pass beyond both Christianity and Hinduism and that that would lead to trouble:

There is no longer any doubt that Shantivanam will very quickly come into conflict with the Church not only on questions of dress and discipline, but over very basic problems. I can no longer take responsibility for it. Add to that the differences of education, character and ideals with Fr Mahieu. The best thing is to let him take my place, that he may make some Cistercian Shantivanam with a bit of India colour, as he wishes. This is what I am gently going to work at from now on. . . . The work of Shantivanam is over for me at least.[17]

He does not refer to the potentially embarrassing fact that the book he and Father Monchanin had written together, *Ermites du Saccidânanda*, was at that very moment being printed and would shortly be published. Nor does he mention the threat to his canonical position if he ceased to do the work for which he had received permission to leave his abbey.

However, he could no longer keep his decision from Father Monchanin, who took it badly, accusing him of egoism, of betrayal, of losing hope, of instability. Abhishiktananda, with a surprising lack of understanding of his friend's point of view, attributed all this to the fact that Monchanin lived in a world of his own and was "knocked off balance as soon as he is confronted by reality."[18] It was no surprise for them both to discover that Father Mahieu, also realizing that he and Abhishiktananda were unlikely to be able to work together, was making other plans: in November 1956, together with Bede Griffiths, who had recently arrived from England, he left Shantivanam to open Kurisumala Ashram, near Vagamon in Kerala.

Somehow the friendship between Abhishiktananda and Monchanin survived these troubles, but the future of Shantivanam looked bleak, and both men must have wondered at the difficulty they would have in finding people to share the venture with them. The one person with whom Abhishiktananda felt he could work was his friend from the community of Siluvaigiri, Father Dominique, who in turn claimed to be happy at Shantivanam or at Arunachala. However, his abbot would not give him permission to join Abhishiktananda.

ABHISHIKTANANDA FEARED that to go to Arunachala, where he had long wanted to be, would not put enough distance between himself and Shantivanam and that he would not be able to dissociate from the ashram completely, so he began to look around for somewhere else to make a new start. He was invited to settle in Trivandrum, a strongly Hindu city in Kerala where he had been warmly welcomed by the archbishop of the diocese. It was a tempting idea, but he decided against it when he learned that Father Mahieu's ashram would not be far away. "I can't settle as a hermit in the same diocese in which Fr Mahieu opens his Trappe,"[19] he wrote, with astonishing and untypical acerbity. (It should be noted that Abhishiktananda and Father Mahieu eventually made peace and worked together amiably on a number of occasions. Bettina Bäumer was present when, in 1968, they met in a mango grove in Rishikesh to read the Upanishads; she found the reconciliation between the two men very moving.)

At last an unexpected windfall, in the shape of payment for articles published the previous year, gave him the chance to look further afield and also to fulfill an ambition he had long held dear—to go to North India. Eventually he persuaded Father Monchanin, who was distraught at his leaving and who wrote later reproaching him for "running away," to release him, and on March 5, 1957, he left a Tamilian priest, Father Dharmanadar, in charge of the ashram and set off. He was not, he insisted, at that point leaving Shantivanam for good; he was simply looking for another way to live out the strange vocation he did not at that time entirely understand himself.

After a brief visit to Arunachala, where he saw Ethel Merston, he went to Madras (now Chennai) to see to his application for Indian citizenship and on to Bombay (now Mumbai) via Bangalore and Mysore, seeing Sri Gnanananda, Harilal, and Dr. Mehta on the way. He must have found the conflicting advice he received rather confusing. Gnanananda did not want him to travel at all, but simply to stay at a temple near Tirukoyilur which he had visited before and where he had dreamt of staying. In like vein, Ethel Merston did not approve of his plan for the Himalayas and thought he should just settle down—the place was unimportant. Harilal does not seem to have come up with any specific suggestions.

Eventually he took Dr. Mehta's advice. Mehta did not want him to go north, but arranged for him to go to his bungalow at a hilltop fort near Poona, for more solitary meditation. He was there for only ten days, but it gave him time to think about why he was always on the move, wondering how to live his life, when he knew—at least with his mind—what the answer was. He knew that what he was or did, even whether he remained a Christian or not, was essentially a secondary matter. All that mattered was "to discover what I am, more precisely, to realize it."[20]

The day after he arrived he recorded the problem in his diary:

The Real is not something to be wanted.
   It just is.
   As long as I have not realized that "I am," anything I want is futile, for being is not something to be wanted; anything I do is futile, for being is not something to be done.
   There is nothing to want, nothing to desire, nothing to seek, nothing to attain.[21]

He also began to face squarely, more honestly than hitherto, his relationship to the church, admitting that it gave him no interior joy, no consolation; it simply gave him a position, a psychological comfort based on long years of involvement and close relationship. Was it honest to remain in the church?

> Am I not merely wearing a mask of Christianity, out of fear of the consequences? Or is it that there is something deep, imperceptible to myself . . . which even so keeps me in the Church, despite my discomfort with formulations, gestures etc.; something that makes me speak of Christ with conviction, makes me (when occasion offers) desire that someone or other should come to the full light of Christ, makes me say the Mass even when nothing obliges me to do so, and when I do not derive the slightest consolation from it?[22]

Yet two days later he was writing: "Christ really is in the very depth of my soul. As he is in the very depth of the cosmos."[23] Clearly his problem was not with Christ or his understanding of Christ; it was with the institutional church. He felt the need to be free of both Shantivanam and from the church authorities; he wanted the total freedom of the *sannyāsi*.

Mehta arranged for him to stay at the hilltop fort for several weeks, but Abhishiktananda claimed to find that the diet that his adviser had recommended was too austere—such an unlikely claim for one accustomed to austerity that it is tempting to assume he was simply restless. At all events he was soon on the move again. He came down to Poona, where he stayed for three weeks, went on to Bombay for a few days, and in the middle of May reached Indore, where he came to know the French Sisters running the Roberts Nursing Home, who nursed him through an attack of fever and who were to be of continuing importance in his life. He was based with them until the middle of August. One evening, when the fever had abated, they sang Breton songs. No doubt the Sisters meant well, but it was too much for Abhishiktananda. His essential Frenchness was never obliterated by his love of India, and sometimes nostalgia overcame him. On this occasion when they sang "Dors donc, mon gars" ("Sleep then, my son"), which quite probably his mother had sung to him, he thought he would not be able to stand it.

There were occasions during his travels that were very positive at a time when he was going through such doubt and loss of confidence. One was the warmth of the welcome he received from priests, for instance, the bishop of Indore; another when he took part in a study week for priests in North India at the hill station of Pachmari; a third when he ended his tour at Banares, staying with his friend Raimon Panikkar, who was at the time a Fellow at Banares University. All affirmed him, the bishop of Indore inviting him to settle in the diocese, Panikkar and the priests at the study week making him feel that he was at last recognized by the church. He was greatly comforted, pleased, and "reinvigorated to feel myself accepted, just as I am, by the Church; it is so hard to feel suspected as a dangerous person."[24]

It was not only the church of his childhood that welcomed him. He also found himself in the role of a popular preacher to the Hindus, talking at Indore to as many as four hundred people at a time and sharing the platform with three or four Hindu *sannyāsi*s, every morning starting with devotional songs to Radha and Krishna. He wrote about this at length to his sister. He told her how to start with he spoke in English, his words being translated, sentence by sentence, into Hindi, but how he was studying Hindi hard, for they wanted him to speak in their tongue. His first talk, about the cave within the heart and of the love needed to dwell in it, was such a success that his audience, delighted that he spoke of the heart while others speak about externals, asked him to speak again—and again. So he spoke to them daily for three weeks, his every need looked after by his devoted followers:

> Here a sadhu does not have to spend anything, people vie with each other to look after him, far more than in Tamilnad. Everyone calls you *"Maharaj," "Gurumaharaj," "Mahatmaji."* In all my life I have never been such a celebrity! I do not know where it is all going to lead, but I believe that God is in control of all that happens.[25]

He had made it clear that he was a Christian, but the news was slow to circulate; in any case the majority of those who did know still wanted him to speak. But he was in a difficult position. He learned later that one of the other *sādhu*s was jealous of his success, but far more important was that he should honestly speak from his own truth, yet do so without upsetting his Hindu audience, and without giving any indication that he was trying to convert them to Christianity—which, of course, he was not. So he was careful to speak always of the presence of God and of love — never to mention Christ by name. His own perilous position, poised between Christianity and Hinduism, was appearing in a new light, even more delicate, as it bore the responsibility of influencing other people.

He must have succeeded in this difficult balancing act, for he was invited to speak to one thousand Hindus at Dewas, just north of Indore.

Then he gave an hour-long address to a group of reformed Hindus, and, amazingly, he was asked to speak to a group who were known to be strongly anti-Christian. Even more amazingly, he was invited again the following week. His bishop could hardly believe it.

Nevertheless, he did not know how to become accepted as a *Christian sannyāsi*, for by definition the *sannyāsi* is free from every bond, just as by definition the Christian monk is dependent on his order, his superior, and his church. When he was asked who his guru was, who initiated him, all he could answer was that his guru lived far away in Brittany. Spiritual progress in India is inconceivable without a guru, and the nearest he could come to answering their question honestly—and in line with his priestly position—was to refer to his abbot. Had he mentioned teachers like Harilal or Dr. Mehta, or his guru Sri Gnanananda, he would not have been acknowledging his Christian heritage. The tension that he had borne since his first meeting with Ramana Maharshi was taking a new form.

Despite these tensions, the trip was rich and eventful, and one of the things it taught him was the difference in attitudes to Christianity in North and South India. In the south, where the church had been implanted since soon after Christ's death, Christians were fairly numerous, forming a conservative, inward-looking minority, whereas in the North the relatively small numbers of Catholic Christians allowed for greater freedom. The warm welcome he had received from both bishops and people, from both Hindus and Christians, must have convinced him that North India was indeed promising ground for him: "You see the call of the North!" he wrote, "I count the days before I can return to pursue my experience among the monks and pilgrims of Benares in a rented room, on the banks of the Ganges."[26]

B UT IT WAS NOT TO BE, not yet anyway. He returned to Shantivanam by way of Madras, where a telegram awaited him, telling him to go immediately to Pondicherry, where Father Monchanin was seriously ill. A deep-seated tumor had been discovered, immediate surgery was needed, and it was to be done in Paris. Abhishiktananda took him to Bombay and saw him onto the flight to Paris, where he died a few weeks later, "serene and lucid to the end."[27] Despite the problems between the two, there was deep friendship and affection. Abhishiktananda had summed up their ambivalent relationship the year before: "Despite all his kindness, his gentleness, his learning, his goodness and his devotion—he is the best of companions, but the worst of partners."[28] Abhishiktananda immediately began to work on a tribute to Monchanin, including some of his articles, contributions from friends and admirers, and even a few of his lecture notes. This was published, anonymously, by the ashram in 1959. Despite the work he put into this book, he suffered from things said about his own role in Monchanin's life. In the early days after Monchanin's death, the period when only eulogy is acceptable, Abhishiktananda was accused of not appreciating his good fortune in living with a saint and his journey to the North was widely condemned as being a desertion of his partner at the ashram. He was, not surprisingly, hurt and upset by these charges: "I should truly need to be a 'saint', not to have my nerves set on edge by all that, apart from everything else."[29]

Would Monchanin's death mean the end of Shantivanam? Many feared so, while Abhishiktananda, of course, was torn yet again. The decision whether or not to leave Shantivanam had been taken out of his hands; reactions to Monchanin's death showed him how important the ashram was to people, and he received much encouragement to keep going. Even so, he felt that if Father Dharmanadar were to stay on, he could accept some of the numerous invitations he was receiving from the North, while coming back at regular intervals to keep an eye on the ashram. However, once he realized that Father Dharmanadar wanted to move the ashram nearer to his own base at Trichinopoly, his immediate future was sealed. His sense of duty to Shantivanam overcame his longing for another sort of life and he realized he must stay. In one of the pieces he himself wrote in the memoir of Father Monchanin he wrote: "The Hermitage of Shantivanam will remain, God willing, what it has been and continues to be, a place of peace and solitary contemplation. Expansion in human terms, success, numbers, are of no importance."[30]

The decision seems to have given him some peace, and before the year was out, even though he still admitted that he would have preferred solitude, there were again signs of movement in the ashram. Two monks were set to join him shortly; a brahmin with an interest in Christianity was coming from Madras, and he expected more Indian lay people to come. He made plans to extend the *mandapa** in the Hindu style and wrote, "The worst moments have passed and the future is no longer purely a matter of stubborn faith."[31] He was even able to write to his sister, Marie-Thérèse: "There, that is the outward news of Shantivanam. The real news—of what is within—that cannot be told. It is joy and it is peace. That is what I would like to convey to you, less by means of words than heart to heart."[32]

---

*An open porch or hall, with a flat roof supported on columns.

Abhishiktananda was to be based at Shantivanam for another eleven years, his solitude frequently broken by his travels and by visits from people drawn to the idea of joining the community. His own ambivalence cannot have encouraged people, for in his heart he did not want the ashram to develop into a community of monks, admitting that he had less desire than ever that others should share his life.

Over the Christmas of 1957 he had a small theological conference, which he found a "grand week," when Father Dominique, Father Bede Griffiths, and Raimon Panikkar joined him for long discussions on *advaita* and Christian mysticism. The next decade was not only to see more friendships, but to see these friendships lead to regular discussions and meetings that were to have considerable impact both on his own life, on the lives of those who took part in them, and even on the life of the church.

13

A Very Active Hermit

1958–1960

Here more than anywhere I am strongly tempted to pitch my tent![1]

THE NEXT FEW YEARS were to see Abhishiktananda developing the great gift of the true contemplative—simultaneously to be in the presence of God and to partake fully in the world. Often he was intensely active, traveling and making friends all over India, yet he was becoming better able to practice what he was later to write: "Contemplation is . . . remaining in the Presence while being present to each and everything."[2] His activity was not the restless whirl of the discontented; he was learning to be present in a very particular way, for he had accepted that "his part is not to have a part, and his function not to have a function."[3]

On the outer level, his indult of exclaustration was indefinitely renewed, which must have been a great relief to him. Though he still loved France, following its affairs closely—for instance the war in Algeria being waged at the time, which he felt had brought the name of his country into disrepute around the world—he had no wish ever to leave India. In fact, the prospect was something he viewed with the greatest dread. After ten years away from his homeland he was able to write to his family:

> I do not understand the missionaries of the past who always felt home-sick for their own countries. . . . It is like a wife, with husband and children at her side, continuing to miss her birth-place. And nothing could ever repay what India gives to everyone who gives himself to her whole-heartedly.[4]

At last, in June 1960, after a process that had started in 1953, he was granted Indian citizenship and wrote proudly to his compatriot Father

Lemarié, "since last Saturday . . . I have all the rights and duties of an Indian citizen."[5] However great his love for France, however true his declaration that he was "terribly, terribly French," he was totally given to India and it was much easier for him to change his nationality than to risk compromising his Catholicism.

By the beginning of 1958 he was more optimistic about Shantivanam's future, and, apart from two short visits to Arunachala, he hardly left the ashram for a year. He had many visitors, his attitude to them interestingly ambivalent. On the one hand, he admitted that he had "less desire than ever that others should come and share my life. The monk is made to be alone."[6] On the other, he admitted to wanting one or two companions, especially if they were Indian. But when a young Malayali arrived, apparently the ideal person, Abhishiktananda did not welcome companionship; he was simply pleased to find someone who might take over the running of Shantivanam, who would be his "relief." "I hope from the bottom of my heart that he will be the seed, the *real* founder of Shantivanam."[7]

His mood swung between peace and anguish, but clearly his energy was not in the running of Shantivanam. In particular his attitude to the liturgical life of the ashram was, to say the least, ambivalent. A diary entry admits:

> I endeavour to hang on, reading, the liturgy, reflection, etc.: and after a quarter of an hour, or at most after a day, all the scaffolding that I have put up in trying to support my faith collapses like a house of cards. And that is the reason for the fluctuations and contradictions in all these pages.[8]

He was still torn "between Arunachala and Rome,"[9] still facing the problems of living "both the cosmic, universal, transhistorical Church and at the same time the institutional, historical, Roman Church."[10] He goes so far as to say, "I often dream of dying, for it seems there is no way out for me in this life. I cannot be at the same time both Hindu and Christian, and no more can I be simply Hindu or simply Christian. So what is the point of living? How little heart it leaves me for living."[11]

In many ways, however, he was more at peace, his life was becoming easier. In one of the few diary entries of 1959 he writes, "As a matter of fact, the anguish is no longer what it used to be; my anguish is like a cyst you get used to and no longer feel, at least as a rule."[12] What had changed to make him better able to live on the frontiers of Hinduism and Christianity? First, he was simply accustomed to the tension; just as the pain of loss eventually lessens, if only slightly, so he was becoming used to his uneasy position between two major religions. Second, he was, at least occasionally, becoming freer from the church, able to talk of being "Free in the Spirit. Be free to say Mass; be free not to say it also."[13] Third, and most significant, was his increasing ability to live in the present moment, to BE. When they founded the ashram, he and Monchanin wanted simply to *be* in the presence of God, without any further objective at all, but that is something that is easier said than done. Now there are passages in his letters indicating that the wish was becoming the reality:

> Westerners are always anxious to be *doing!* but we come to India, and there we learn simply *to be;* and be-ing is the most intense form of action. No external movement in the physical world is so intense as the movement at the heart of the atom, through which indeed it exists. So it is with us; and that is our essential vocation as monks, nuns, contemplatives.[14]

And to one of his Carmelite friends he wrote:

> the soul which has lost its footing in penetrating into the depths of itself and, as it becomes more and more aware of its own "I am," discovers that in the end there is only one "I AM," that which God uttered at the Burning Bush, that which Jesus three times repeated to the Jews in chapter 8 of St. John.[15]

Abhishiktananda is often at his most effective in his shortest statements. The full force of his longing to live in the present can be felt in these few words:

> There is only one thing that is real, the present moment in which I am face-to-face with God. . . . I have only one sermon: "Realize what you are at this very moment."[16]

Two others aspects of his life contributed to his less anguished mood. One was that he was finding more people with whom to share his vision. The success of the theological conference he had held at Shantivanam in December 1957 led to another at the end of 1958, slightly larger: for someone so torn apart and distanced from the church of his childhood, the company of like-minded people must have afforded great comfort. Second, there was travel. In contrast to 1958, which he spent almost entirely at Shantivanam, during 1959 he hardly stayed in one place longer than a few weeks.

A BLOW-BY-BLOW ACCOUNT of Abhishiktananda's travels, by train, by bus, by rickshaw, and by foot over twenty-five years in India would make confusing reading, but a detailed itinerary of one trip gives a sense of the nature of the journeys he set himself, their extensiveness, and something of the hardship he endured and the deep pleasure he enjoyed. His travels during eight months of 1959, typical of many that he made, provide a good example.

On February 12 he left Shantivanam for Bangalore, the capital of the state of Karnataka, a modern bustling city and an important industrial center, popular not least for its pleasant climate. He stayed at the Bangalore Carmel, where he gave spiritual direction, heard confessions, and instructed a would-be Catholic. From there he visited Harilal, undeterred by the seven-hour bus journey to the manganese mine where his friend was working, then back to stay with the Ingles, friends of Father Monchanin's, enjoying the luxury of a European home and hearing music on a recent introduction to the world of recorded music—"Hi-Fi." He also went to Kengeri, a suburb of Bangalore, to visit the Asirvanam Monastery, the name by which the Siluvaigiri community, to which his friend Father Dominique belonged, had been known since it moved from Salem in 1957; then on to spend Easter with the Little Sisters of the Sacred Heart, where he gave retreats and spiritual direction, before returning to Shantivanam at the beginning of April.

Three weeks later, on April 26, 1959, he left Tiruchirapalli, the train station nearest to Shantivanam, stopping first at Nagpur, well over one thousand kilometers away and close to both Sevagram, the ashram Gandhi built in 1933, and the ashram of his famous follower Vinoba Bhave. He went another four hundred kilometers to Indore, where he stayed with the French Sisters at the Roberts Nursing Home, then on to meet some friends of Raimon Panikkar's near Bareilly. From there it was just 150 kilometers to Almora, stopping just before at Kalimat. At last he was in the Himalayas, at least in the foothills, able to see the great peaks towering above him. He went to Pithoragarh, on the border of Nepal, to Pindar, famous for its glacier, three kilometers long and nearly half a kilometer wide, and to Karnaprayag, the confluence of the Pindar River and the Alaknanada River. Then down to Rishikesh, Haridwar, and Solan. Back to the plains, to Delhi and Agra, then another visit to his new friends near Bareilly. August saw him back in the Himalayas, at Kalimat and Almora, until, sick with herpes, he had to stop a while before returning to Shantivanam in the middle of October. All this, at a conservative estimate over five thousand kilometers and staying at more than a dozen different places in under six months—and all by third-class train, by bus, or by foot. No wonder he had no time to write his diary—there are only four entries during this period. No wonder he became famous for his knowledge of Indian rail timetables, no wonder there has been speculation about the effect of his travels on his health. But among the noise and bustle and detail that are an inevitable part of travel, two events stand out: his first view of the high peaks of the Himalayas and the forming of new and important friendships. It is hard to overestimate the importance of friendship in Abhishiktananda's life, and some of the most significant of his friendships were to have their roots in the next few months.

The first of these, which in fact led to many of the others, was when, at the suggestion of Raimon Panikkar, he stopped to visit the Jyotiniketan Community near Bareilly. As accounts of just how Abhishiktananda met his numerous friends are rare, it is worth recounting the rather unusual occasion of his first meeting with Father Murray Rogers.[17]

It was a dark night, and the community were ending Compline as they always did, facing the door of the chapel and blessing the neighbors in the adjoining villages. They saw a strange figure, patiently waiting in the surrounding mango grove. He was wearing the saffron robes of the *sādhu*, the wandering monk, and the bags containing all his worldly possessions were slung around his neck. It was Abhishiktananda, who had traveled over seven hundred kilometers from Indore with no apparent notice of his arrival (the postcard he had sent had not arrived) and with little idea whom he would be meeting. He had lost his way until he saw the lanterns shedding light on the little chapel. It was, in some ways, typical of the way Abhishiktananda traveled and socialized, and it was to lead to one of his closest friendships, with the whole community, but particularly with Father Murray Rogers, its founder. It was also to open his eyes to Christian denominations other than Roman Catholic.

Murray and Mary Rogers had come to India as traditional Anglican missionaries, but their experience of life there, together with the influence of the Gandhian movement, had made them rethink their ideas. They wanted to share the poverty and daily grind of village life in North India, following their instincts that "God is with us in the mud and the suffering and that is where we too wanted to be."[18] So they started the Jyotiniketan Community, near the village of Kareli, and they later resigned from the Church Missionary Society. They also had a vision of finding God beyond the different religions, beyond the clothing of name and form, and a longing to return to the "source" where all is one.

Despite their different nationalities and denominations, the two men shared a vision, neither belonging completely to their own traditions and both feeling, as Murray put it, "blessedly at home with a fellow eccentric."[19] The early days of their friendship are, however, interesting also for what they could not share because of their denominational differences. At first, when he was staying with his new friends at Jyotiniketan, Abhishiktananda would say Mass standing in his room, wearing the crumpled Roman vestments and using the portable Mass kit and Latin missal that he never traveled without. After his recent declaration that he was "Free from Mass and no-Mass," it is surprising to learn that he was still in thrall to the way Mass was customarily said before the Second Vatican Council.* Not to be able to celebrate the Eucharist with his friends, though one of them always sat with him, could hardly be called freedom. It still mattered to him that he was seen to be a Christian and a Roman Catholic and that he should not be out of step with the authorities.

There is also in this meeting a glimpse of how insulated Abhishiktananda had been from Christian faiths other than Roman Catholic, for though he quickly saw the work at Jyotiniketan as a real contribution to the church, he initially had difficulty in accepting that a priest could be married. It was not long, however, before he appreciated the value of a married priesthood, even referring to "the sacerdotal value of the couple." In a few weeks he was to expand this sympathy, when he met the Bakers, friends of the Jyotiniketan Community who were living nearby. Laurie Baker was an influential architect, and his Indian wife, Kuni, a doctor; together they ran a hospital at Pithoragarh on the border of Nepal; they were Quakers. Abhishiktananda was deeply impressed by them and wrote to Anne-Marie Stokes, a fellow Breton living in New York: "What Pharisees we Catholics often are, and how the Lord sometimes delights in making us aware that Love (the essential thing) is sometimes found in greater measure outside the Church than within it."[20]

The same awareness was to strike him in August, when he was afflicted simultaneously by herpes and neuralgia and spent two weeks being cared for in the Bakers' hospital. "The Lord has willed to make me realize that the Spirit also works beyond the frontiers of Rome. . . . A disturbing problem which is set to the Church by the presence of the Spirit outside Rome and even apart from the Christian faith."[21] Later he refered to the Bakers as the people in India he had found to be taking the Sermon on the Mount most seriously, despite being "a Quaker family who do not even recognize the necessity of baptism."[22]

---

*The Second Vatican Council did not open until 1962.

ANOTHER HIGHLIGHT OF THIS TRIP was his first sight of the Himalayas. The lure of place is strong, elusive, and ultimately intangible. Why should God seem to be more present in one place than another? Abhishiktananda never ceased to love France, sometimes bursting into tears at the sound of a Breton song. He had barely understood his passionate wish to live in India, though over the last decade of living on the subcontinent his instincts were to be fully confirmed. He wrote to a Carmelite friend that in India he had "made direct contact with the fundamental sources, those which speak—or rather, stammer—about the experience of the seers. . . . There is here a sense of being which it appears has not been experienced in any other part of the world with such intensity, such crystalline purity."[23] The use of the word stammer is significant, for not only was he, more than most, in touch with the inexpressible, but he also suffered from a slight speech impediment.

When Abhishiktananda first arrived, he was intoxicated by the whole of India. Then he gave his heart quite specifically to Arunachala, seeing in it a symbol of all that stands for the wisdom of India and setting it against the position Rome has for Roman Catholicism. Now the Himalayas held him in thrall:

Behold the great peaks of the Himalayas, the summit of the world, Earth's supreme effort to reach up to Heaven! Thrusting upwards to the greatest possible height, they soar towards the sky, as if to lay hold of the "waters above the firmament," of which Genesis speaks —to lay hold of them, and cause them to fall back upon the earth, first as raging torrents which devastate the mountain sides, and later as placid rivers, winding across the plains and making them fertile for the well-being of mankind.[24]

And just as the holy mountain of Arunachala is sacred to Shiva, so are the Himalayas a "sanctuary not made with human hands which nature itself had raised up to the glory of Shiva."[25]

Though on this trip Abhishiktananda did not reach the High Himalayas, he traveled widely in that area known as the Deva Bhumi—the Land of the Gods—going first to Almora, one of the few hill stations not created by the British, from where he first saw the great peaks, up to eight thousand meters high. He then walked twenty kilometers on the mountain road to Binsar, where he had been given an introduction to a Punjabi Hindu, a former philosophy graduate and businessman, now a solitary, with whom he hoped to stay. Abhishiktananda's tension between

Hinduism and Christianity emerged in a personal way in this encounter, for the two understood each other at a deep level, the Hindu being a man who loved Christ yet was appalled by the church's claim to be the only way to God. Abhishiktananda felt that here was a man who had "authentically realized that incredible experience of being (the 'I am' of John 8) which is at once the axis and the summit of Hindu mysticism."[26] Yet, again the chasm opened between them. "We understood each other immediately and felt each other strangely close, but at the same time so distant that tears came to our eyes. . . . He put to me the most pressing, existential questions about my own experience."[27]

Unable to go farther north, as he had not got the necessary permit,* he traveled, mostly by foot, to Karnaprayag, the confluence of the Pindari River and the Alaknanda, and to the great towns of ceaseless pilgrimage, Rishikesh and Haridwar, where he met "*sadhus* of every kind of dress and in none at all, in every shade of orange and ochre—but not a single Christian!"[28] Then into the state now known as Himachal Pradesh, to Solan, where his friend Father Christanand was the parish priest: from there he wrote most movingly to his sister Marie-Thérèse about the joys of traveling on foot along the Ganges:

> You are free, instead of being jammed together in trains or buses. There are enchanting solitudes and wonderful times of silence. Think of it, no noise of engines, no motor-horns, no trains, no radios or loudspeakers, etc. The solitude of Shantivanam is nothing compared to it. You cross hills and valleys, climbing up and down. Sometimes you follow beside a river, one of the streams which join up to form the Ganges, along a narrow valley beside the swift torrent . . . sheer cliffs on either side, maybe 500–1000 metres high. Then with the Ganges you descend towards the plain. The Himalayas open up, hills are less high, the Ganges spreads out, divides up and enters the plain to make it fertile.[29]

He then spent ten days in Delhi, seeing many people, including his two young friends Shri Ram Swarup and Shri Sita Ram Goel, who were militant members of a right-wing revolutionary party, their anti-communism based not on political but on religious grounds. Abhishiktananda was touched when, after two hours of fierce discussion about Christianity, they asked for half an hour of silent meditation. He was also received as a *sādhu* by a government minister who asked him to assist India by helping with a spiritual parallel to the Five Year Plans, which were

---

*Permits were necessary because of the proximity to the Chinese border.

intended to improve India's material circumstances. Then, after a visit to Agra, the city of the Moghuls, Abhishiktananda was back in the mountains, this time with a permit to go higher.

On the way he returned to Almora, where a Russian painter wanted to paint his portrait. Abhishiktananda's reaction to the two paintings shows great insight on the part of both painter and sitter. Both sensed two aspects, the man resting in pure being, the other "coming down again":

> These two portraits are shatteringly and profoundly true. Behind the mask (is) what I ought to be, showing through. One is the "pure being," neither dead nor alive, neither (in?) time nor space . . . the other is in some fashion the resurrection, the return to the world, in a form that again is shattering.[30]

His travels were interrupted by the sickness that took him back to the Bakers' to be cared for; then he was off for his first experience of Himalayan pilgrimage.

HE INTENDED TO WALK to two great Hindu pilgrimage centers, Kedarnath, for him the third point, along with Arunachala and Elephanta, of the sacred triangle of places especially sacred to Lord Shiva, and Badrinath, close to the Tibetan border and the legendary home of Lord Vishnu, in his incarnation as Narajan. He longed to go; "the Lord himself was expecting me there."[31] He set off from Rudraprayag, the cascades and waterfalls swollen by the September rains.

Untypically, he admitted the physical difficulties he met, and it was indeed a tough journey, over eighty kilometers and trekking from just under eight hundred meters in height to over thirty-five hundred meters. He was walking during the rains, and he was nearly fifty, not a great age, but he had just had three weeks of illness, including emphysema, which is not a helpful condition for climbers. It was the end of the season, so there were not many other pilgrims, and for three days he followed the river alone and in silence. Conditions were poor, with the path in bad repair, as he climbed, then descended a little, only to climb higher. The rains meant that many of the streams were in spate and he was forced to make frequent detours.

As the world receded, even memory becoming faint, a deep peace possessed his spirit:

> With every step that I took on this arduous climb, soaked to the skin, breathless, bowed under the weight of a bag that grew heavier

by the minute, and enveloped in the mist which everywhere rose from the ground, it seemed as if I was all the time penetrating more deeply into myself and drawing closer to the source of my being.[32]

As he approached Kedarnath, the going became even harder as the path steepened and he was constantly having to stop, put down his bag, and recover his breath. He even hallucinated mildly, thinking that he glimpsed houses or temples and imagining that he would soon be able to rest, only to find that they were mirages—merely rocky outcrops outlined in the mist. It was late afternoon when he arrived, and Kedarnath was wreathed in fog. He went to the temple for evening worship and then wandered around the village looking for food and shelter for the night. Eventually he found a room and slept.

Later that night, he woke and looked outside. The fog had cleared and the full moon shone directly overhead, lighting up the village and mirroring the temple in the water running across the meadow. Now the snow-capped peaks and the great amphitheater of rocks, the torrential waters meeting at the foot of the temple, could be seen in all their glory:

> It was overwhelming both outwardly and inwardly. Everything is a sign, a sign of the one unique Mystery. It was a coming to the inscrutable mystery of the birth of the *self*—at one and the same time at the foot of this ring of snow-covered mountains and at the summit of the remorselessly climbing path—at one and the same time in the original source from which everything comes, and in the fulfilment towards which everything tends, where the road ends and all is gathered into one.
>
> One may truly say that the only Lord of Kedar is Christ. There is only one Birth, at the very heart of Being, the birth in which Being is revealed to itself, in that "place" beyond all place, from which all comes and to which all returns.
>
> There is but one Source. . . .[33]

Sunrise the next morning was so beautiful it was painful. He went down a few hundred meters along the main stream, for the pleasure of climbing up again to the village. He was reminded of Saint Briac as he scaled the rocks, fearful of falling, fearful of stones falling on him. "Climbing back again to the source, in solitude, source of Self, source of being. . . . The Presence which comes down to BEING, for it is so full and vital that there is no longer any room for who—or what—ever here might be of the feeling of ONE in the Presence."[34]

He RETURNED TO THE PLAINS to see the bishop at Meerut, who was in charge of the Himalayan area. The bishop, along with many Hindu friends, had already encouraged him to lay the foundations of a hermitage at Haridiwar or at Deva-Prayag, the place of the confluence of two rivers where the Ganges takes its name. (A confluence in India is always considered particularly divine.) This visit sealed the arrangement for him to settle, at least experimentally, among the mountains. The Himalayas had conquered him; here he was tempted "to pitch his tent," and it looked as if he would not have to resist the temptation.

But once again he was caught in the opposites, his feelings about Shantivanam ambivalent. He wrote to Mother Françoise-Thérèse, the prioress of Lisieux: "I have just returned to Shantivanam and am caught once more by the charm of this solitude, I now find it difficult to cope with the appeals which come to me from the North, urgent as they are."[35] For four months he remained in solitude, even spending Christmas alone, and for the whole of the following year, though he made several visits to religious communities, he remained in the South, the outer landmarks being another ecumenical study week at Shantivanam and a hernia operation in February. The year 1961, however, saw him traveling to the North several times; it was also the year in which he met someone who was to be the springboard and catalyst to an aspect of Abhishiktananda's personality that had thus far had little direct expression—the expression of religious experience through discussion and an attempt to formulate it in theological terms.

14

Pioneers in Dialogue

1961–1963

Only in the cave of the heart can true dialogue
between Christianity and Hinduism take place.[1]

THOUGH ABHISHIKTANANDA WAS A COMPULSIVE WRITER, by the 1960s, past his fiftieth birthday, he had published nothing that really tackled the theological and spiritual problems confronting those drawn to both Christianity and Hinduism who felt they had a double spiritual heritage. In two books written with Monchanin, *An Indian Benedictine Ashram* and *Ermites du Saccidânanda*, he had only touched on the questions arising from the meeting of the two religions, and his self-effacing memoir about Monchanin appropriately gives little idea of what he himself was thinking and feeling. Fewer than a dozen of his articles had so far been published, and *The Secret of Arunachala*, though it had been drafted in 1956, had to wait another twenty-three years to be published.

In this reluctance to put his thoughts on record Abhishiktananda was unlike many who rush into print before their thinking has left the nursery. It was as if he could not admit just how far he had gone beyond the normal constraints of the religious understanding of the time, nor could he expect readers to follow him. His one attempt so far to express himself in depth, *Guhantara*, had been banned by the Paris censor,[2] and, apart from one chapter published in 1963,[3] it was not until after his death that some extracts were made accessible to a wider public.[4]

Abhishiktananda had tried to communicate honestly in the *Guhantara* essays and had been deeply hurt by the censor's rejection and by the criticisms of theologians. He knew he was still far from finding a synthesis between Christianity and Hinduism that satisfied him, let alone one he could present convincingly to others. He felt very alone, with few sympathizing with his position. But 1965, 1966, and 1967 were to see the publication of some of his most significant books—*Saccidânanda: A Christian Approach to Advaitic Experience*; *The Mountain of the Lord: Pilgrimage to Gangotri*; *Hindu-Christian Meeting Point: Within the Cave of the Heart*; and *Prayer*. What had changed to enable him to express himself with more confidence?

This release of his undoubted ability as a writer owes much to his spending more and more time with other people on the cutting edge of twentieth-century spirituality who shared his vision and understood something of the internal struggles he was enduring. There had been a few people he had been able to talk to, for instance Monchanin, Bede Griffiths, and Francis Mahieu, but the relationships were sometimes uneasy and communication was not free and complete. In fact Bede Griffiths once said he "went too far" toward experiencing *advaita*, a remark that cannot have endeared him to Abhishiktananda. There were others with whom he had been able to share his thoughts, such as Sister Thérèse de Jésus, a French Carmelite at Shembaganur; his great friend the quiet, eremitic Father Dominique, the Benedictine from St. André; and, since the late 1950s, he would regularly spend time with Raimon Panikkar, finding him one of the few people with whom he could talk at a theological level. (This was, of course, made easier by the fact that Panikkar has referred to himself as a Hindu-Christian priest.) Nonetheless, Abhishiktananda often felt that he was a lone voice, crying in the wilderness, and in a sense this was true. He was a powerful example of what anthropologists and theologians have come to refer to as "double-belonging"—at once Hindu and Christian, finding joy and truth in both, unable to reject either in favor of the other. At the time few shared his predicament. In fact some Christians, especially those who had read *Guhantara*, thought that he was a heretic, an accusation that hurt him deeply, for it was far from the truth.

In the 1960s this small circle expanded as Abhishiktananda made friendships with other like-minded people. These included the Jyotiniketan Community at Bareilly, with whom he felt totally at ease and two of whose members, Mary Rogers and Heather Sandeman, were to translate his books into English; the Bakers, who had introduced him to their Quaker way of life; and Sr. Térèse de Jésus, a Carmelite nun from Lisieux (not to be confused with Sr. Thérèse from Shambaganur, mentioned above); and another remarkable nun, Sara Grant, a sister of the Sacred Heart who taught in Bombay and who was later to translate *Hindu-Christian Meeting Point*. There was James Stuart, who translated much of his writing and was later to edit his letters in the invaluable book *Swami*

Abhishiktananda: His Life Told through His Letters, and Odette Baumer-Despeigne, with whom he carried on an intense correspondence, though they met only once, at the end of his life. He also had many young followers, including a group of people who were to play an important part in keeping his memory alive, Caterina Conio, the Italian scholar who founded the Centro Le Saux in Milan, the indologist Maria Bidoli, and the distinguished Sanskrit scholar Bettina Bäumer, currently the editor of *Setu*, the bulletin of the Abhishiktananda Society, whom Abhishiktananda once referred to as "the best of the bunch!" He crossed denominational bridges easily, forming relationships not only with Hindus of every caste and shade of belief and with members of the church of South India, but also with Christians such as John Taylor, later to be Anglican bishop of Winchester, England; Klaus Klostermaier, a member of a German order, the Society of the Divine Word; Ilse Friedeberg of the World Council of Churches, a Lutheran who never gave in to her longing to become an Orthodox and through whom Abhishiktananda met Russians such as Bishop Anthony Bloom, Head of the Russian Orthodox Church in England and Scotland. There was the South African bishop Alphonse Zulu; two American Methodists, Bob and Mary Petersen; and the first Western teacher of Tibetan Buddhism, the German-born Lama Govinda. Abhishiktananda himself saw the irony of having so many relationships, admitting: "The hermit should bury himself in solitude and here he is widening his acquaintance more and more."[5]

These people supported Abhishiktananda in friendship and understanding, but one man played a particularly important role, as their association led to a series of formal discussions in which Abhishiktananda took a leading part. This was Dr. Jacques-Albert Cuttat, who had worked at the League of Nations and been Minister to Ecuador and Colombia. Cuttat was the Swiss ambassador to India, a post that he must have been delighted to hold, as for thirty years he had studied the relationship between Eastern spirituality and Christianity. He was fifty-two when he met Abhishiktananda and only the year before had published *The Encounter of Religions*, with an introduction by Prime Minister Pandit Jawaharlal Nehru. Cuttat was a deeply spiritual man, insisting that his secretary gave him at least five minutes' space between interviews, to give him time to be silent. He also had an instinctive ability to find like-minded people: Murray Rogers talks of "his uncanny way of smelling out contemplatives and deep spiritual characters in government."[6] This deep level of Christianity owed something to his contact with Hindu interiority, so it was no surprise that there was an immediate sympathy between him and Abhishiktananda.

It was January 1961 when they met, when Abhishiktananda, on his way to another trip to the Himalayas, had stopped in Delhi to see friends. He and Cuttat spent six hours together, during which they had lunch with some of Cuttat's friends at the Swiss embassy. It was one of several occasions on which Abhishiktananda was tempted by the life he had renounced. Here he was looking like a Hindu ascetic, yet somewhere inside him flickered the yearnings of a Frenchman—the son of a grocer at that—for good food and drink:

> They naturally served rice and vegetables to me, while a meat dish made the round of the table. That was nothing; but on the table there were two very attractive bottles of Burgundy, a Châteaneuf, and, after the excellent coffee there was a bottle of Martell Three Star, something I had not seen for many years. . . . I said firmly I would content myself with looking at them . . . and enjoying them "by proxy" only![7]

The exchanges between the diplomat and the swami/monk were fruitful, and they agreed to hold a series of theological-spiritual discussions, based loosely on the meetings Abhishiktananda had already held at Shantivanam in 1957 and 1958. They decided to bring together a group of priests and theologians concerned with the relationship between Hindu and Christian experience, something that for readers of the twenty-first century may seem predictable enough, but this was 1961 and they were pioneers in a field that had been little explored.

They agreed that they had no intention of trying to formulate resolutions or arrive at final conclusions; the territory was too unfamiliar for that, and in any case they did not want premature attempts at definition to destroy spontaneity. They also agreed that the discussions should be centered in the heart rather than in the head, in experience rather than in theory. They did not want people participating out of speculative curiosity—Abhishiktananda had met many people who did not know the real India yet who "missionize like Don Quixote and fight with windmills, unaware of the fact that India at one and the same time awaits Christianity and guards itself against it."[8] A true meeting of Hinduism and Christianity could only come about in the Spirit, so this meeting must happen first in their own hearts.

Both Cuttat and Abhishiktananda had accepted that the participants should all be Christians—meetings between Christians and Hindus would, they hoped, follow. Though ecumenism was not assumed in those days—indeed it was rare—Abhishiktananda insisted that it should not be only Roman Catholics priests and theologians, but that members of other churches would be included. The first meeting was arranged for April 1961, and the subject was to be Vedantic and Christian experience: Cuttat financed it, acted as host, and made the arrangements; Abhishiktananda was the animator.

A year after their first meeting, some ten people—Cuttat and Abhishiktananda, several Catholic priests, two Anglican priests, and a Russian Orthodox monk—met in Almora, the hill station in the Land of the Gods from where Abhishiktananda had, for the first time, seen the Himalayas. The venue was the home of the Methodist bishop of Delhi, and their theme was Christian and Hindu religious experience; "Christians were gazing at Christ in the mystery of India, where Christ was gazing at them in his eschatological glory."[9]

Their morning Eucharist took place under an immense deodar tree "having as 'backdrop' for the altar the breath-taking sight of snow-clad Himalayan peaks, touched with the light of the rising sun. . . . We were conscious of being in the Presence."[10] They were in the land of the *rishis*, contemplating the mountains in which the holy men of long ago first heard "the imperceptible murmur which sounds in the depth of the heart, like the murmur of the streams which wind along the higher slopes, but swelling continually as one descends towards the torrent, until at last it drowns every other sound in its overwhelming thunder."[11] No wonder they found it such an exhilarating occasion: they were living with a deepening sense of the ultimate mystery, sharing their most profound beliefs in sympathetic company.

The experiential approach was honored from the start, as they devoted an entire day to the effect India had had on their spiritual lives. Abhishiktananda writes of them anonymously—of one who had been reminded of his true monastic vocation by the witness of Hindu *sannyāsis*, another of meeting India first through books and forsaking the bourgeois Christianity of his upbringing until he found the truths that India had taught him revealed in the Jesus Prayer. Grace had come to him through India. Another (Abhishiktananda himself?) had found, after an initial sense of losing his balance on the edge of a great abyss, that the Upanishads had revealed to him that the soul and God are "not two." "The Vedantic night" he concluded, "is certainly a royal road by which to enter into the ultimate secret of the mystery of the Blessed Trinity."[12] Another had been inspired by the lives of Hindu monks, comparing them to the fathers of Christian monasticism, while yet another, arriving in India steeped in preconceptions of the Christian missionary, found new light shed on the gospel of Christ through contact with disciples of Mahatma Gandhi, so touched by the authenticity of their lives that he changed his lifestyle to live in poverty among India's poorest.

Abhishiktananda flourished in this environment. He was finding corroboration, through other people, of everything he had come to believe, especially in his instinct that the experience of India could lead to a mystical deepening in the church. This was something that he had shared with one of his Carmelite friends, about eighteen months before the meeting at Almora:

> This pearl of India will only be discovered by contemplatives. For all others it remains a sealed book. . . . What India essentially needs are contemplative Christian souls who are ready to plunge into the depths of her mystical experience, to lose their foothold, to disappear in it from human sight, trusting in the grace of the Lord who will enable them to bring to light the marvellous pearl of Saccidananda which the Spirit has hidden and sustained there.[13]

Despite their intention not to make resolutions, they did come to some conclusions. The first was rather surprising: "that the Lord is already in India, and we need not imagine, poor feeble creatures that we are, that it is we who make him present."[14] That this was a new discovery says much of the arrogance of Christianity at the time; for all our weakened spirituality in the twenty-first century, there are few who believe anything at all who would doubt that the Lord is indeed in India as in the Far East or even Europe and America. The second conclusion was a renewed awareness of the gift of interiority that is India's; the message of the resurrection could have no impact in India unless it is revealed in its essential interiority. The third was to discover each other as Christians, across denominational boundaries; they met at a level beyond the opposites, where all apparent differences were transcended. "This is like the *anamnesis** of the early church, before the divisions," said Dr. Cuttat,[15] thus hitting on the paradox that in order to go forward, one often has to go back.

The success of the first meeting at Almora led to another the following year, this time rather larger, held at the Christian Study Centre in Rajpur, at the foot of the Himalayas. The focus was one of the conclusions of the first meeting, the importance of interiority—could Hindu interiority be integrated with Christianity? Abhishiktananda had little difficulty persuading his fellow participants that papers should be given

---

*A Greek word meaning "memory" or "memorial."

on the great contemplatives of Hinduism and Christianity. The representatives of Hinduism were Sankara, Ramana Maharshi (the paper given by Abhishiktananda himself), the Bhagavad-Gita, and Aurobindo. Meister Eckhart, Hesychasm, St. Gregory of Nyssa, St. Teresa of Avila, and St. John of the Cross were the topics of Christian mysticism. Through these great messengers of the divine, the experience common to both could be seen and experienced.

The third meeting of the "Cuttat group" was in Nagpur, in northern Maharashtra. It was held immediately after Christmas 1963, and this time the group, the largest so far, planned to read the Bible in the morning and the Upanishads in the evening. They wished to give the Hindu scriptures the meditative attention that they were accustomed to giving Christian scriptures by reading the Upanishads in the spirit of the monastic tradition of *lectio divina*, contemplative reading "in the Presence." "Above all no one would seek to be the centre of attention. Each person, rather than speaking, would want to *listen and ask questions* of the Spirit in his brothers."[16]

Their discussions were free and informal. They sat cross-legged in a circle under a great tree, only moving when they lost the protection of the shade, reading from the Psalms, from Isaiah, from the Isa and the Kena Upanishads. And as they read they came nearer to understanding some of the deepest mysteries. How, for instance, "the wise man who finds himself in the ultimate retreat in himself has at the same time reached the very centre of the universe. All in self, self in all."[17] How the door to this experience does not stand open, but only opens from the inside, to him who begs to be admitted. "When at last the door opens, he is no longer the contemplative, his body has gone to ashes, his breath to wind. Indeed, this marvellous face which appears to him, is it not himself?"[18] The last two Bible readings were from the Fourth Gospel, a glorious crowning of the mystery at the heart of both traditions. "The secret that had been divined by the *rishi*s, John unveiled to us; very clearly from then on, that of the Word; in great depth also, that of the Spirit."[19]

Abhishiktananda's concern was that Indians should see the glory of the Christian Gospels, something he was convinced would happen only if it was preached "in the manner of St. Francis of Assisi, in poverty, simplicity, humility and prayer."[20] He was not surprised that priests and bishops had had so little success with the Hindus, for "the sauce with which they serve up the Gospel is so insipid. It is like inviting someone to a banquet, and then offering him nothing but boiled noodles!"[21]

Once again it is important to realize what an unusual path they were taking. In those days few Christians read the Hindu scriptures, and the idea of reading them alongside the Bible was revolutionary, and, for those wishing to keep contact with the church, dangerous. Abhishiktananda was treading a delicate path and he knew it, as was clear when he wrote to Murray Rogers, "Like you I feel a little nervous. Let us be good *advaitis*, and not mind what people may think of us, but go straight on our way, seeing only the 'atman' in everything, and being so void of everything inside that the Spirit may use us at his own free will."[22]

Abhishiktananda—for he was the guiding force behind their discussions—was years ahead of his time. The Second Vatican Council was sitting, but it was to be two years before the proclamation of *Nostra Aetate*, the document that encouraged dialogue between Catholics and other religions and declared, "The Catholic Church rejects nothing that is true and holy in these religions." While he was wearing the clothes of a *sādhu*, sitting cross-legged discussing Hindu scriptures in India, in the West the term "interfaith studies" had not yet been coined, indeed "comparative religion" as it was then called, was based on the assumption that everything was seen in relation to a basic model of Christianity, not the relationship of two faiths speaking from the same central truth. It is even conceivable that the Cuttat meetings had an influence on the Vatican deliberations, for some of the participants were attending the sessions of the council and making courageous interventions in the discussions. Murray Rogers feels that the church has still not caught up with the vision that Abhishiktananda was encouraging over forty years ago; he even feels that he himself, though present at the time, is still digesting the implications of Abhishiktananda's vision and of their discussions. Abhishiktananda himself seems to have shared this diffidence, for he once said to Murray, "Only the one who knows in the heart has experienced the mystery and that one seldom returns from the silence."[23] The little group shared something with the Celtic saints who went to sea in rudderless boats with no idea where they would arrive, but knowing that God would steer them.

At last Abhishiktananda felt he was not struggling alone. The loneliness of the visonary had been hitting him hard, as he admitted to close friends like Canon Lemarié:

It is wretched to live amid such lack of understanding on the part of one's neighbours. I avoid dining at the Bishop's house, so as to avoid stupid questions. (The Bishop himself is fortunately more sensible.) I avoid ecclesiastics whom I do not know to be specially sympathetic. How happy I am to be in purely Hindu surroundings. . . .

With no one to ask, How many "conversions"? or How many postulants?[24]

So now, in the company of others who shared his vision, they struggled toward the understanding of complex issues, for instance, that *advaita* did not go *beyond* the Christian experience, as Hindus sometimes believe, rather that it is the very foundation of Christianity. The participants immersed themselves in the Vedantic tradition, agreeing "to bow before the magnitude of this experience, the spiritual experience *par excellence* of India."[25] Abhishiktananda ended his reflections on these meetings with what is surely an oblique reference to his own anguish: "Christian salvation is reconciliation. It implies pain and salvation, agony and tearing apart. It cannot be otherwise in the *passage* from advaita to the spirit, or rather from the recognition at the very depth of advaita of the mystery of the Spirit."[26]

Though everyone agreed that this meeting had been fruitful and successful, it was the occasion of a remark being passed that cast doubt on Abhishiktananda's Christian integrity, stirring up his familiar agony and wounding him to the depths of his soul. Though the remark came from Dr. Cuttat himself, who Abhishiktananda must have known respected his integrity completely, Abhishiktananda was so deeply hurt that he never attended another meeting and the "Cuttat circle" continued without him. The degree of his hurt says much about the tensions in which Abhishiktananda lived; if even his close friends could not understand his complete loyalty to both Hinduism and Christianity, could not understand the depths of his Christian faith or his dedication to the truth that lay at the heart of both traditions, how could he himself accept the "double-belonging" in which he found himself?

What was worse, and perhaps what Abhishiktananda knew in the depths of his being, was that however innocently the remark was delivered (and we do not know exactly what was said), there was a real problem at its heart. Dr. Cuttat wrote about this some years later. This problem is so central to Abhishiktananda's difficulties, both with himself and with others, that it is worth quoting from his letter at length. Cuttat is responding to Abhishiktananda's account of his meeting with Gnanananda in *Guru and Disciple*:

My first impression was outstandingly excellent. Dear Swamiji Abhishiktananda-ji explains the most difficult and subtle things in a remarkably simple and clear way. I felt surrounded again with the deeply contemplative atmosphere of India. Again, thanks to Father

Lesaux I had the priviledge* to experience the fact that Brahman is the *unique reality*.

After several days of contemplating in this line of Shri Gnanananda-ji, I felt a strange sadness. Suddenly, I realised that something essential was lacking in this jnanic[†] way to the Supreme. Everything whatsoever was pervaded with joy and bliss centred in my own Self, the whole reality was luminous and transparent, yet all this happiness was without *love*. There is in this way neither love for God nor love to the other, both are not loved as *others*. Swami Abhish. lives in a happy world of *sacred solitude*.

I hoped first, reading the book, that something of Christ's love to God would appear towards the end. In vain. The Christian reader is cut off from *every* Thou, divine or human, and assembles all felicity within himself. Nothing is more opposed to the Christian holy Mass, where—in the Eucharist—I am the victim offered in Christ to the (illegible) Father for the sins of the world.

I became incapable to follow again the way of Swami Abhish. I only can pray for him, for the moment of death when he will be face to face with Christ.[27]

This letter shows the anguishing predicament in which Abhishiktananda lived for so long, misunderstood even by his friends. It also, as Bettina Bäumer points out, shows a typical and painful misunderstanding between Hindus and Christians:

It shows that the Christian emphasis on the love of God is more often based on an underlying dualism, and the misunderstanding of Vedanta as a solipsistic monism. Both are wrong. The "love of God" has to take seriously the Gospel of John and the oneness expressed therein. The advaitic experience, on the other hand, cannot be understood without love—and bhakti[‡] and advaita are not contrasts but complementary. It is here again where theology has to be based on experience.[28]

Ironically, Abhishiktananda was later to have his own differences with Dr. Cuttat, finding an article by him, published in 1966, to be misleading

---

*English was not Dr. Cuttat's first language, but the letter is left as it was written.
[†]From *jnani*, "a sage," one who was awakened to reality, realized the Self.
[‡]*Bhakti*, loving devotion.

and fearing it would prevent rather than help understanding of the very real problems at the heart of Hindu–Christian dialogue.

P ERHAPS, HOWEVER, IT WAS NOT only Cuttat's remark that caused him to stop attending the meetings. Murray Rogers suggests that Abhishiktananda came to feel a "spiritual foreigner in such learned meetings. . . . His own inner dialogue in the advaita of the Spirit had carried him on; he ceased to believe in the value of such discussions."[29] Indeed his attitude to the things of the mind, particularly theology, was ambivalent. On the one hand, he did not hold the discipline in high regard; he was distressed that so many professional Christian theologians "refuse to perceive the *gold* in the crude ore which is offered by the Hindu philosophers"[30] and grieved that even the best European theology rings hollow in the face of "the Hindu discovery of '*I am*,' the only support that abides when everything collapses."[31] He once rhetorically asked of a priest friend, "How can he expect that theologians lead the band! As Athenogoras rightly put it, they are made to follow."[32] On the other hand, he was no mean theologian himself; he was respected by professional theologians, and he could not, and did not, dismiss the importance of theology. Indeed, he saw one of the church's most urgent needs as theological renewal, believing that without a theology of the meeting of religions the crisis confronting the church could never be resolved. Toward the end of his life his thinking was to take another turn, when he wondered whether a theology that went too deep should not be written down at all, for fear of misunderstanding.

It is ironic that one of the results of these meetings, with their explicit favoring of the heart over the mind, was that they helped Abhishiktananda to express himself theologically in two books that have been widely read over the last forty years. One was his account of the Cuttat meetings, which was published in 1966 in French and three years later in English as *A Hindu-Christian Meeting Point*. He gives a lively account of the meetings and tackles the theological problems of their conversations:

> . . . above all to discover the relation between the experience which the Hindu regards as ultimate and the experience of the Christian mystic. Must not the ultimate experience of God be an experience of the mystery of the eternal generation of the Son in the depth of the Godhead and of the inexpressible "non-duality" of Father and Son in the Spirit?[33]

Abhishiktananda admits that there is no solution if thinking is confined to concepts of Christian theology, but that we must seek to know this "double experience" from within, "trying to realize simultaneously in the depths of our own being both that experience of the ultimate 'nonduality' which the Vedantin regards as the final goal of human life and the experience of divine sonship in the unity of the Spirit which lies at the heart of our Christian faith."[34] While this was familiar thinking to anyone knowing Abhishiktananda's thought, to new readers it must have been received with either a shock of delighted recognition or in horrified dismissal. Those in the former category often wrote to him, many of his friendships beginning in such a way.

From the evidence of his letters and diaries, however, the book that most concerned him, widely regarded as his major work, is the one he referred to simply as *Sagesse*. It was published in French in 1965 and, after his death, in a revised English edition, *Saccidananda: A Christian Approach to Advaitic Experience*. Any comment on Abhishiktananda's books is complicated by the fact that he changed his mind about what he had written, sometimes even before it was published. Indeed, the only books with which he remained content were those based on personal experience, such as his accounts of meeting Ramana Maharshi and Sri Gnanananda, or his books about pilgrimage and prayer. Like any profound thinker, he was always growing and changing, so by the time the text of *Saccidananda* had rolled off the printing presses, he had moved on, not at all sure he agreed with himself any longer. For instance, James Stuart points out[35] that when Abhishiktananda started the book he found the "theology of fulfilment"—the idea that all religions find their fulfillment in Christ— helped him hold together his advaitic experience and his Christianity. By 1971, however, when he wrote the introduction to the English edition (he was keen for it to be available in English, despite not being entirely happy with it), he needed to qualify this, removing any suggestion that Hinduism, or indeed any other religion, was simply a preparation for the ultimate truth of Christianity and admitting that "the theology of 'fulfilment' is unable to do justice to religious pluralism."[36] He felt that neither his books nor Raimon Panikkar's were intended for Hindus, but that their role was "to sensitize Christian thought to the treasures that await it here; and to prepare Christians for dialogue."[37]

The book was an attempt, greatly influenced by Ramana Maharshi, to give a trinitarian Christian response to advaitic experience. In the first pages he established the universality and namelessness of God and the similarity of those who believe in him, before embarking on theological argument. In his introduction to the book, James Stuart tells of how the publisher, enthusiastic though he was, insisted that "much clarification of the style and presentation was needed if the book was to make its full impact."[38] So for eight months Abhishiktananda wrote and rewrote, argued amicably with his publishers, anguished, and, like any author in such a position, considered giving up the whole project. But he persisted and, apart from being hurt by a review in Taizé's *Verbum Caro*[39] suggesting that his theology was syncretistic, found the reactions rewarding. As stalwart a representative of Christianity as the *Clergy Supplement* said the book "may well become a classic of Christian Indian spirituality,"[40] and, to his even greater delight, he received several responses from contemplatives in the West who found the book helped them to understand their own experiences. He shared these with his friend Raimon Panikkar:

> At noon today I received another shattering letter on this subject. Even John of the Cross, said the writer, had not been able to explain so clearly the interior stripping (nudity) and the passage from the "self" to the "Self." . . . Yet another letter from Europe strengthens my conviction that the advaitin experience underlies all true mysticism, Christian included. All these letters in short say this: "Your book has taught me nothing new, but for the first time in my life I have understood what was happening in my soul." That consoles one for many things, doesn't it? It is just one more proof that we are not heading in the wrong direction.[41]

So the 1960s were full and rewarding in terms of discussion, theological expression, and, at last, publication and enthusiastic response. These activities did not, however, rule out other aspects of Abhishiktananda's life, not least the physical expression of the spiritual journey, pilgrimage.

15

To the Source of the Ganges

1963–1964

A pilgrim on his way up to God.[1]

DURING THE BUSY YEARS of the Cuttat meetings, Abhishiktananda was making plans for his future, trying to find a place where he could live in solitude on the banks of the Ganges. In April 1961, while he was at Almora, his wish to "pitch his tent" in the Himalayas was granted when he was given a few hundred square meters of land near the Ganges at Uttarkashi on which to build a hut, a *kutiya*. It was bought for him by Raimon Panikkar; the land was acquired in the names of Abhishiktananda and R. Panikkar jointly and he could have it for life. Ever since his first sight of the high peaks in 1959, he had been drawn to the Himalayas like an unfaithful lover changing his allegiance from Arunachala. The decision to spend more time there was influenced both by the Cuttat meetings and by the depth of his encounters with Hindus at Uttarkashi and in Delhi. He was more and more convinced that "only by the way of *interiority* will the Church be able to make contact with India, except at a superficial level."[2] It also suited him personally, for his love of silence and solitude was growing, though he knew how easy it was to find distraction, even to plead the excuse of good works: "Thus the Lord has to come and seek us out in the last nook and cranny of our being, in the very place where, without realizing it, we seek to escape from him, to be on our very own, even making the wonderful excuse that he needs us and that we must work in his service."[3]

It would be a mistake, however, to think that he found solitude easy, even though he longed for it.

> The solitary is all alone face to face with himself, all alone face to face with God, in the depth of himself, but with a God who draws

him beyond all signs, all forms of manifestation, all symbols, all images, all concept; and in the last resort, there is nothing in which he could "embrace" this God, or touch him, or see him, whether he be the one God experienced by the *bhakta*, or the triune God of the Christian's faith-experience. So it is a solitude in which nothing answers the call, or rather in which no response to the call is heard. For in every response, I know that it is from myself that it is welling up. And, in the end, who is calling? Nothing any longer exists but the kevala, the totally blank page in the Ten Pictures of Zen.[4]

Solitude allows for no distraction. Whereas someone in regular employment—a factory worker, a teacher, a priest—has a task, a pattern of life that takes one outward, if the solitary gives himself a task, he would risk forgetting his real task, which is to be without any task in this world but to be: "a witness to the End [*eschaton*] from the Christian viewpoint, to the permanent [*nitya*] from the Vedantin viewpoint. Fulfilled, completed in *kevala*."*

By November the *kutiya* was completed, but he had decided not to live there permanently. At the moment he wanted to keep both ashrams, for not only had he responsibilities in Shantivanam, but there was much that still drew him there: "The mountains are beautiful, but in the plains there is a brightness of colour which opens you up and 'expands' you wonderfully. Mountains concentrate you, limit your horizons, but make you go deep."[5] So long as he could afford the expense he would keep both ashrams, spending as much time at Gyansu as he could.

MEANWHILE HE TRAVELED the length and breadth of India, meeting people and taking part in study groups. He visited Father Mahieu in Kerala, his great friend Father Dominique in Bangalore, the Jesuits at Dindugul, a leprosarium at Anandavanam and various Carmels, including those at Kareikkal and Bangalore. When he was at Shantivanam (he spent less than six months a year there during this period), he received many visitors, including Max Thurian of the Taizé Community, the Orthodox theologian Olivier Clément, his friend from Jyotiniketan John Cole, the priest-writer Jean Sulivan, and Ilse Friedeberg, who worked for Christian unity.

There were also meetings and conferences. In the years of the Cuttat meetings, between 1961 and 1964, there was a study group on Teilhard de Chardin at Jyotiniketan, a theological meeting at Bangalore, an exper-

---

Kevala is applied to one who has attained to unity in total isolation. Abhishiktananda also called it "the solitude that has no name" (*Further Shore*, 125).

iment in contemplative reading of the Upanishads in Delhi, a eucharistic conference in Bombay, and, arguably most significant, the Assembly of the World Council of Churches, a ten-day meeting that took place at the end of November 1961. This was held in Delhi, the welcome he received giving another boost to his always rather tenuous hold on confidence; he was becoming accepted by the church, and whatever his criticisms of the institution, that was important to him. And he enjoyed it greatly, writing that there was a real longing for unity and that it was

> a most impressive atmosphere. All nationalities, all kinds of dress. Lay attire predominates (and there are many women). . . . Five official Catholic observers and 10-20 unofficial. . . . Relaxed, simple, fraternal atmosphere, I wish some Roman cardinals were here incognito to take note of the atmosphere.[6]

The early 1960s were a busy time in Abhishiktananda's life, but perhaps the most significant single event of that period was that he fulfilled a long-held wish to make a pilgrimage to one of the sources of the Ganges. More than most people, Abhishiktananda's whole life was a pilgrimage, in the sense that it was totally devoted to seeking God, but, in keeping with his passion for experience, he also lived out pilgrimage physically, for though not a particularly strong man, and nearly forty by the time he arrived in India, he often journeyed to places believed to be especially sacred, places of pilgrimage, and some of these journeys were very strenuous.

The power of the sacred place is mysterious, demanding, unreasonable. If God is within, why do we look for him in the outer physical world? And if he is everywhere, why do we travel to sites where he is thought to be especially present? These are questions that every pilgrim must ask, and no doubt Abhishiktananda asked them. We have no record of his answers, but we cannot fail to realize that Abhishiktananda had a boundless curiosity to visit sacred places, perhaps partly because he had so keen a sense of place.

France, or rather Brittany, beloved land of his birth, the country in which he lived for nearly forty years, was naturally enough the place he felt deep in his bones even after he had become an Indian citizen. Gazing at the crashing waters of the Ganges, he saw the waves of the Côte Sauvage. Hearing the rocks clatter down Himalayan slopes, he remembered the rocks of Saint Briac falling under his childish feet. He eyed the food and wine of his country with controlled longing, and even after living in India for over twenty years he could still be affected by a French song or an old family photo; a letter from Brittany could still make him dream and "relive those things I usually push into the background in order to be able to live my life in peace."[7] Whatever wonders he found in the Himalayas, in Arunachala, he never forgot "the sea of my Emerald Coast. . . . All this belongs to the depth of my being. It is like those Tridentine Masses and the Gregorian chant of the monasteries, which I would doubtless put on again like a glove."[8]

This love of his homeland is natural enough, but why, loving it as he did, did he never think of returning? Why did he only consider returning to France if, for any reason, things became impossible in India? Why did he never visit his family? So well did he cover his feelings that it comes as a shock to realize that what stopped him from returning to the land of his childhood was his very love of the place: "Perhaps behind all the high-sounding reasons that I give for refusing and arguing against any possibility of returning there, is my fear of not being able to bear it emotionally, and the great difficulty I would have afterwards in taking up my 'role' again."[9]

So India became the place he loved, the home of his heart. But again comes the question—why was he so restless? India is a huge country, and he never stopped traveling its length and breadth, loving Arunachala and the Himalayas especially, but never staying long in one place. Did he think the full advaitic experience for which he so longed might be more available to him in one place than in another? It was not until the end of his life that he seemed to lose the longing to be in a special place and to feel that in being there he was closer to God. Then, at last, he could say: "Every place is sacred, because sacredness comes from the Self and is radiated by it. Every place in which the renouncer sits is his ashram. Every stream in which he bathes becomes for him the Ganges."[10]

What did he feel about his restlessness? Was he worried by his continual desire for travel? He came near to facing this when he recounted an occasion when he was asked why he did not simply remain in the Himalayas.

> Why reopen this old wound? . . . How dearly I would love not to return with you to the plains, to remain here hidden in some mountain cave, lost in the mystery of the Father and the Spirit. . . . Why indeed are there so many things which hold me back and prevent me from staying here?[11]

So travel he did—and sometimes these travels took the form of pilgrimages, a journey to a place believed to be sacred in a specific way. His first Indian pilgrimage was in 1956, just before his visit to Sri Gnanananda, when he and Monchanin went to Nerur, not far from Shantivanam, to visit the temple of Sadashiva Brahman, the eighteenth-century yogi who never spoke a word and wore no clothes at all, not even a *dhoti*. Many miracles have been experienced at the shrine, and the villagers of South India still tell strange stories about the man. One relates how the yogi wandered into the tent of a Muslim chieftain. The ladies screamed, the warriors attacked him, and Sadashiva Brahman departed quietly, appearing not to notice that he had lost an arm in the fracas. The chieftain picked up the arm and followed the yogi, who simply placed it back into the bleeding stump of his shoulder. When the Muslim, not surprisingly deeply impressed, asked for spiritual intruction, Sadashiva, saying nothing, wrote in the sand, "Do not do what you want, and then you may do what you like." (Sadashiva so impressed Abhishiktananda that it was his example of nakedness and silence that he had promised to follow, should Sri Gnanananda have asked such a thing of him.) A gentle pilgrimage, this.

Some of his explorations of Arunachala were more strenuous. During his numerous visits there he explored every inch of the holy mountain, both climbing to its summit and walking round it. The ritual circuit of a mountain is known as *giri-pradakshina*, and in India it is considered to be a genuine penance; to do it is to gain great merit. The pilgrim, who is supposed to wear new clothes, starts by taking a bath in one of the sacred tanks and then walks some thirteen kilometers around the mountain, preferably barefoot. The ritual ends with a *pūjā* in the temple.

Abhishiktananda at first regarded all this as pure superstition, a relic of ancient lore; but while he was living in the cave of Vanatti he discovered a timeless wisdom in the practice and felt a longing to make the circuit himself. So he would set out, usually alone, often by night when there was not even starlight to guide his steps, sometimes with the moon for light. Once he reached the far side of the mountain as dawn approached and "came round to its eastern slopes just as the rising sun was flooding them with the rosy tint from which the Mountain derives its name."[12] Pilgrimages may be arduous, backbreaking, and sometimes even boring, but there are moments of glory, and these moments make up for everything.

He also climbed to the summit of Arunachala,[13] something he admitted was quite an ordeal. It was a three-hour climb, with only goat tracks to follow, and even they were not always clear. He found himself scrambling on hands and knees, and on his first attempt had to admit defeat; he returned accompanied by a young guide. He once made the climb in January, when he had another of those moments of joy in the midst of physical hardship. He and his friend were caught in a thick mist, cold and damp; by the time they reached the summit they could only catch momentary glimpses of the view they knew stretched beneath them. But there was a surprising compensation, for they "found that when Arunachala was shrouded in cloud and impregnably solitary, its secret was more mysteriously revealed than it could ever be on days of bright sunshine."[14]

Most people seeking to make a pilgrimage in India would go to the Himalayas, to the Mecca for all pilgrims to India, one of the sources of the Ganges. The Ganges, known as Ganga Ma, Mother Ganges, is loved and worshiped as the holiest river in India, the river whose water sustains towns, villages, and cities such as Allahabad and Banares and gives life to more Indians than can be counted. The Ganges of whom India's first prime minister, Jawaharlal Nehru, who was born on its banks, wrote,

> The Ganga, especially, is the river of India, beloved of her people, round which are intertwined her memories, her hopes and fears, her songs of triumph, her victories and her defeats. She has been a symbol of India's age-long culture and civilization, ever changing, ever flowing, and yet ever the same Ganga.[15]

Such is her supernatural status that epic poems regard the Ganges as a consort of the God Shiva.

Abhishiktananda had already, in 1959, walked to Kedarnath, one of the sources of the Ganges and one of the holiest places of pilgrimage for the devout Hindu. Now he set his heart on walking to Gangotri, a tiny village at over thirty-one hundred meters, where there is a temple of the goddess Ganga. It is believed the Ganga, the stream of life, touched earth for the first time here, where it is known as the Bhagirathi River, before it goes on to become the Ganges. But Abhishiktananda had his own thoughts on whether this really is the true source:

> In fact, the sources of the Ganges are not so much the glaciers from whose lips trickle her first waters, as those great peaks pointing to high heaven. There is the meeting point of the world above—that inaccessible world from which none the less we come and to which we go—with the world below in which for the time being we lead our earthly life.[16]

In 1963 and 1964, Abhishiktananda made two pilgrimages to Gangotri. He wrote about these in a short book called *The Mountain of the Lord*. The accounts are poetic rather than precise; creative writer that he was, Abhishiktananda took liberties with facts and gave no dates, changing the order of events and the name of his companion, but joyously sharing the experience in every line. The details of how he traveled can be clarified in his letters, and shaking the kaleidoscope between the various versions of his travels reveals a glimmer of the importance the experiences held for him.

In May of 1963 he traveled with a young postulant, Anand, who had come from Madras to spend a month with him. They walked from Uttarkashi to Gangotri, romantic ideals knocked into place by harsh reality: "65 kms on foot by very bad tracks, climbing up and down the hills; unbelievable lodging places at night, unbelievable the food also."[17] Their fellow pilgrims included the rich, riding on mules with coolies in attendance, their wives and children carried in litters, but the majority were poor, many barefoot or wearing ill-fitting sandals, some blind and lame— "the poor and humble, those whom the Gospel calls blessed."[18] Abhishiktananda was deeply impressed by the faith of his fellow pilgrims, braving difficulties in their hundreds. He was happy to be able to say Mass every day, in particular to celebrate it at Gangotri itself.

In hindsight this trip seems, however, to be a preparation for the one he was to make in June the following year, when his companion was to be Raimon Panikkar.* They followed the pilgrim route from Uttarkashi, from Gangotri climbing up to Gomukh, the very point where the stream issues from the glacier and the river begins its life as water. There, on the feast of the Sacred Heart, they celebrated Mass at the source of the holy river.

They first plunged, naked, into the icy river, thus symbolically both returning to the womb, the source of Being, and recalling the rite of baptism. They then chose a hollow place, with a flat stone from the riverbank for the altar, laying out the linen cloth, missal, and chalice they had brought with them. They had also brought chapattis made of unleavened wheat flour, and they drew pure water from the river beside them. The wind prevented them from keeping candles alight, but their incense sticks survived, the scent wafting around them. The sun, high in the heavens, was their only witness as they sat cross-legged, facing each other, a meter from the river.

Before beginning the liturgy, they chanted first some verses from the Upanishads, and then a Sanskrit litany "to Christ, the Saviour, the Son of God, and Son of Man, the only Lord."[19] The Eucharist, "the cosmic rite beyond compare,"[20] took its leisurely course, their voices drowned by the roar from the river, "as by a mighty organ accompaniment." This obliteration of their human voices signified mystically for Abhishiktananda "the

---

*In *The Mountain of the Lord* he calls his companion Sanat Kumar.

voice of the Spirit who 'fills the whole world,' in which is said everything that is said about God or to God."[21] The full and final oblation had been made on the banks of the Ganges, at its very source, it was "the Eucharistic fulfilment of all the prayers, offerings and austerities which over the centuries have mounted up from here to heaven."[22] These were not Abhishiktananda's final thoughts on the subject, but at this point what he called his "visceral Christianity" was asserting itself.

So the pilgrims descended, while the Ganges thundered toward the plains, at first a fierce torrent, sweeping earth and rocks from the high peaks, but before long a wide and placid river, bearer of fertility and grace.

THE TWO PILGRIMS RETURNED to Uttarkashi, where Panikkar left him, and, after a week's rest, Abhishiktananda returned to Gangotri alone, spending three days walking with a pack on his back and a bamboo staff in his hand. The paths were stony, muddy, and slippery, and the pilgrims slept close-packed on the narrow verandas of unfurnished wooden huts provided for them. The huts lacked all privacy, and the pilgrims ate only when they could find something to eat. It was a crowded and colorful occasion, for it was June and the pilgrim season was at its height. Travelers swarmed up and down, greeting each other with "Glory to Mother Ganges," to which the *sādhus* replied "OM." There were suckling children, old women leaning on their sticks, and *sādhus*, "ranging from those who are totally naked to those covered in unimaginable cast-offs as a protection against the cold."[23]

So for three weeks he was over three thousand meters high, in the heart of the Himalayas, stripped bare and trying to understand the interior silence of the *munis*, those ascetics living lives of perpetual silence. He took no books, making it "a complete fast of the mind."[24] He did not even have a breviary, but simply recited the Psalms and repeated the sacred mantra OM.

> Not allowing myself to locate God anywhere outside me, but recognizing that within as well as without there is only He alone. For, if there were God plus an "other," he would no longer be God, the Absolute! Nothing is left but he who says: I AM! Then what does it matter where I "myself" am? It is his business! But how to say "Him"? "Who" is there to speak of "Him." Nothing is left but He who says "I" "*aham*," from eternity to eternity. OM is precisely the word of the one who in the presence of the mystery can do no more.[25]

He was vowed to silence; he had no books. How did he actually spend the time? He admitted that climbing in the opposite direction to the current of the river toward the source, the "silence in which everything began," was in a sense symbolic of the feeling he had of "going against everything in me that wanted to run away towards externals, against desire and thought itself, continually leaving a little further behind me the world and its allurements, my anxieties and preoccupations. My longing to know, to theorize, to understand things fully."[26]

He stayed in a wooden hut facing the high peaks of the Himalayas, surrounded by pine trees. Every morning he followed the custom of *sādhus* and had a bath in the Ganges, immersing himself three times. It was so cold that he said it was like "being stung by a scorpion," but it was "a symbol of contact with the 'Source,' for who can endure a direct contact with the archetypes in the depth of his being? One who dares to *think* or to *speak* about God will surely be petrified when at last he finds himself confronted with the reality of God."[27] Then, the sun warming his body, with just a saffron cloth around his waist, a patched blanket over his shoulders, and a towel around his head, he went with the other *sādhus* to receive alms for food, silently holding out a piece of cloth for rice and chapatti and a pot for lentils or split peas. Then he would return to his hut, where he spent the day wrapped in blankets, or, if it was warm enough, sitting outside. Opposite him were the high snow-covered peaks; below the hut the falls of Gaurikund, where the waters thundered through channels in the solid rock, the spray rising a hundred feet in the air.

> The chaotic roar of the waterfalls blended into a vast pandemonium, in which all the sounds were included without any being lost —the sound of rushing water, of water dashing against the rocks, of boulders being hurled along, the sound of waves in conflict, as some hurled forward while others were driven backwards by some obstacle, as if they were engaged in a cosmic battle.[28]

In his silence he was surrounded by sound, drowning in it. It was sound that preoccupied him, sound that filled his mind and his life.

> The Ganges fell in cataracts which became more and more violent as the melting sounds swelled it, a noise literally stunning in my intellectual void. I don't think I could have stood it much longer. It was cathedral choirs, psalms, mantras from here with diverse but relentless rhythms, often sometimes like Honegger's *Joan of Arc at the Stake*.[29]

It was as if voices were pouring out of the mountainside, rising from the waters of the Ganges crying "Shiva, Shiva. . . ." He was relieved to come back to the repetition of OM, "refreshingly contemplative and penetrating my consciousness more deeply than any other sound, which calmed, expressed and released the silence of my spirit."[30]

THE VEDIC MANTRA OM, symbol of the ineffable mystery of God, is chanted and meditated on throughout India. It was Abhishiktananda's lifeline, the still center at the heart of his prayer, the ineffable sound from which everything comes and to which everything returns. It is the chief mantra of every *sādhu*:

> Wherever he goes the OM wells up from his heart, just as it does from the river, the mountains, the forests and from every living creature that he meets on the way. It is the OM that makes itself heard in the roar of the Ganges, the rustling of leaves, the chirping of birds, that is ceaselessly thrown back from the rocky cliffs, and that arouses in the sadhu's heart, as it were, an infinite echo, since there it unites with the primal OM in that silence from which all words have come.[31]

So the pilgrim whispers OM with every step he takes. "He quietly chants it when his weariness is not too great, and even then he struggles to repeat it in order to forget how tired he is. And so, when he meets other pilgrims, he only has to raise his voice a little to reply to their greeting and to bless them in the name of God."[32]

Abhishiktananda loved the sacred syllable OM and wrote about it with a rare passion and insight. One of his best passages on this subject is in the little book on prayer that he began to write around the time when he made this silent retreat in Gangotri. His words are especially valuable in the twenty-first century, when the use of the sacred syllable is so widespread in the West yet the depth of its meaning is not always understood.

He begins by explaining that OM is not a name for God; like the names of Rama or Shiva, it has no special meaning. It does not stand for an event, rather "it stands for the ineffable and unsearchable nature of the abyss of the divine Being. . . . It is a kind of barely articulated exclamation, which is uttered when anyone finds himself personally confronted with the infinite mystery of God."[33] It is traditionally considered to have three elements, *A*, the primordial sound at the origins of language, the vowel sound in words like Mama and Dada, merging with *U* to make the diphthong *O*, ending with the resonant *M*. This symbolizes all the triads in the universe, for instance past, present, and future, finally that which is beyond all things. It is said, he continues, that there is a fourth part, and that is the silence in which OM finally disappears.

OM is the first sound heard by the newborn babe, the last sound uttered by the dying soul:

> OM is the primordial word uttered by God in creating. OM is *Vag*, the eternal Word. OM is the beginning of God's self-manifestation. OM is at the origin of the universe. OM is also at that centre of the soul from which arises the awareness of being oneself. All the possible sounds that our lips could utter, all the words which will ever be derived from them in the languages of mankind, are already contained in this primordial OM, the *shabda-brahman*, brahman in the form of sound, as it is also called.[34]

Christians drawn to reciting OM need have no problems, though Abhishiktananda did not recommend the use of OM by people of other faiths indiscriminately, because it will be a meaningless sound if it is uttered by people who have not begun to have the inner experience to which it corresponds. But the one who "has been initiated into the Indian tradition, and above all if he has accepted the Gospel message in its fulness . . . has as much right as his Hindu brother to murmur the OM, the ultimate symbol of the abysmal depth of God and the self."[35] Christianity is expressed in its three elements; this gives it a trinitarian resonance and "introduces us to the mystery of the Spirit, the Person in God who is neither uttered nor begotten, yet the One who alone reveals the mystery of the Son."[36] It is identical with the Word of the Fourth Gospel, as is the Tao, the Way. Indeed, Dr. Wu, a Catholic convert, translated these lines as "In the beginning was the Tao, and the Tao was with God and the Tao was God."[37] "It is in that same Word, made human flesh, mind and word in Jesus Christ, that all our prayer and worship ascends to the Almighty."[38]

During his silent retreat at Mauna Mandir, Abhishiktananda wrote one of his strange prose poems, where it is almost as if prose could not contain the intensity of his emotion. A section of one of these poems is a hymn to OM:

> The OM which our *rishis* heard resounding in their souls,
> when they descended to the greatest depths in themselves,
> deeper than their thoughts
> and deeper than all their desires,
> in the existential solitude of Being.

The OM which sounds in the rustling of leaves
shaken by the wind,
the OM which howls in the storm
and moans in the gentle breeze,
the OM which roars in the rushing torrent
and the gentle murmur of the river
flowing peacefully down to the sea,
the OM of the spheres making their way across the sky,
and the OM that throbs at the core of the atom.

That which sings in the song of birds,
that which is heard in the call of beasts in the jungle,
the OM of people laughing and the OM of their sighs,
the OM that vibrates in their thoughts
and in all their desires,
the OM of their words of warfare,
of love, or of trade,
the OM that Time and History utter on their way,
the OM uttered by Space when entering into Time.
This OM suddenly burst out, whole and entire,
in a corner of space and at a point of time,
in its indivisible fullness,
when in Mary's womb was born as Son of man,
the Word, the Son of God.[39]

During this time in silence in Gangotri he made only one diary entry:

The solitude of the Alone. An advaitic retreat. I do not allow myself any prayer, except for the Psalms which take the place of my Breviary; recited conscientiously—generally Lauds at 8.00, Matins at 11.00, Vespers and Compline at 3.00—not accepting any prop; no support, no appeal, no request. Solitude *with* God is not solitude. Accept being alone, infinitely alone. Alone in my eternity. This is the royal road that leads to the real face-to-face with the Father. Jesus was alone in his death; *Eloi, Eloi, lamma sabachtani.*[40]

16

Overcoming Opposites

*The deepening of the spiritual sense is the one
and only cure for the present crisis in the Church.*[1]

MANY PEOPLE WHO SEEK the experience of *advaita*, who long to transcend the opposites, are drawn on this path partly because they themselves, in their own lives and personalities, are caught between opposites. Ever since his arrival in India in 1948, Abhishiktananda had been torn between Hinduism and Christianity, between India and Europe. Now, as he approached his sixtieth year, he found himself more than ever torn between solitude and company. He was, as always, ambivalent about solitude, continually seeking it, in the course of his life spending months at a time in total solitude, but also loving people and talking. For instance, when visiting Jyotiniketan, Murray once asked whether his friend would prefer to be left alone for a while. The answer was immediate: "Why do you think I've come here? I've come to talk!"

This ambivalence, however, took an added twist as the pressures on Abhishiktananda's solitude began to come from without as well as from within, for he was increasingly in demand and had friends all over India. To his own surprise he was becoming a well-known personality, and though there were those who, as James Stuart comments, were "merely curious to meet this unusual person,"[2] whatever their initial motivation might have been, anyone who met him always wanted to meet him again. So these years saw him traveling as much as ever, seeing old friends and making new ones, with mixed feelings about his way of life. Though he declined invitations to travel, for instance, to talk to a Christian yoga group in Canada or to attend a candlelit dinner at the French embassy, he was uncomfortable with the contrasting lifestyles he experienced, "alarmed at the number of different environments through which I have

200

to pass"[3] as he mixed with Protestants, Catholic bishops, Americans, Europeans, Hindus—including his Hindu extremist friends who were anti-Christian, anti-Muslim and anti-West.

So his first response was nearly always to refuse, to try to keep his solitude. He knew very well that "the monk is not called to go running round the world"[4] and politely tried to avoid European visitors, finding it "a nuisance to be so well known."[5] By 1967, unsure whether this reaction was wisdom or egoism, he felt he had become "such an old buffer, an unsocial 'bear,' that I no longer dare to accept any involvement."[6] He could not, however, escape. He was all too familiar with the kinds of friends who urged him to keep his solitude—except, of course, when it was they who wished to see him.

If being torn between solitude and company was an uncomfortable situation, how much harder was it for him to hold the tension between Hinduism and Christianity. We are by now familiar with the anguish this caused him, but as his contacts with people widened he saw that his pain could have value for others. He began to regard himself as a bridge,* and

It is precisely the fact of being a bridge that makes this uncomfortable situation worth while. The world, at every level, needs such bridges. If, to be a Hindu with Hindus, I had become a complete sannyasi, I would have been unable to communicate either the Hindu message to Christians or the Christian message to Hindus.[7]

This, particularly communicating the Hindu message to Christians, was what he was in India to do. He wrote to Raimon Panikkar that he saw both their roles as preparing Christians for dialogue, sensitizing Christian thought to the treasure that awaits it in India: "We have to be among Hindus, both physically and spiritually, so as to *gather* the honey for the Church and to pass it on, while awaiting the hour when Christians as a whole will be capable of gathering it for themselves."[8]

Abhishiktananda was frequently critical of the church, saddened that it had given India "so much evidence of worldliness that its spiritual and contemplative character has often almost disappeared from sight,"[9] wondering what could be done to wake up those in charge, indeed finding it extraordinary that people remain in the church at all. It is easy to assume that he himself had left the church behind, that he was seeking, and had almost found, a God beyond the church, beyond the opposites, beyond

*The Sanskrit word for bridge, *SETU*, is the title used by the Abhishiktananda Society for their newsletter.

the need for human structures and institutions. It comes as a surprise to discover how important he still felt the institutional church to be and how much he cared about its future. It was as if he was caught between another pair of opposites—one familiar to many Christians today—exasperation with the shortcomings of the church and the recognition that it has a role to play, that structures can have value.

Abhishiktananda's concern for the church was particularly evident in this period of his life, as the years between 1963 and 1965 saw the Constitutions, Decrees, and Declarations of the Second Vatican Council being issued. At one level he was excited by the news that was coming from Rome, and he admitted that "there is a breath of the Spirit such as the Church has rarely known in the past."[10] Murray Rogers, who knew him as well as anyone and spent a lot of time with him during this period, remembers him as optimistic, full of hope, and animated, finding the council "splendid." And yet he wondered . . .

> And yet, who has anything to say about what is essential? . . . Does anyone reflect that the Church is she who continually abides in the *Presence*, included in the Son's presence to the Father in the unity of the Spirit? Or that the Church needs that summons to what is essential, which "contemplatives" by their vocation precisely are.[11]

His letters contain numerous references to a sense of turmoil in the church that sometimes made him "feel giddy."[12] He felt that they were approaching "a nuclear explosion in the realm of religion"[13] and that 1968, the year in which Pope Paul VI issued his controversial encyclical *Humanae Vitae*, ruling against artificial contraception, was "a year of terrible mistakes."[14] Indeed, Abhishiktananda saw the encyclical as a crisis of authority that "only an explosion will resolve."[15]

He was quite clear what was needed—the only cure for the increasingly agonizing crisis of the church was the deepening of the spiritual sense. The need, he insisted, was for more monasteries like Taizé and Solesmes; for centers of nonduality; for "advaitin ashrams to 'point' uncompromisingly toward the Beyond"[16]; for "'Christian Vedantin Centers,' which, helped by the 'advaitin rope,' may draw up water from the well of Christian experience; for the Church of the West must deepen itself."[17]

More surprising was his wish to see some structures emerging.

> It is a matter of deciding the main themes to be worked out by the Church—to prevent it becoming "the grave of God"! Above all I

should like to see some structures coming out of it which would be able to guide the aggiornamento*—a "brains trust," a "study group," an official commission, call it what you will, but something with authority.[18]

F ROM ABHISHIKTANANDA'S POINT OF VIEW, one of the most significant outcomes of the Second Vatican Council was the National Seminar on the Church in India. This seminar, which took place in Bangalore in February 1969, saw the continuation of the renewal process started at the council and applied in depth to the Church in India.

Abhishiktananda was involved in the preparations for the seminar, which were countrywide. He took part in a meeting in Andheri, near Bombay,[†] which set the tone. He wrote articles and a booklet,[19] as well as continuing his attempts at an Indian liturgy. Sadly, he wrote to Raimon Panikkar that "the time for enthusiasm was past"[20] and that though he was not yet sixty, his strength and vitality were diminished. Nevertheless, the Andheri meeting found him full of enthusiasm, his paper coming as a revelation to many of the twenty-five people present. Sara Grant found it exhilarating to watch Abhishiktananda sitting cross-legged on a chair, "his balance rendered precarious by the vehemence of his utterance and the vigour of his gestures."[21] However, another meeting, at Agra, proved disappointing. Though the participants were well disposed, they were largely unaware of the serious nature of the crisis and were not thinking in the revolutionary terms that Abhishiktananda felt were, at least in some areas, essential. The few progressive leaders who might have been able to promote some action were held firmly in line by two bishops who were present.

Though Abhishiktananda recognized that his articles had helped prepare the ground for the seminar, his lack of confidence is apparent in his surprise at being invited, since he "represented an ideal recognised so far only by a tiny minority of the Christian community in India, either as concerns the ideal of contemplative and monastic life or the integration of Hindu values on spirituality, liturgy and theology."[22] In the event he was surprised and thrilled, finding the seminar successful beyond his highest hopes and regarding it as an important stage in the awakening of the church in India. He was delighted that the bishops mixed with the people with "perfect courtesy, simplicity and discretion"[23] and with the resolutions, which emphasized spiritual renewal and interior silence; his

*Act or process of bringing up-to-date.
†Now Mumbai.

call for a renewed theology was taken seriously and his amendments, calling for ashrams of prayer and silence and for liturgical renewal, were passed with large majorities. He was particularly pleased that Archbishop Pignedoli, secretary of the Congregation for the Evangelization of Peoples, endorsed practically everything that he had stood for over the last twenty years: the seminar confirmed his optimistic expectations for the future of the monastic and contemplative ideal in India.

In fact, Abhishiktananda's personal contribution was considerable and he knew it. He led his own workshop and was consulted both during the seminar and in projects resulting from it. He made numerous contributions to the discussions, one of which was recalled by Sara Grant, one of the other delegates:

> No one who was present will ever forget the vision of Swamiji at the mike, addressing himself to it from a respectful distance of several feet and totally absorbed in the effort to enunciate a to him all-important amendment insisting on the need for a deeply interior spirit in the celebration of the Indian liturgy, if it was to be true to the age-old contemplative tradition of the country. Noting the gap between speaker and microphone, the moderator asked gently: "Could you come a little nearer, Father?"—whereupon, after a moment's puzzled reflection, Swamiji meekly and firmly seized the mike and advanced several paces up the centre of the hall, to the immense delight of the Assembly![24]

He was not only an endearing figure; he was now a serious participant in the struggle for theological renewal and, for him, the answer lay in the meeting of Christianity with the experience of the East. His personal experience of being torn apart was becoming universalized in his contribution to this meeting, a subject that, with the honorable exception of his friend Raimon Panikkar, he felt was scarcely being addressed by Western theologians. But in addition to his wish to bridge the two religions, many of his public statements showed his concern to spread Christ's message in India:

> There is no place for double-dealing among the followers of the Gospel. Their duty is to carry the message of Christ, a duty which springs from the very fact that they are by baptism sharers of Christ's death and resurrection and has to be fulfilled by them both by their word and by their life. Their sole task is to tell the Gospel, to express the "good tidings" by word and lip.[25]

Was he once again donning the clothes of the missionary? Emphatically not. As Murray Rogers says in the preface to *The Church in India*, Abhishiktananda's concern was to rebuke Christians who ignore the spiritual riches of Hinduism and to emphasize that spiritual renewal in India must come from the depth of the Hindu experience. After all, Hindus are content with their own tradition: it is Christians, not Hindus, who seek dialogue, and that can develop only once a common ground has been established.

Abhishiktananda argued that ecumenism is not simply "a matter of discussion meetings, even less of cheap social or religious gatherings";[26] it should arise spontaneously. The Christian seeking ecumenism should not have a specific aim, either of giving or of gaining, but should simply join with members of other religious faiths to express fellowship and love. "The Christian goes to his brother without any trace of paternalism, without any inferiority or superiority complex which blurs the best of his intentions. He meets him at the very level, material, intellectual, spiritual, in which he lives."[27] This was a far cry from the attitude of Christian missionaries at the time, and when this little booklet was published in 1969 it was considered both unusual and disturbing. Here was someone who associated OM and Christ and who was convinced that the solution for the world and for the church lay "in becoming aware of that fundamental experience of the human being whose best formulation until now seems to have been given by the Upanishads."[28] He was able to make these contributions only because he had lived it himself, suffered the anguish of "double-belonging." He knew all too well that he ran the risk of not belonging finally to either side; his calling, however harrowing it might be, was to belong wholly to both sides. And he was beginning to see the value of his experience for other people, as he wrote to his sister Marie-Thérèse:

> What contrasts! I do my best to be at ease everywhere, but there is an inevitable tension. But it is precisely this being torn apart between India and Europe, between Vedanta and Christianity which enables me to live the fundamental experience and to express its mystery to some extent.[29]

ABHISHIKTANANDA'S GROWING SPIRITUAL STATURE and the influence he was coming to have on people were born of his lifestyle and closely integrated with it. His spirituality, radiating from him more and more, was the fruit of the life he led; it came from his insistence on learning from experience rather than from theory; it had its roots in the long hours he spent in solitude and silence. By 1968, the year before the Bangalore Seminar, he found that he needed more of that silence and solitude, and at last the decision was made: he would leave Shantivanam and spend as much time as he could in the hut that was now built for him in Gyansu, near Uttarkashi.

This was not an impulse. The Himalayas, the place where seven years ago he had said he was "strongly tempted to pitch my tent," had finally won his heart. His Kergonan dreams had never been fulfilled in the ashram, and now he was finding Shantivanam an intolerable burden and a great anxiety. In August he and Father Mahieu met to discuss the ashram's future, both finding the other changed and able to appreciate each other and their differing monastic vocations without the strains that had sometimes divided them before. (Abhishiktananda rejoiced that "Fr Mahieu has changed enormously, entirely for the good"[30] apparently unaware that he too had changed over the years.) It was agreed that Father Mahieu would take charge of Shantivanam and that it should either be a new foundation, related to his ashram in Kurisumala, or an independent house of prayer for those seeking a truly contemplative life.

In the event it was decided that Father Bede Griffiths would leave Kurisumala and take over Shantivanam. On August 28, 1968, he arrived with two young brothers from Kurisumala, surprised to find the ashram empty. Abhishiktananda had already left, claiming later that he thought it would be better if he were out of the way, but the truth is, almost certainly, that he found the parting hard and needed to make a private departure, unwilling to witness the new party's excited arrival, longing for the new challenge they saw in Shantivanam. He admitted that leaving the ashram moved him more than he had expected and that he found it "a severe strain, both physically and morally."[31] After eighteen years, he had to accept that his dream of founding an ashram had failed. He could not have known at the time that though it had failed in that it had attracted no vocations, Shantivanam was eventually to be regarded as the fertile soil in which the meeting of Christianity and Hinduism first began to grow.

So ABHISHIKTANANDA MOVED to a place where he hoped that the world could be forgotten and nothing would distract him from the one essential, his longing for "Being there, simply."[32] Gyansu is near Uttarkashi, north of Rishikesh on the pilgrimage route to Gangotri. (Gyan, from *jnana*, means "knowledge, wisdom"; *su* is a suffix meaning "village.") His *kutiya*, his hut, was one of ten little houses built for *sādhus*, close to the bank of the river; it was essentially a one-room house, the Ganga thundering past only three or four yards away. It was built of stones covered with mud plaster, with large untrimmed slates, carried down from the mountainside, for a roof. The main room was filled with the books and papers that accompanied him everywhere, there were a few necessities including a lantern, essential for the dark lonely nights, a screw driver and a hammer—remember Abhishiktananda was a practical man, quite capable of putting things to rights himself—and basic supplies such as flour, rice, and dal. There was a tiny lean-to kitchen and a cell made of bamboo matting, which, with the addition of a *charpoy*, a string bed, doubled as spare room and study. The walls of this little room were so full of holes that to keep out the draft Abhishiktananda had filled them with rolled up pages of *Informations Catholiques*, stuffing them in with a screwdriver. Up a rickety ladder was a small attic room that served as both box room and chapel. It was "wonderfully Heath Robinson."*[33]

In October 1968, soon after the ambivalent sadness of his departure from Shantivanam, he settled in his *kutiya*, firmly believing that this would be his home, though as so often he was caught between those people who told him never to move from Gyansu and those who insisted he make an exception to go and see them—and of course only them. His friends' contradictory advice echoed his own ambivalence, but for the rest of his life he did manage to stay at Gyansu for at least half the year. There he found nothing distracted him from the essential; there, and he once said there *only*, he felt fully alive. Soon he made it not only a retreat but a home, as he planted fruit trees and vegetables—beans, marrows, cucumbers, pumpkins. For lunch he would mostly have rice, split peas, potatoes, and marrow, and at first he also allowed himself half a liter of milk a day, something which he later gave up, so that he could save the money and send it to some poor people he had supported for many years.

Once again the opposites were in play as he indulged his compulsive need to write, yet was not entirely happy with the arrangement, asking one correspondent, "Where is the beautiful freedom of the sannyasi who never has any obligations whatever, the glorious freedom of the children of God?"[34] and exclaiming to another "What a false sadhu, un-free, all this business makes me!"[35] Perhaps a remote and beautiful place is not enough to ensure peace.

His book on prayer had just been published in English, and soon he himself translated it into French, while others did Italian and German

*Heath Robinson: a phrase commonly applied to ingenius contraptions, after Heath Robinson (1872–1944).

translations. Abhishiktananda's wish was that it should "awaken people to real prayer, that of silence in the heart, repeating the name of Jesus, or the Abba, or else the OM of the silence of the Spirit. Life is so good, despite everything, when you are awakened in the depth of the heart."[36] The popularity of *Prayer*—of all his books, it has been the one with steadiest and highest sales—probably contributed to his receiving numerous requests for articles. So he wrote on Hindu symbolism, on Gandhi, a meditation on the Trinity, on women hermits and a syndicated article called "Theological Commission Needed for Indianization of the Church" as well as several on religious archetypes and the contemplative message of India. Many of these were substantial essays that were eventually to be published in *Intériorité et révélation* and *Initiations à la spiritualité des Upanishads*. And of course there was more writing, as he kept up his wide correspondence and expressed his innermost thought in that classic of spiritual diaries, *Ascent to the Depth of the Heart*. He was now convinced that the more he wrote from his own experience the better the writing. "All is biographical!—and nothing is! Everything comes from the experience of this tension, but everything has been rethought by the mind, in the halo of a double culture. The 'I' naturally is literary. Who has the right to say 'I', when he speaks of advaita?"[37]

HOWEVER, IF NOT ENTIRELY FREE from work and obligations, at least he now had the solitude and the silence for which he yearned, and he reveled in his periods of "blessed solitude," at one point claiming, "In the last six months I have done nothing but say No to my friends."[38] He realized that his withdrawal to the Himalayas added a mythical touch to his personality, but he resisted all invitations to the West, certain that to accept such invitations would be:

> a betrayal of all that I stand for, solitude, silence and monastic poverty. I have no more sought poverty than Amos sought the role of a prophet, but once placed in that position, nothing else remains for me but to be a hermit for good, and not a mere salesman of solitude and monastic life.[39]

Murray Rogers was one of the few people privileged to be invited to Gyansu (and lucky enough to get permission from the authorities). One of the high points of every day was the Mass. They would carefully select an altar stone from the river and clamber up the ladder to the attic chapel, for all its roughness and lack of Anglo-Saxon order more perfect, perhaps, than any cathedral I have been privileged to experience. We sat side by side on our mats on the floor—no man could have stood in that cathedral. The altar was a rough box raised some 6 inches from the floor under which Swamiji kept many treasures (relics, I called them), little brass dishes for the arati, camphor, and water, a sandal wood rosary from Hardwar, papers on which he had typed many Sanskrit verses from the Vedas and Upanishads without which no Great Thanksgiving would be complete. . . . Everything served, the sound of the river which sometimes almost drowned the words, the little vessels and papers and saffron cloths, the stone chalice and paten discovered with joy in the bazaar in Hardwar. . . . There followed an unmeasured time of silence, a silence from the depth of which one could almost audibly, tangibly, sense the emerging OM.[40]

The Mass would sometimes go on for hours, but to Murray it always seemed too short. Abhishiktananda's deep Christian roots were at last in harmony with his love and knowledge of Hinduism; anyone who sampled the honey this marriage yielded must count themselves fortunate.

Liturgy was, not surprisingly, another thing that had found Abhishiktananda with divided views. Nourished as he was by nearly forty years of the Tridentine Mass, how could he not have its rhythms deep in his bones? He grew up on it as on his mother's milk; how could he ever cease to be nourished by it? Yet by the 1970s he was free of any dependence on the rites of his mother church, for the simple yet quite extraordinary reason that he was living in the presence of God every minute of the day. He did not need special reminders; he saw no need to single out special times for special forms of worship. "To keep Advent as I formerly did," he wrote, "I should have to escape from the blazing Presence and imagine that it was still 'to come.'"[41] "Christmas is every day, when you have discovered the non-time of your own origin! Each moment is the dawn of eternity in the explosion of the joy of Being."[42] "Every day is Good Friday, every day is Easter, for the dawn of eternity is present in every moment."[43] Many have had glimpses of this experience, but for Abhishiktananda it had at last become not only a reality, but a continuing reality.

After long periods when he had compulsively said Mass every day, others when he refrained altogether, now he was free. Liturgical details had become secondary, and he could celebrate in the strictest Tridentine tradition, should anybody desire it, or in a "spontaneous style, when people ask for that."[44] So the rites were a glorious expression of love and being, they

> recover their value, and the man who is "realized" cheerfully takes part in the rite without inhibitions. One day he will celebrate the rite, the next day he will not even think of it. For him the rite is not a means of obtaining something, for there is nothing to be obtained. All is given from the beginning.[45]

Abhishiktananda no longer felt *bound* to the Eucharist. "But so long as the Lord grants us the Eucharist, we should be very mistaken if we did not avail ourselves of it to the full. We are human and have need of signs."[46]

From the early sixties he had been making "discreet and timid attempts at an Indian liturgy"[47] at first alone, then in a group, often with Murray Rogers at Jyotiniketan, with the Little Sisters of Jesus and with a group of friends at Banares. The Mass was sometimes "polyglot," using Latin, Greek, Hindi, English, and of course Sanskrit; on every occasion flowers, incense, and lights were offered as part of the ritual, not simply present on the altar as in Europe. There were experiments in a spontaneous liturgy. Soon he was in touch with others who were thinking seriously about an Indian rite, including Father Amalorpavadass, who was at the time in charge of the National Commission for Liturgy. As the green light was given to the development of indigenous forms of worship by the Vatican Council and more people began to think about liturgical renewal, so controversies began. These ranged from the parish priest in Banares, who, hearing that Abhishiktananda had celebrated an Indian liturgy, dismissed him as a "hippie," to a more serious confrontation when Abhishiktananda heard that some Christians were infuriated by the simple greeting with joined hands practiced all over India and annoyed when people bowed and prostrated instead of genuflecting. Uncharacteristically, Abhishiktananda picked up his pen and joined the battle, writing to the editor of a Catholic weekly that if joining hands is pagan, then we are all saying Mass in a pagan fashion, and if prostration is pagan, then so had all their ordinations been pagan.*

However, beyond debate about gesture and language and the use of flowers lay the deep central issues. Abhishiktananda was adamant that liturgical renewal must spring from spiritual renewal and that a "'mod-

---

*Total prostration is part of every ordination ceremony.

ern' liturgy should spring out of a 'modern experience' of the deep things of God and the Paschal mystery."[48] He was no instant improviser, seeking to make theatrical gestures. He was longing to share the riches he had found in Hinduism, to share the honey he had gathered. How this man had changed. The strict Roman Catholic liturgist of twenty years ago now saw the prohibition of intercommunion as artificial and openly celebrated Mass with an ecumenical study group

> all seated in a circle on the floor of the chapel, the bread and wine on a brass tray, with incense and lights offered in Indian style. Upanishadic and Sanskrit hymns, Gélineau Psalms for Introit and Gradual etc. And a second chapatti on another tray for distribution as (at least) "blessed bread" at the end of the Mass.[49]

He rejoiced in this newfound freedom in celebrating Mass, the priest at the service of his people:

> And while the Gregorian liturgy has an excellence beyond compare for those who have the necessary education to understand it, there are other forms that are humbler and more within the reach of the new generation, as I discover even in my infrequent meetings with young people from Europe. I at last begin to accept the fact that other people think differently from me![50]

And on his own, where any small inhibitions he might have had in the company of others could be blown away as the chaff he was seeing them to be, he would say his own long slow Mass:

> Every morning I begin my solitary Mass with Vedic mantras, appeals to the earth, the elements, fire water, infinite space, an appeal to the Purusha, adoration of the Purusha* under the form of Christ, appeal to and adoration of the Trinity, then Upanishadic reading. We must integrate all that with the richness of the Christian experience; but will advaita allow itself to be integrated or to integrate anything whatever? The insoluble problem.[51]

What was crucial was the spirit in which the Mass was said. For Abhishiktananda it must be said thoughtfully, in a deep interior spirit, and

---

Purusha is the primordial, archetypel man.

very slowly. Liturgical renewal must spring from spiritual renewal, then the Eucharist can resound with its full cosmic glory. Toward the end of his life the content was so concentrated that his Mass needed only three words—"*Om tat sat*"—the great Upanishadic mantra, "Indeed, That [*brahman*] is the Real."

As he spent hours alone in his *kutiya* at Gyansu, had he at least reached a reconciliation of the tensions that had waged war within him for so long? He was certainly learning about silence. He had long loved it and sought it, long realized that the choice of silence had little to do with personal virtue, for there is "as much latent egoism in the choice of solitude as in choosing to meet people."[52] So too he knew that, though silence was the last mantra, "at the other side of the spaces of the heart"[53] it could be "as dangerous as speech, if one is attached to it; for silence is equally a sign, and the Unique is beyond silence—no less present in speech than in silence, neither within, nor without, nowhere."[54] His reflections were becoming ever deeper as he found that the language of silence was "the only real solution,"[55] the only way to teach, that "it is a secret that only the Spirit tells to the spirit."[56] We need to share the interior silence of Jesus.

The conflict he felt between silence and conversation was at a relatively outer level, easy to understand and even to joke about; the old tension between Christianity and *advaita* was at an incomparably deeper level. But here too there is now a perceptible maturity, an increased confidence in his thoughts on the subject. He is beginning to sound less like someone struggling in the grip of an insoluble dilemma and more like one who has arrived and can tell others of the journey and the arrival. How else can he write that anyone who still has some sense of himself as an individual should not even mention *advaita*, that *advaita* is "a royal secret, only to be revealed at the last moment by the guru who knows . . . to the disciple who is ready, ready to know"?[57] Now he knows that the words of the advaitin are to awaken, not to instruct. And now, for him, the Upanishadic road is sufficient:

> Its end must be the awareness of the Presence, and when that is experienced, one is free, one needs nothing else—not even God, as Gnanananda would say, because God no more has to be attained or possessed. He is my "I AM"—but what theology is still possible on the basis of this fundamental and unique non-dual experience . . . ?

It is curiously wonderful that he wrote those words during a period when he was involved with the church as never before, sharing the depth of his Christianity revealed in his passionate concern that it should reflect the Christ he had come to know; his conviction that only through the grace of *advaita* could the church survive its crisis. The great awakening of his life was still to come, but surely, by his sixtieth birthday, he had reached a level of understanding, through experience, attained by few.

17

A True Disciple

Whoever has not disappeared in the light
cannot testify to the light.[1]

MANY PEOPLE WHO HAVE HAD A GREAT EXPERIENCE or who have mastered a difficult art form long to share it, so it is no surprise that, after a few years living as a *sādhu* in India, Abhishiktananda began to want to have disciples, to pass on what he had learned, to have spiritual children. Some wonder whether he was almost desperate to have disciples, perhaps forgetting the great *sādhus* who waited literally years, alone, before acquiring the status of a guru. His longing was also complicated by some initial ambivalence, as he worried that to have disciples would put an end to his travels. Most crucial of all was the constant question—had he reached enlightenment, was he ready to take this responsibility?

The work of the guru is the gentlest, subtlest teaching, aware at a level almost beyond awareness, loving beyond normal concepts of love. He* teaches his disciple to silence the mind by withdrawing it from all external objects of sense and imagination and fixing it on a single point, watching and waiting until the disciple is ready for the next stage. Most of all he is alert to any signs of too strong a sense of ego.

So long as a man has a strong sense of his own ego (*ahamkara*), God is necessarily "another" for him. To him therefore advaita can only be an intellectual concept and not an actual experience, and can have the disastrous effect of enhancing his self-conceit and lead to a monstrous development of the ego.[2]

---

*There are, of course, also female gurus, but I use the masculine to reflect Abhishiktananda's experience.

214

So when the disciple knows the bliss of inner silence, then, not by words but by the subtlest communication, the guru can teach him what he longs to learn: "To a pupil who comes with mind and senses in peace the Teacher gives the vision of Brahman, of the Spirit of truth and eternity."[3] To be able to do this means, of course, that the guru must speak from experience; he must be someone who has found the living God in the depth of his soul and who "from that moment onwards and throughout the rest of his life is marked by the scorch of this encounter."[4] He must not, however, refer to his own experience, for that would show that he had in fact missed the experience. He wrote to some German friends, "Whoever has not disappeared in the light cannot testify to the light. You must surely know the Persian proverb: 'No one knows the secret of the Flame.'"[5] The guru's work must be one of the subtlest and greatest challenges faced by any human being, for it is nothing less than attempting to communicate the mystery of God. And the medium for the teaching must be silence:

The Word proceeds from Silence, as Ignatius, the great bishop of Antioch, taught. And it is only in the silence of the Spirit that the Voice can be heard. And only the Spirit can make the Word understood, as Jesus affirmed. When the Voice became silent on the earth, the Spirit appeared in tongues of fire on the heads and in the hearts of the disciples. The knowledge of the mystery of God is transmitted only by means beyond words.[6]

ABHISHIKTANANDA HAD BEEN A DISCIPLE, living wholeheartedly through experience, only allowing himself theological expression when occasion demanded it and experience inspired it. He had, in subtly different ways, learned from Harilal and Dr. Mehta, but most crucial was the influence of Ramana Maharshi and Sri Gnanananda, perhaps the only one who would qualify as a true guru. Abhishiktananda had also come to the decision that, however much he learned from these people, in the end it was Jesus who was his *sad-guru*, his "root guru," his true master: "It is in him that God appeared to me, it is in his *mirror* that I recognized myself, by adoring him, by loving him, by consecrating myself to Him."[7] Had the moment arrived when he was ready to take the other side of this most subtle of relationships—to be a guru himself?

For some time people had been approaching Abhishiktananda, wanting to be his disciples, but none were suitable, or even completely serious. There was, for instance, a young Hindu who insisted that he saw his putative guru with a green halo. Abhishiktananda's first serious attempt at being a guru was in 1961 and it was not a success. A young Indian *sannyāsi* came to him, asking fervently for baptism. He stayed at Shantivanam for two and a half months, proving to be a difficult character, stretching Abhishiktananda's patience to the limit. Finally, Abhishiktananda baptized him, only to find that he was a liar, but one who played the disciple game cleverly and with determination, going from priest to priest, from Catholics to Protestants, and to all the Protestant sects, pretending to be converted. He had already managed to deceive Father Mahieu and Father Bede Griffiths, who had both baptized him. Later the three-times-baptized fraudster used Abhishiktananda's name to get himself accepted in various houses in Bangalore. When he was finally exposed and handed over to the police Abhishiktananda took it philosophically, saying, "The Lord has his own ways of playing games with us!"[8]

Nevertheless, Abhishiktananda learned from this experience, finding that his spurious postulant knew his part as a disciple rather better than he himself knew that of a guru and confessing ruefully, "It is no small thing to be 'projected' without warning into this kind of fatherhood."[9] Perhaps it was a sign "that all my desires for expansion are unacceptable to the Lord, and that all he asks of me is simply to remain for ever in solitude."[10]

There were also serious young people who sought him as their guru, but somehow, though Abhishiktananda was filled with warmth and affection for them, the relationships did not acquire the subtle resonance that vibrates between guru and disciple when the relationship is really working. There was Anand, a postulant who was later to give a paper about Abhishiktananda at a conference in Hauterive* and who stayed with him for some weeks, sharing in his life and his prayer on the banks of the Ganges; but there is no indication that a relation as between guru and disciple resulted. Abhishiktananda found him a "choice spirit"[11] and recognized that Shantivanam needed people with personality, but he was not happy that they could work together—he himself was, he admitted rather enigmatically, "pretty stubborn."

Then there was Ramesh Srivastava, who came to Uttarkashi in 1965. He spent hours a day singing the name of Rama; he also read the Gospel and wanted to be a Christian. Here was just the sort of person Abhishiktananda longed for the church to welcome, someone with a sense of Christ beyond all forms, an understanding of *advaita* in no way opposed to Christianity. It must have seemed as if a new angle on his own anguish was there before him: "Ramesh would like to be a Christian, but the

---

*Hauterive Conference, December 21, 1999.

Church cannot accommodate him. My dream is that he should be the starting-point for Christ lovers, who out of their Hindu depth love and serve him. . . . What is it that the Spirit wants to show me through this?"[12]

The next year he met a young brahmin aged eighteen, Lalit Sharma, who had been dreaming of living a life of total renunciation for some years and who begged Abhishiktananda to take him to Uttarkashi. Abhishiktananda liked him and found his spontaneity and simplicity refreshing, but he was not sure if this was a real vocation. Was it "a momentary spark—or the start of a fire?"[13] He insisted that the young man complete two more years of study.

The two young Hindus, Ramesh and Lalit, were a joy to him. They loved him as a father, and he regarded them as his two big children and when they stayed with him he would wake them every morning with a kiss. They would go off to work, and in the evening they would have supper together. In fact, they were as much children as disciples, they "make me a guru in the deepest sense of the word, a human relationship which realizes the deepest meaning of fatherhood. It is what I felt with Gnanananda, and what Ramesh makes me realise, when he takes all from me without depriving me of anything."[14]

He loved them, they loved him and revered him; yet it seems that something was missing, for he admitted that though the relationships warmed his heart, he found the solitude all the more beautiful after they had left. Perhaps he was slightly ambivalent about the close relationship demanded of the guru? Perhaps he still needed to be independent? Most probably the spiritual chemistry between them was simply not right.

IF THERE WAS ANY AMBIVALENCE, it was to disappear when he met Marc Chaduc, a French seminarian from Bourg and an immensely impressive young man. Bettina Bäumer later met one of his theology professors, who told her Marc had always been an ecstatic. She herself knew him well and found him extraordinarily gifted spiritually, humanly, and intellectually— a unique combination:

There was a radiance about him . . . he was so totally one-pointed. He just didn't want anything else but God. He didn't care about outward circumstances, whether he had anything to eat or not, but it was not an artificial asceticism, it was just that he was so full of that divine search that he didn't care for anything.[15]

He was no prude; he was also able to laugh and tease, for instance, joking if they were sitting under the bodhi tree in Bodh Gaya* that they might become enlightened.

Abhishiktananda's first reference to Marc is laconic; he simply includes his name among those approaching him for teaching, along with an Argentinian Trappist and countless Italians, as one among various potential disciples with whom he corresponded: he simply wrote, "Last month it was a seminarist from Bourg."[16] However, Abhishiktananda must have spotted that this was no ordinary seminarian—who was barely twenty when he first wrote—for he responded encouragingly and they corresponded for two years before Marc finally attained his great wish of coming to India. Perhaps remembering his own missionary tendencies when he was young, Abhishiktananda warned the young man:

> Without a contemplative "sense," to come to India is absolutely useless. Come to receive; don't seek to give, any more than the rose or the lily. Your interiority will radiate of itself, whether the surroundings are Christian or Hindu. Be concerned to *be* and not to *do* . . . or even to understand intellectually. . . . Give a sabbatical year at least to your Mind![17]

Marc clearly took his advice, for the next year he set off to do voluntary work in Niger, with more advice from Abhishiktananda, who encouraged him to be open to the many voices of the Spirit, who could for instance be heard through animism and Islam, and who was speaking to all, even "to the arrogant members of the western Church, indeed to the West as a whole."[18] The real work was to help people to hear the voice of the Spirit. He also warned the young Frenchman that he would find the depth of the experience awaiting him in India "as shattering for theology as is the monsoon for ships crossing the Indian Ocean."[19]

Marc Chaduc was not deterred, and at last his long-held ambition was realized; he arrived in India on October 21, 1971, and Abhishiktananda's life underwent a revolutionary change, reaching a peak of fulfillment he had never before experienced. The young seminarian and the sixty-one-year-old French *sādhu* quickly found they were living the fullness of the guru–disciple relationship. Abhishiktananda spent less and less time in Gyansu, instead devoting himself to his disciples, above all to Marc. The disciple was ready for his guru and Abhishiktananda was ready for him. "Guru and disciple are a dyad, a pair, whose two components call for each

---

*The bodhi tree was the tree under which the Buddha attained enlightenment.

other and belong together. No more than the two poles [of a magnet] can they exist without being related to each other."[20] He had experienced one side of this extraordinary relationship between guru and disciple; he was about to experience the other.

His original intention was to give Marc two weeks of concentrated initiation and then to leave him to discover India for himself, but such was the power generated by the meeting of the two that his plans dissolved and he allowed events to take their course. Silence seemed impossible, and for the first few days there was ceaseless talk, of which Marc said, "By the second evening Fr Le Saux (Henri) had 'volatilized' all my questions. He plunges (me) into the Source, beyond *logos* [the level of reasoning]."[21] (In the light of this comment from Marc it should be said that Abhishiktananda was later critical of himself for allowing so much talk: "I have talked to you too much and have put ideas into your head—*ideas* of silence! If I had been silent, I would have led you beyond ideas.")[22]

At the time Abhishiktananda was also keeping an eye on his Carmelite disciple, Sr. Térèse de Jésus, who had just arrived from Lisieux to start her life as a hermit, but Marc came first and Abhishiktananda found time to introduce him to many of his friends, including Ramesh and a Japanese friend, Minoru Kasai, now a professor at the International Christian University in Tokyo. They also traveled to Hardwar and Rishikesh, where they had charismatic meetings and endless conversations on the banks of the Ganges. Before three weeks had passed, the two had an experience of such depth that it has to be mentioned, even though to write about it defies words. It took place at Phulchatti ashram on November 8, 1971.

Phulchatti ashram lies on the mountain road that runs beside the Ganges between Rishikesh and Badrinath, four miles upstream from Lakshman Jhula. The two were walking along the path beside the Ganges, on the way to the ashram when it happened. Marc left a diary,* in which he records this occasion, when, as he puts it, "grace erupted." It was Abhishiktananda who was first "seized by the mystery of the acosmic one who leaves all in response to the burning invitation from God." Abhishiktananda told Marc that the one who receives this light is paralyzed, torn asunder, unable to speak or think. Marc's diary continues:

He remains there, immobile outside of time and space, alone in the very solitude of the Alone. Absorbed in this way the Father relived —lived again—the sudden eruption of the infinite Column of fire

---

*This was given to Odette Baumer-Despeigne, who later became a disciple of Marc's. It is not yet published.

and of the light of Arunachala, that myth which was the source of that interior awakening which had flashed forth in him in 1953. For a brief moment, he could only stagger under the excess of the interior drunkenness, and I had to support him. At that moment there opened within myself an abyss which had been hidden to that point. Later we realized that this experience was the beginning of the mauna-diksha, the initiation by silence, which is the work of the Spirit alone. One does not have any awareness of being guru; if words spring forth, they come from the source.[23]

It is hard for Westerners to understand the relationship that now developed between Marc and Abhishiktananda. It was as if there was only one "I," *advaita* experienced by these two people at the same time. It was a relationship of total love yet of total non-attachment, the communion between guru and disciple taking place at the very center of the self, drawing on experience springing from the deepest level of being. Later he wrote to Marc that he remained incapable of understanding what had happened: "this non-dual diad of which I spoke in Gnanananda, we have lived out with such intensity. In discovering you as son, I have found myself."[24] It had become a relationship of which Abhishiktananda wrote a few weeks later: "I am now following you (on your way); or better, I am you here, and you are I there."[25] Now Abhishiktananda knew, without a shadow of doubt, that he had found "a true total disciple."[26] He was very aware of the responsibility he carried and was frightened by it, wondering if he was handling Marc well, nervous that perhaps he was not.

Abhishiktananda had long held that there was a point beyond which theology could not be expressed in words, and both he and Marc had reached that point. He recommended three weeks of silence to his young disciple, writing to him regularly—words were all he had, and he used them carefully: "The door of the *guha** has been opened to you! You have glimpsed its depths, now enter within, from depth to depth, to ever deeper centres, in a constantly deeper passing beyond of yourself and of God, which has neither beginning nor end, in that mystery which is no more either not-one or not-two."[27]

Apart from the joy of passing on the truths he had so long sought, there was another side to this relationship. After years of celibacy and childlessness, Abhishiktananda had found an outlet for his affectionate nature, probably for the first time since he was a child and living in the warmth of a close family, yet unlike so many who find themselves with

---

Guhā—cave, the secret place of the heart.

the influence of a guru, he was resolutely non-attached; there was no sen-timentality, no exclusiveness. Like any father, he said that both Ramesh and Marc drove him crazy, "How you 'empty' me, as you fulfil me. I can only allow myself to be led, to embrace, be embraced, to give, be given, to receive, be received."[28] His strongest advice was that Marc should learn to "simply live in the eternity," to learn the importance of "being lost"[29] within. His intellectual training, ordination to the priesthood and the like, would come later. Despite his ambivalence toward his own time at Kergonan, Abhishiktananda strongly recommended a monastic forma-tion for Marc and admitted that he himself gained from it enormously.

The heart of his message for his disciple was what he had for so long been trying to do himself—to "lay hold of eternity in the present moment,"[30] to have the blazing experience of God's presence in the actual situation in which we find ourselves. That only is real, "the present moment, in which I am face-to-face with God."[31] So he urged Marc, "The Espresso bar on the corner of the ghats is no less 'brahmic' than the *arati* or the ecstatic Mass. This is precisely what you have to discover and live now; the expression of the inmost and unique mystery in the most commonplace action or meeting."[32]

After Marc's three-week silence, Abhishiktananda sent him on pil-grimage, including, naturally enough, a visit to Arunachala; he was not surprised when the Holy Mountain played one of its "tricks" on Marc, in an incident curiously similar to what he himself had experienced.* Marc's room was burgled and all his papers and money were taken; he was unable to leave the Holy Mountain. The young man responded in a way that must have delighted his guru: "Perfect," he tells me: "Stuck at Arunachala, unable to stir!"[33] Abhishiktananda himself had regarded the occasion when he was burgled as an important step in his understanding of the importance of surrender, but it was another matter when the same thing happened to his beloved disciple:

> I cried out to Shiva: What have you done to my child? And he answered me: It is you who has done it to him, it is he who has done it to himself. Was it not just that which he himself *wanted* most deeply in his heart, where he is nothing else but Myself? . . . Now there is no longer any question whether I should join you or not . . . you may equally think that Shiva wants you there by yourself, with-out even this form of his presence that I myself am.[34]

---

*See chapter 9 above.

How DOES ONE EVALUATE THE WORK of the guru and his disciple? The disciple has no exams to pass, no tests to endure; he, like his teacher, can only testify by his experience. For those who know him, the most reliable thermometer is what radiates from him. One thing is certain: by the end of 1971, at the time of the overwhelming experience he shared with Marc at Phulchatti, Abhishiktananda himself was a long way along the path of enlightenment. We cannot dare to evaluate his progress in objective terms. He had no guru himself at that time, he did not belong to a discipline that endorses experience and measures it with the weight of long years of tradition and knowledge. We can measure his progress toward enlightenment only through the reactions of those who knew him at the time and with our own imprecise and unreliable tools of perception as we read his words. And these judgments cannot be certain, for not many are so far along the path he traveled with such courage; we can only offer his thoughts and words, and wonder. Yet even though there are no scales to measure enlightenment, no precise definition of an enlightened person, is it not undeniably true that by now Abhishiktananda was a truly enlightened man? Let his own words speak for him. A month after the experience at Phulchatti he wrote in his diary:

> The solitude of one who has found God, for there is no longer any God to be with: God is only with himself and one who has found God exists only in the Self. It is the Self that he finds everywhere, in God, in his fellow human beings. Just as it is this very Self, *atmanam*, that the Father finds in the Son and the Spirit, and vice versa. And to discover oneself everywhere, what a draining out of oneself it is, what an emptying, *kenosis*. Everything is taken away from me. Supreme solitude, which is supreme emptiness, for how can the one who is Alone still define himself; no coordinates left by which to situate himself.[35]

Surely these are the words of an enlightened man. Or these, which, at the beginning of 1972 he wrote to his sister Marie-Thérèse,

> when you have discovered this *I am*, scorching, devastating, then no longer even (can you say) *God is*—for who is there to speak of God? This is the great grace of India, which makes us discover the "I am" at the heart of the Gospel (John 8). May the devastating joy of this "I am" fill your soul.[36]

And the telling image of fire appears again when he writes, "it is in the actual situation in which we are placed . . . that we meet God and have the scorching experience of his Presence."[37] Perhaps most profound of all, a diary entry made soon after his experience with Marc at Phulchatti, "A being lost in my source, a being lost in my fulfilment. And in this very loss, I am . . ."[38]

Let us then look at the effect he had on people. A collection of articles published several years after his death gave many of his friends and disciples a chance to recall their most precious thoughts about him.[39]

In her foreword, Vandana Mataji points out that he was "so utterly human and simple, there was nothing exotic or elitist about him."[40] This surely draws us to the heart of holiness—ordinariness, the ordinariness of a Brother Lawrence, of a St. Teresa of Avila, the deceptive simplicity of becoming a full human being. In her opening article, Mataji points to the aspect of Abhishiktananda that alone secures him a place among the significant spiritual people of his time. It was he, she writes, who helped those who knew him to learn that "one was *able to live in deep communion* with men and women anywhere in the world, *beyond all religions or differences of religion.*"[41]

Another contributor to this book, Bettina Bäumer, reminded her readers of one of Abhishiktananda's most piercing questions, heartrendingly relevant to many: "Is there any place in catholic christianity (or in any institution) for people who have gone beyond name and form?"[42] She also responds to a criticism sometimes made about Abhishiktananda and people like him—are their lives centered too much around their own spiritual progress rather than helping others?—by recording an occasion when he said to her, "You see, I have time and quiet to study and to go deep into the Upanishads. I do it for myself, but also as a kind of service to those who are too busy to have time for this kind of contemplation."[43] Another contributor, Verghese Kottu, who met Abhishiktananda at the All-India Seminar in 1969 states without question that Abhishiktananda was an enlightened man:

The simple prayerful, humble, sweet and silent way he moved about among us made a deep impression on the hearts of the people present. The smile he had on his lips proclaimed the inner bliss of his heart. He seemed to breathe out the peace he possessed, through his being rather than through his doing. His sparkling eyes beamed forth the illumination of his inner life.[44]

T HERE WERE MORE GREAT EXPERIENCES ahead of Abhishiktananda and Marc. The second was on the night of the Ascension, in May 1972, when they were spending three intense weeks studying the Upanishads at the ashram at Phulchatti. Marc asked Abhishiktananda whether it was possible to split *anya*, the "other." Abhishiktananda said it could not be split. "It's like the number 23."[45] This was for Marc a shattering awakening:

> A sudden and overwhelming vision of *param jyotir*, of the Great Light, for three hours; engulfing the total depths of myself, in the ineffable light which I am. An experience of annihilating, beatifying death, an awakening to Self! At the same time I had the definitive revelation that Henri (Le Saux) is my guru. I saw him in his blinding glory, transfigured in the Light. But he experienced the terrible anguish of not knowing if I was going to "return," and if so, if it would be with all my faculties.[46]

So overwhelming was this experience that Marc let out a shriek, audible to the head of the ashram, who came out from his room to see if anything was wrong. Abhishiktananda simply said, "Go away." This was not something that demanded witnesses or could bear explanations. It could only come to one who will "be taken all the way to the end whatever the cost, even the cost of risking death or losing his head!"[47]

Again this was an experience shared by the two men, guru and disciple, and of blinding importance to them both. "This Light of 'great death' overwhelmed us both equally."[48]

Abhishiktananda knew that what he had experienced was beyond theology: "It is too overpowering to feel onself in the presence of the True, and how can one express in words that which words would only betray?"[49] Nevertheless he tried, in a complex passage of his diary.[50] The words that sing through are his declaration that "the experience of the Upanishads is true, *I know it!*"[51] This declaration was followed by the great words from the Svetasvatara Upanishad:

> I have come to know the mighty Person,
> golden like the sun, beyond all darkness.
> By knowing Him a man transcends death;
> there is no other path for reaching that goal.[52]

This day, the feast of the Ascension 1972, was, he wrote, the day Marc "became unborn," the day he was enlightened; it was also the day when

Abhishiktananda "understood that the Upanishad is a secret which is only properly given in the secret communication of guru to disciple."[53] He knew as never before that guru and disciple cannot be taken apart; they are one.

On the last night of their time together, on May 28, they had a third extraordinary experience. They were at Shivananda Ashram, an ashram near Rishikesh whose *acharya** was Swami Chidananda. They held each other in the greatest respect: "The mutual relationship of these two holy men was a joy to behold."[54] Abhishiktananda and Marc were on the terrace when, once again simultaneously, they experienced what Marc called "the night of Pentecost" and Abhishiktananda called the "upanishad of fire." "Of the fire that I am, of the fire that anyone is who has even had only a glimpse of Brahman. A fire that burns—slowly perhaps but inexorably—in all the names and forms of whoever comes near him."[55] James Stuart writes that they were both so shattered by this experience that the next morning, Trinity Sunday, they were unable to celebrate Mass.[56]

It was around this time that Abhishiktananda began to write of what he called "correlations," or "correspondences" in the Upanishads, "which go beyond all the words employed and pierce the living flesh like electric shocks."[57] "Correlation causes the spark of experience (*anubhava*) to flash, that alone gives fulfilment."[58] He wanted Marc to live the Upanishads so deeply, beyond all names and forms, that he would be able to take it to Europe "stripped of all its exotic oriental trappings and springing directly from the Source."[59] It is curious that he who himself refused all invitations to Europe or beyond should be eager for his disciple to spread the teachings of the Upanishads.

Abhishiktananda at last felt he had come to a new level of understanding, his anguish transcended, his taste only for the Upanishads and the Gospels. Now he knew. It was, in a way, as simple as that. And what he knew was beyond words. It could be communicated only in parables, and when true prayers did emerge they "came from too great depth and shatter everything!"[60] He could talk to Marc, who had shared the Phulchatti experience and who he felt had received the essential heart of what he had to pass on to him, but he encouraged him not to read the Upanishads for more than six hours. "Your head would not stand more . . . nothing can take the place of a slow walk on foot along the tracks which follow all the windings of the Ganges."[61] Then, slowly, the wisdom of the *rishi*s will reveal itself.

On June 30, 1973, Marc and Abhishiktananda shared another great experience, Marc's initiation. *Sannyāsa-dīkshā* is an initiation into the life

---

Acharya—master, teacher, head of an ashram.

of renunciation, and it can be given only when the guru feels confident that the disciple really *knows* and has the spiritual strength to follow the ascetic life and to practice the acosmic way.* Following tradition, the days before the ceremony should be spent in silence, culminating in a day of fasting, a night of prayer, and in this case, at four in the morning, there was to be a celebration of the Eucharist, after which the stone plate and cup would be thrown into the Ganga, symbolically showing the end of all signs. Afterwards the newly intitiated *sannyāsi* should renounce all possessions and have a long period of wandering and living on alms.

There has been much argument about who is qualified to initiate another person, and there is no doubt that it has sometimes been given too easily. However, in this case there was no problem, as it was to be an initiation into a double tradition, Swami Chidananda, the *acharya* of Sivananda Ashram, transmitting the Hindu tradition of *sannyāsa*, a tradition going back through countless *sādhus* to the *rishis* themselves, Abhishiktananda honoring the call of Christ, heard by men and women since the time of the Desert Fathers and Mothers, to leave all for the sake of the kingdom. Honoring that tradition, the ceremony was to end with readings from the Gospel as "uncompromisingly radical" as those in the Upanishads. In *The Further Shore* Abhishiktananda lists some of these, showing the unity between the Upanishads and the Gospels:

> The Son of Man has nowhere to lay his head . . .
> Go, sell what you have . . . and come, follow me . . .
> Leave the dead to bury their dead . . .
> No man who puts his hand to the plough and looks back, is fit for the Kingdom of God.
> If anyone . . . does not "hate" his father, mother, wife, children, brothers, sisters, and even his own life, he cannot be my disciple.
> Take nothing for your journey—no staff, bag, bread, money, no change of clothes . . . (See Luke 9:58; Mark 10:21; Luke 9:62; 14:26; 9:3; etc.)[62]

This ecumenical *dīkshā* spoke from the heart of Christian teaching.

The preparation had been long and painstaking. The event, on June 23, 1973, was to be one of the highest points of Abhishiktananda's life. He wrote to Murray Rogers, the unusually short sentences indicating the inadequacy of words:

---

*The word "acosmic" is often used by Abhishiktananda. It means literally "denial of a universe distinct from God."

Deep in the Ganga he [Marc] pronounced the old formula of renunciation. I join him; he plunges into [the] water; I raise him up, and we sing our favourite mantras to the Purusha. He discards all his clothes into [the] water, and I receive him as from the maternal womb. We envelop him in the fire-coloured dress. We communicate to him the *mahavakyas,** and I give him the "envoi": "Go to where is no return . . . ."[63]

So, dressed simply in the fire-colored dress, the *gerua vastra*, with no money, no possessions, carrying only a begging bowl, Marc Chaduc, the young French seminarian now known as Ajatananda, the bliss of the Not-born, walked away. To where, no one knew.

Abhishiktananda was overwhelmingly moved, as so often when overcome by emotion, expressing himself in a loose poetic form:

> You are no longer the child
> begotten by me
> whom I love extravagantly
> but you were transfigured before my eyes
> as I was before yours.
> In you I had had darshana (vision)
> of the Unbegotten
> Ajata.
>
> Your diksha [monastic profession]
> as your flight of May
> shook me to the depths of my being
> stripping me of myself
> losing myself in infinite spaces
> where I no longer knew anything
> where search in vain.
> OM.[64]

Curiously and touchingly, he admitted to envy. He passionately wished that he too had gone to the lengths demanded by the dress he wore, that he who in the eyes of most people had given up so much had not given up more, for the true *sannyāsi*, he was convinced, should have nothing. But at least he could rejoice in his role: "I shall at least have had the joy

---

*One of the great sentences of the Upanishads, like *"aham brahma asmi,"* "I am brahma."

of awakening this child, and of realizing through him the ideal of which I have talked so much in my books and articles, but which alas, I have lived so little."[65]

He was also worried. He worried that he himself dared to wear the orange robe, when he could not do completely without money, could not live by alms or wear only a loincloth. He worried that he had no right to give *sannyāsa* when, as he felt, he did not live it fully himself. Most of all, like any father, he worried about Ajatananda. Ten days after the *sannyāsa-dīkshā* ceremony he wrote in his diary:

> Have felt terribly anxious for the last three days about what is happening to my child. What is he eating, where is he sleeping, has anything happened to him? and the rain? I cannot eat without wondering if he is able to eat . . . : no appetite for any food.

But he was honest enough to admit the nature of his pangs of envy:

> And the torment is that he has left me, not just physically, but that he has passed into a sphere of the sacred to which I have no access.
> . . .
> The one who was after me has gone ahead, and I can no longer join him. . . .[66]

18

The Final Explosion

The Awakening alone is what counts.[1]

ABHISHIKTANANDA HAD FOR MANY YEARS been living dangerously. He had given up his country, his family, and most material comforts; he had put his physical health, his relationship with his community, his relationship with the church, sometimes even his own sanity, at risk as he accepted challenges and opportunities that came his way in his search for God, for enlightenment, for awakening, the Holy Grail—the names may vary but the goal is the same. His goal was humanity's highest aspiration, involving the harshest deprivation, the most risks, in search of the greatest reward.

After he met Marc, Abhishiktananda rejoiced in being able to accompany him on a similar path. He had plans for him to become a Master, even to take the message West—something he had never been able to bring himself to do. In traveling this path there were risks to both men. While no one can criticize someone for where they travel in their own personal lives, when it involves someone else the criteria are rather different. Some of the experiences he shared with Marc, like the events of the *sannyāsi-dīkshā*, were, as he well knew, "too strong" even for him, a mature monk with years of experience: "Who can bear the glory of transfiguration, or man's discovery as transfigured; because what Christ is, I AM! One can only speak of it after being awoken from the dead."[2]

Some of his friends wondered if Abhishiktananda was wise to lead a young and sensitive man toward such powerful, explosive experiences. These doubts were strengthened when, in 1977, Marc, or Ajatananda as we should now call him, disappeared, without word, without leaving a message of any sort. What led him to act in such a manner? Still no one knows—or if they do they do not share the knowledge—what happened to him. The day before his disappearance he is known to have sent a message to Swami Chidananda, who had shared the giving of the ecumenical *dīkshā* to Ajatananda. The Swami went to visit him, but the privacy of that conversation has always been respected.

So the question has to be asked—was Abhishiktananda a wise guru? Bewildered by Marc's disappearance, doubts were raised. Murray Rogers, close friend and fervent admirer of Abhishiktananda, was among those who wondered:

> If these experiences were too strong for Swamiji, with his long years of monastic life, with so many years of maturation, physically and spiritually, would it be surprising for Ajatananda, in his 30s and with no years of monastic training and experience, to have been over-whelmed by what had happened to him in the deepest depth of his being? Had Swamiji, for whom this area of spiritual fatherhood was also an unknown mystery, for whom his hopes had been more won-derfully fulfilled than he could have dared to hope and pray, failed to give sufficient weight to the danger, human and spiritual, laid on Ajatananda?[3]

Indeed, Abhishiktananda was not uncritical of himself, for when Marc went off on his own after the *sannyāsa-dīkshā* he not only worried about him but admitted doubts about how he had guided his young disciple: "He is calling me there where he is. There where I have shown him the path without having ever thought he would take it so seriously!"[4]

The joy and the ecstasy were also tinged with a feeling of his own inad-equacy in the face of Ajatananda's extreme austerity. Abhishiktananda was facing yet again the harsh truth that the real *sannyāsa*—and monks and nuns come to that—should possess nothing, absolutely nothing, not even a typewriter or a book. In his diary he expressed this ascetism in hard, practical terms:

> For food—even when prepared by oneself—just food received from begging, what people throw to a beggar.
>
> For clothing, what is most ordinary, worn out, what the rich leave for the poor when they no longer want it.
>
> For shelter, what is lent to the passer-by, what people allow a beg-gar to use. The minimum of indispensable equipment, and not a compromise with what is more practical.
>
> But, what about that which is supposedly necessary for work?
> My work is to be.[5]

The ascetism of his life, his continual travels—always, remember, in third-class trains, by bus, or on foot—coupled with the rich spiritual diet, took their toll on his health. He rarely complained, but over the years he had had his share of physical problems. In 1957 he came to know the French Franciscan Sisters who ran the Roberts Nursing Home at Indore, and he was to stay there regularly, both as friend and as patient. They first looked after him when he spent a few days in the Nursing Home with fever, exhaustion, and a high temperature. On his first visit to the Himalayas in 1959 he contracted the skin disease herpes; in March of 1960 he had an operation for hemorrhoids, which he approached with "the emotions and fear of a criminal about to be handed over to the executioner"[6] but which in the event proved a painless experience, indeed he found it delightful, as for the first time in years he reveled in sleeping for ten days between clean white sheets. In 1965 he spent ten days suffering from an abscess in his foot.

Given his slight build and his relentlessly ascetic lifestyle in a hot country not his own by birth, this is not a bad record. But there seems little doubt that the events shared with Marc had affected his health, for after the extraordinary experience of "the night of Pentecost," he had a serious attack of breathlessness, the first indication that he had heart trouble. He had felt for some time that an "impulse to death"[7] had been pursuing him; even that he was living "under the sign of Death." He tells most movingly how, on June 29, 1973, the day before the *dīkshā*, a *sadhaka** sang to him and Marc; he chose the "Arunachala Siva," the funeral chant that had been sung when Ramana Maharshi was dying. The chant stirred emotions Abhishiktananda could hardly bear, and as he left he was seized with giddiness and had to lean on the handrail of the stairs for support. Soon afterwards he wrote a "will," headed "TRUE COPIES OF INSTRUCTIONS LEFT BY SWAMI ABHISHIKTANANDA DULY SIGNED ON 9.7.73," asking for six friends and disciples to be informed in case of accident and including instructions as to the disposal of his few worldly possessions.

I⊤ WAS AS IF WITH THE END OF HIS LIFE in sight Abhishiktananda was becoming increasingly refined, concentrated, one-pointed. On the level of solitude he was refusing most of the invitations with which he was overwhelmed; he was being invited to seminars in Bangalore, to give lectures at Vidya Jyoti, the Jesuit scholasticate in Delhi, to assist with Jesuits

*One who practices spiritual exercises.

who were training as novice masters and spiritual fathers—there was a never-ending list of demands on his time. Occasionally he was tempted to accept; for instance, he was drawn by a suggestion from his friend the Jesuit Tony de Mello, and by another from the Sufi Master Pir Vilayat Khan, whom he had recently met unexpectedly and delightfully near the Ganges. But however much he enjoyed talking and meeting people, he knew that he had gone beyond the point where what he had to say could be communicated in talks and seminars:

> The place of the hermit is in his cell. A little hard to swallow, but true, isn't it? Some would like me to give up writing. And in fact what remains to be written is impossible to write. Everything explodes when you have reached the fourth *matra** of the OM.[8]

So too he was coming to terms with the thought of leaving his *kutiya* at Gyansu. This was partly because he realized his health was no longer up to living alone, partly because his position was being questioned by the church authorities in charge of the mountain districts, who had sent two priests with a curious brief—to find out whether Abhishiktananda was well known as a Catholic priest. At around the same time, with an interesting synchronicity, he was abruptly told, with no explanation, that he could no longer use his *pied-à-terre* at the School of Prayer at Rajpur. Abhishiktananda never ceased to care about his position in relation to the church, and these two events must have worried him.

Ajatananda, knowing his guru needed to move from Gyansu, had found a *kutiya* that he thought would be ideal for him, so ten days after the *sannyāsi-dīkshā* he sent a note to Abhishiktananda, who decided to go immediately to see it. By one of those chances that is not really chance, the two met there, spending a few days in a small deserted Shiva temple at a place called Ranagal; they referred to this as "the great week." Yet again guru and disciple lived at the outer edge of normal experience, spending three days, apparently without food, which James Stuart says "can only be called a 'holy inebriation' like that of the *keshi* (hairy ones) of the Rig-Veda."[9] Marc's diary† reveals that this included some sexual expression, probably almost inevitable given the highly charged atmosphere; it does not seem surprising that such ecstatic union should need to take physical form.

---

*Element; especially of the sounds *A*, *U*, and *M* making up the OM. The fourth element is the silence beyond *A*, *U*, and *M*.

†This impression came from one of the passages Odette Baumer-Despeigne read to Murray Rogers.

It is impossible to enter into their experience, but an extraordinary entry in Ajatananda's diary gives a vivid idea of this week and how it affected his guru:

> During these few days Swamiji was as if driven by a force which went beyond him. They were lived out through certain great symbols such as the taking up of the Prophet Elias in his fiery chariot, that of Dakshinamurti, the manifestation of Shiva as a young guru teaching by his silence. Or finally the myth of the Column of fire which had neither base nor summit of Arunachala-Shiva.*
>
> On July 11, under the influence of the Spirit, there issued from the mouth of the Father, unexpectedly, words which stammered the inexpressible, suggesting that he who was after had been before; that there was no longer either master or disciple. . . . What was spoken cannot be remembered. . . .
>
> Suddenly a flash of lightning illumined the nearby mountain and in this light Swamiji lived again the irruption of the Column of fire and light of Shiva-Arunachala. The very depths of his being shook and trembled to the point of snapping. . . . The rain fell in torrents, it ran down to the mandir.† We remained seated for a long time in silence. An extraordinary power emanated from everything. Finally we curled up as best we could to pass the long night around the linga (the upright stone which is a symbol of Shiva).[10]

As dawn broke the next morning, July 12, it was still raining: "A power —a shakti—of total stripping away reigned in this place, man could no longer cover himself with any rag, there was nothing other than the Absolute who shone forth in his dazzling radiance."[11] Still under the influence of this dazzling radiance Abhishiktananda intoned the OM in such a way that the fourth, silent, syllable resonated; then he slept again.

In one important respect the two men reacted in different ways. For Ajatananda the night at Ranagal was the night he realized that his vocation was silence. Abhishiktananda, on the other hand, reminded him that silence was not the final goal, the final goal was the "taking up of ordinary life, without any exterior manifestation, whether of word or of silence."[12]

The mystery of the guru–disciple relationship had reached an extraordinary peak, touching, in Ajatananda's words, "this profound mystery of

---

*See chapter 6 above.
†*Mandir*—temple.

the son who 'engenders' the father, in the very act in which the father engenders the son as his own, with both awakening the Unbegotten." Abhishiktananda told him he was to transmit this mystery: "All that has been given is received in order to be given anew."[13]

These few days of searing intensity were to prove too powerful for the frail Abhishiktananda. But at least they must eat, so he left Marc to his solitude and returned to Rishikesh, intending to stock up with some food and to return to Ranagal. It was not to be.

HE HAD BOUGHT HIS PROVISIONS and was running for the bus when it happened—a full-scale, serious heart attack. He lay helpless on the pavement for, he thinks, half an hour, when a French woman from Sivanandam Ashram was passing in a taxi, which happened to stop right beside him; she recognized Abhishiktananda and called the doctor. He was taken back to the ashram, where Swami Chidananda arranged a bed for him and Nirmal, a young brahmin boy, looked after him.

He was seriously ill, but this physical illness was to be the great climax of his life. Over the next months he talked and wrote about it gratefully, sometimes ecstatically, always with a sense of wonder. "Really a door opened in heaven when I was lying on the pavement. But a heaven which was not the opposite of earth, something which was neither life nor death, but simply 'being,' 'awakening' . . . beyond all myths and symbols."[14] He had reached his goal. Ajatananda called it "the definitive Awakening beyond all else, the final explosion."[15]

Nearly two months later Abhishiktananda made a long diary entry, in which he wrote of the first few days after the heart attack. His central intuition was that "the Awakening is independent of any situation whatever, of all pairs of opposites. . . . One awakes everywhere and once and for all."[16] It is a change of consciousness, and Abhishiktananda had at last experienced it. But it was not all easy. The first night was filled with dreams that he called "difficult," though they were not nightmares. He was being led from cave to cave at different altitudes, and all the times he was saying, "The awakening has nothing to do with 'testing oneself' against increasingly difficult life situations. It comes about in any circumstances. At every moment in life, in fact in every circumstance, *I wake up*."[17] He also had disturbing experiences of being acutely aware of the smallness of the human body and wondering how it was enough to support consciousness.

Meanwhile Ajatananda waited in the jungle, agonizing over what had happened to his guru. The only person who knew where he was was Abhishiktananda, and he was not strong enough to write for four days. As soon as he could he wrote a note, imparting the news with a piece of his inimitable poetic prose. Nirmal set off to find Marc/Ajatananda and give it to him:

MARC,
Shiva's column of fire
brushed against me
Saturday midday
in the bazaar at Rishikesh,
and I still do not understand
why it did not carry me off.
Joy, the serene one,
OM *tat sat (That—Brahman—is the Real)*
ekadrishi (the one-pointed gaze)
ekarshi (the unique rishi)
Oh!
The crowning grace
OM!
With my love.[18]

Marc traveled immediately to the ashram, where he found his guru "simply transformed into the radiance of the Lord."[19] On July 30, he took Abhishiktananda to some Quaker friends in Rajpur and three weeks later, Abhishiktananda for the first time in his life traveling as a first-class passenger, on to the nursing home at Indore, where he was cared for by his good friend Mother Théophane. Here he knew he would find a homely atmosphere and would be well looked after and given suitable food.

The doctor's initial prognosis was hopeful. After only two weeks he said his patient was already 70 percent cured and in three months he should be recovered, but there was no escaping the fact that he would no longer be able to travel alone, carrying his few worldly possessions with him. Nor would it be safe for him to live alone—he was confirmed in his instinct that he had to say goodbye to his *kutiya* at Gyansu, indeed that he would have to forgo any ideas of a totally solitary life.

IT WAS NOT, HOWEVER, HIS PHYSICAL HEALTH and his future lifestyle that concerned Abhishiktananda, nor did he think that the cause of the heart attack was entirely physical. He was sure it was not running for the bus that had caused the attack; it was the explosive experiences that he and Marc had been through in the preceding two weeks. For him this was not a physical tragedy but "a marvellous spiritual experience," and he rejoiced. At last he was free to be, simply to be, and along with this realization he knew that this grace was not only for him; it was for others. He longed to share the experience that had eluded him for so many years; to say to others, as others had said to him: "in this quest you run about everywhere, whereas the Grail is here, close at hand, you have only to open your eyes."[20] Whatever time he had left was an unexpected extension; he must not misuse it—he must use it for others, though he had no idea how. He knew better than most that words were not enough; nevertheless he would try using them. He would say, "Look, it is in the depth of yourself, it is that very 'I' that you are saying in every moment of your conscious life, even in the depth of your consciousness when you dream or sleep."[21]

His excitement was such that, whenever he had the strength, he wrote to his friends telling them of his marvelous adventure. These were not the letters of a sick man; they were written by someone who had had the most important experience of his life and who was rejoicing in it. They are astonishing letters:

> The discovery that the AWAKENING has nothing to do with any situation, even so-called life or so-called death; one is awake, and that is all. While I was waiting on my sidewalk, on the frontier of the two worlds, I was magnificently calm, for I AM, no matter in what world![22]

That to his sister. And to a friend, he used the analogy of the sea: "It seemed to me as if I was navigating between two 'shores' of being that man calls life and death, and to discover myself in the middle of the great current of Being Itself which has nothing to do with either life or with death."[23] It was "like the marvellous solution to an equation":

> I have found the Grail. And that is what I keep saying and writing to anyone who can grasp the figure of speech. The quest for the Grail is basically nothing else than the quest for the Self. A single quest, that is the meaning of all the myths and symbols. It is yourself that you are seeking through everything.[24]

For years he had longed for this moment, lived for it, suffered for it; yet now it had arrived and it was so simple. "The discovery that the AWAKENING has nothing to do with any situation, even so-called life or so-called death; one is awake, and that is all."[25] "It is at the same time a wonderful experience of 'cruising' between death and life, discovering that one IS!"[26] Sometimes he expanded his thinking, for instance, on the distinction between notion and experience and how even after his own awakening experience

> I can only aim at awakening people to what "they are." Anything about God or the Word in any religion, which is not based on the deep I-experience is bound to be simply "notion," not existential. From the awakening to self comes the awakening to God—and we discover marvellously that Christ is simply this awakening on a degree of purity rarely if ever reached by man.[27]

Mostly it was sheer joy that he wanted to communicate. "It is wonderful to pass through such an experience which makes you find full peace and happiness beyond all situations, even of death and life. Life cannot be the same any more, because beyond life we have found the Awakening."[28] Sometimes a single phrase was enough: "The awakening alone is what counts."[29]

IF THERE WAS ONE THEME, apart from his overabundant joy, that concerned him, it was Christ and the church. During twenty-five years of seeking the unifying point between Christianity and *advaita*, Abhishiktananda had often found it a struggle to remain a Christian and was increasingly disenchanted with the church. He felt that the current crisis in the church was even deeper than was generally thought, but "when seen from the Himalayas, how mean and petty sound the arguments of radicals and reactionaries alike!"[30] He saw *advaita* as "the specific, if not the only, way by which the Church may survive its appalling crisis."[31] Yet, as early as 1956 he had written that true *advaita*, "blows up the institutional Church of the Vatican."[32] The frequency with which he writes of the church shows his concern, yet he was curiously indifferent to its fate, for instance, saying: "The structures will blow up, but what does it matter? There are plenty of tracks leading to the summit of Arunachala!"[33] It depended partly who he was writing to—that last comment was to Marc, who would have understood him very well on the subject.

But he never wavered in his love for Christ. His "double-belonging" had cost him bitterly, but eventually he was rewarded with dazzling revelations of the truth beyond the opposites; he had also found the reconciliation, in himself, of Christianity and Hinduism. In 1972 he was able to write: "the Christian experience is truly the Advaitic experience lived in the human communion."[34] Now, these few months after his heart attack, he was flooded with new understandings about Christ, many of them contained in two letters to Murray Rogers, at the time living in Jesusalem and unable to visit him in the nursing home.

The catalyst to these thoughts was the invitation he had received earlier in the year from Pir Vilayat Inayat Khan. The Sufi was keen for Abhishiktananda to attend a youth camp in Chamonix and Abhishik-tananda was under pressure from some of his friends to go. Clearly now his health ruled out acceptance, but the idea, accompanied, he admitted, by some slight temptation to accept, seems to have clarified his thoughts on Christ. He realized how concerned he was that he could no longer speak for the average Christian:

> The further I go, the less able I would be to present Christ in a way which would still be *considered* as "Christian." . . . I am interested in no Christo-logy at all. I have so little interest in a word of God which will awaken man within history. . . . The "Word of God" comes from/to *my* own "present"; it is that very awakening which is my self-awareness. What I discover above all in Christ is his "I AM."[35]

A month later he wrote, "The Christ I might present would be simply the 'I AM' of (every) deep heart, who can show himself in the dancing Siva or the amorous Krisna! And the kingdom is precisely this discovery . . . of the 'inside' of the Grail!"[36] So what happens to Christian theology? Are all christological theories blown apart? Did he feel confirmed in his long-held doubts about the value of theology?

Now, over thirty years after his death, there are many who would hear this message with exhilaration and relief, but at the time he was probably right not to address a group of Christians. Like anyone who has broken barriers, Abishiktananda was ahead of his time, and few were ready to receive such insights; they could have caused pain rather than joy and he had no wish to shake people's belief. He could "use the Christ-experience to lead Christians to an 'I AM' experience,"[37] for that is what matters and in that knowledge all Christ-ology disappears, but were people ready to hear that? He used to say that the cover of his next book would be an "atomic mushroom," because:

> The discovery of Christ's "I AM" is the ruin of any Christian theology, for all notions are burnt up within the fire of experience. Perhaps I am a little too Cartesian, as a good Frenchman. And perhaps others might find a way out of the atomic mushroom. I feel too much, more and more, the blazing fire of his I AM, in which all

notions about Christ's personality, ontology, history, etc., have disappeared. And I find his real mystery shining in every awakening man, in every mythos.[38]

For a while, in the constant care of the nursing home, there was some improvement in Abhishiktananda's health, and at the beginning of October the doctors gave permission for his diet to be varied, and, probably for the first time in twenty-five years, he ate some fish. For a while he got a little stronger and put on some weight, though he did not like having to desert his vegetarian ways and Sister Théophane notes that the Hindu servants refrained from comment. Abhishiktananda began to feel that perhaps the tide had turned, even to think in terms of returning to the South.

But the improvement did not last, and he was still pathetically weak. Sister Théophane says, "At that time he symbolised for me the suffering Christ. It was as though he had been broken by the Lord, left unable to read or pray or do anything at all; it was an utter spiritual nakedness, together with complete physical prostration."[39] She wrote that he took his medicines but did not like the oxygen that was available and wasn't able to eat the food he was offered.

He had not, however, lost his sense of humor. Chatting with him, Sister Théophane once said, "'Father, you're groggy . . . you'll be the first groggy saint, it's wonderful.' To which, laughing with delight, he replied with a litany of groggy saints: 'From getting up early, good Lord, deliver us—From taking cold baths, good Lord, deliver us—From making an effort, good Lord, deliver us—From eating tasteless pap, good Lord, deliver us. . . .'"[40] And when the sisters talked about taking him south by air, he imagined them all in a crate, or he conjured up a beautiful icon representing the chariot of fire of Elijah. At other moments they would read from the Upanishads or from John of the Cross.

In his longing to share his experience he probably did not even consider just how much he gave through his letters, nor would he have known the significance that the radiance of his presence held for others. The person who saw most of Abhishiktananda at this time was, of course, Sister Théophane, a true contemplative, who nursed him devotedly from the time he arrived in Indore on August 21 until his death, and who deeply admired "the simplicity and complete docility with which he received my every suggestion for his wellbeing and health."[41] It was as if he was living out his own thought, written when he was very ill and felt concentration was beyond him: "And then the Lord takes you seriously, removes every fine thought, and leaves you there, capable of nothing more than simply being there! And that is what is most real!"[42]

He had many visitors. He had so impressed people that all the doctors attached to the nursing home wanted to meet him, friends like Father Dominique came, the local priests, the superior and the bishop, European priests, Indian priests, especially the parish priest Father Gratian Aroojis. He enjoyed their visits but found them very tiring and was upset that he couldn't give more to people, some of whom had come some way to see him.

One visit must have been curious for both patient and visitor, and that was from Odette Baumer-Despeigne, with whom he had a long and profound correspondence but whom he had never previously met. She and her son Christopher came to see him on October 10, and she wrote to the abbot of Kergonan about her impressions. She found him physically very weak; he could only walk for a few minutes a day and had a persistent cough, but the effect of the man she had hitherto only known by correspondence was overwhelming:

> It is difficult to describe the days spent with him, what the conversations were about, the moments of silence—his silence in particular had a very special quality—and the celebration of the Eucharist. His entire person and all his actions literally radiated the presence of God, he was totally transparent to the Lord . . . his whole personality gave out a serenity and very subtle joy, his own mind was 100% alert, and at no moment did he lose his good humour, nor his sense of humour.[43]

All agree that his whole being was transparent to the divine Presence; many saw the radiance of his smile, his countenance glowing with light, his eyes wide open with wonder. "His entire being was total transparence to the inner Mystery, joy and peace radiating in his penetrating regard which reduced one to silence, to an amazing silence."[44]

AT THE BEGINNING OF DECEMBER, Abhishiktananda seemed to be better, but the fifth and the sixth were difficult days. He couldn't sleep and was increasingly breathless; it was as though he had a weight on his chest. He didn't take easily to the oxygen that was offered; he wasn't hungry, and in the evening of December 7 he had a short, but very bad, attack of breathlessness. The doctor came and prescribed medication, should it happen again. As he was taking his medicine he said to Sister Théophane,

"'As God wills,' smiling sweetly and moving his hands as though to say 'all is finished, nothing matters any more.' Then he said to me: 'I am ready. As God wills.' He murmured something about 'the chariot of Elijah'; it was as though he knew he was on his way."[45] (Sister Théophane could not have known that the chariot of Elijah would also have reminded him of the experience at Ranagal, "the mystery of the disappearance of the guru in the very act of total transmission.")[46]

After supper they had the exposition of the Blessed Sacrament, Sister Théophane sitting with him, determined not to leave him alone for a minute. At eight o'clock he had another attack, after which Abhishiktananda said to Sister Théophane: "'What a story, finally, when one has done all that one can, this will be as God willed, I am ready.' With a beautiful smile he added: . . . Behold, as God wills! What trouble I have given you!'"[47] Later that evening he had yet another attack, and the sisters came at once and gave him injections. Sister Théophane sent word to the fathers and they came at once. "He was calm but didn't seem to be breathing, although his heart was still beating. He was anointed and slipped quietly away to the Lord. It lasted perhaps seven minutes in all. It was eleven o'clock on the evening of December 7."[48]

ABHISHIKTANANDA'S DEATH WAS ANNOUNCED at the first Mass the next morning, and all day long people filed through to see his body, lovingly dressed in saffron robes and a white stole. "He looked wonderful, with a supernatural beauty, and seemed to be lying at rest, about to look at you and smile."[49]

The funeral Mass was said that afternoon, conducted by Father Gratian, and Abhishiktananda was buried in the graveyard at the House of Studies run by the Society of the Divine Word at Palda, four kilometers from Indore.* The cathedral was full, the liturgy beautifully sung, and Father Gratian gave the panegyric for him, showing a real understanding of Abhishiktananda's unusual mission and the pain it cost him. He was one of those who appreciated his search in a way that perhaps only an Indian Christian could do. Recalling the way Abhishiktananda was appreciated at the Bangalore Seminar of 1969, he wrote later:

---

*In 1995 Abhishiktananda's mortal remains were transferred from Indore to Shantivanam, where they now lie next to Fr. Bede Griffiths. Their unceremonious removal (there are no laws against grave digging in India), while understandable in terms of the wishes of the church and the ashram—indeed done with the full agreement and participation of Shantivanam—is a source of sadness to his friends, who felt that the most suitable last home for him would have been the Ganges, the sacred river that was so important to him.

So the long quest for the Soul of India—in the tradition of Dandoy
and Johanns, in the path of De Nobile—was finally ended. He who
had been so often ignored and so often misunderstood in his own
church was finally vindicated in the National Seminar. He took
great comfort from that.[50]

It was left to Sister Théophane to contact Father Dominique and
Marc, who cleared up his guru's few worldly possessions, as his friends
wrote letters and obituaries. A moving tribute came from his old friend
Father Francis Acharya:

> He was a giant "in the spirit." He was astounding by the depth as
> well as by the vivacity of his insights. At the same time he always
> preserved the insights of the child, his sense of wonder and sensi-
> tivity, with marked likes and dislikes. But when a man has crossed
> over to the shores of the world beyond, he takes on his true dimen-
> sion, that of eternity.[51]

Here was someone who risked everything, who reached his goal and was
able to say, in the last entry in his diary:

> The Awakening at the level of anyone who has consciousness is pre-
> cisely to lose oneself, to forget oneself. The Awakening is the shin-
> ing out of the splendour—in splendour—of the non-awakening, of
> the eternal non-born. The non-awakening, the not-born, is mani-
> fested by a—what!—a brilliance, a light, a glory that envelops every-
> thing. A sense of *Beyond*, of the Beyond. . . .[52]

Abhishiktananda was a pioneer who had the courage to break boundaries and to forge a path that inspires and illumines people today, when
as church going declines, interest in spirituality grows. Over his sixty-
three years he himself was transformed, but the significance of his life has
not stopped there. This was a man who has joined the small group of people whose lives have changed our perception and reminded us that we are
all capable of simply "being" and that the Awakening is there for us all.

Abbreviations

AF	Mrs. Antonia Fonseca
AMS	Mrs. Anne-Marie Stokes
BB	Bettina Bäumer
F	Le Saux Family
Fr M	Father Jules Monchanin
FT	Mother Françoise-Thérèse
L	Canon J. Lemarié
M	Mr. and Mrs. Miller
MC	Marc Chaduc
MR	Murray Rogers
MT	Sr. Marie-Thérèse Le Saux
OB	Mme. O. Baumer-Despeigne
RM	Father R. Macé
RP	Dr. Raimon Panikkar
RW	Brother Robert Williamson
SA	A Frenchwoman living as a hermit
Th	Mother M. Théophane
TJ	A Carmelite of Lisieux, later in India
TL	Sr. Tĕrèse de Jésus (Lemoine)

ABBREVIATIONS OF BOOK TITLES
[*For complete citations, see selected bibliography. Books quoted only occasionally are cited in full in the notes.*]

Diary	*Ascent to the Depth of the Heart*
Guru	*Guru and Disciple*
Mountain	*The Mountain of the Lord*
Meeting	*Hindu-Christian Meeting Point*
Message	*Swami Abhishiktananda: The Man and His Message*
Lettres	*Henri Le Saux: Lettres d'un sannyasi chrétien à Joseph Lemarié*
Life	*Swami Abhishiktananda: His Life Told through His Letters*
Secret	*The Secret of Arunachala*
SPAA	*Swami Parama Arubi Anandam*

COLLECTIONS OF LETTERS

A. le B. Coll.	Collection of letters in the possession of Abhi-shiktananda's niece Agnès Le Bris
MR Coll.	Collection of letters in the possession of Father Murray Rogers
LS&T	*Letters Spiritual and Theological*, Kergonan Archives

Notes

Preface

1. L, April 24, 1954, *Lettres*, 113.
2. AMS, February 9, 1967, *Life*, 213.
3. Odette Baumer-Despeigne, "The Spiritual Journey of Henri Le Saux, Abhishiktananda," *Cistercian Studies Quarterly* 18, no. 4 (1983).
4. MT, November 28, 1971, *Life*, 288.
5. MT, August 21, 1960, *LS&T*, 129.
6. TL, November 24, 1973, *Life*, 360.
7. Reverend Mary Lewis to author, November 14, 2001.
8. Shigeto Oshida, *God's Harp String* (unpublished).

Chapter 1: Roots in Brittany

1. Abhishiktananda to MR in conversation.
2. May 2, 1964, *Diary*, 273.
3. Interview with author.
4. Interview with author.
5. Interview with author.
6. Interview with author.
7. Interview with author.
8. Véronique to author.
9. AMS, August 3, 1971, *Life*, 11.
10. To author from recteur, December 3, 2001.
11. F, October 31, 1962, *Life*, 166.
12. Ibid.
13. FT, December 15, 1964, *Life*, 187.
14. To his novice master, December 4, 1928, *Life*, 3.
15. Ibid.
16. Ibid.
17. To his novice master, January 4, 1929, A. le B. Coll.
18. To his novice master, May 27, 1929, A. le B. Coll.
19. To his novice master, December 4, 1928, *Life*, 3.
20. To his novice master, April 23, 1929, *Life*, 4.
21. RM, June 3, 1929, *Life*, 4-5.
22. RM, July 17, 1929, *Life*, 5.
23. His sister Marie-Thérèse says that he entered "for Teresa of Avila," whose feast day is October 15. The date given in the Kergonan archives is October 18.

Chapter 2: An Irresistible Call

1. RM, October 27, 1929, *Life*, 6.
2. Interview with author.
3. RM, October 27, 1929, *Life*, 6.
4. Louisette, October 26, 1929, A. le B. Coll.
5. E-mail to author, December 2001.
6. From *Swamiji: Un voyage intérieur*, a film by Patrice Chagnard, Inner Quest, Paris, 1984.
7. Ibid.
8. Ibid.
9. From a letter read to the author by Agnès le Bris.
10. Interview with author.
11. RM, May 15, 1930, *Life*, 7.
12. RM, May 9, 1935, *Life*, 7.
13. Ibid.
14. Interview with author.

Chapter 3: The Second World War

1. F, September 23, 1940, A. le B. Coll.
2. Much of the information about Kergonan during the war comes from Guy-Marie Oury, *L'abbaye Sainte-Anne de Kergonan: Un siècle d'histoire* (Paris: Sarment/Fayard, 1997).
3. Author interview with Sr. Marie-Thérèse, 2003.
4. F, June 11, 1940, A. le B. Coll.
5. Marcel, October 13, 1939, A. le B. Coll.
6. Marcel, November 2, 1939, A. le B. Coll.
7. F, October 18, 1939, A. le B. Coll.
8. F, June 11, 1940, A. le B. Coll.
9. From a letter to the author from Agnès le Bris, November 18, 2001.
10. F, February 4, 1947, A. le B. Coll.
11. RM, June 23, 1941, *Life*, 8.
12. Quoted in Oury, *L'abbaye Sainte-Anne*, 125.
13. Interview with Murray Rogers.
14. F, September 23, 1940, A. le B. Coll.
15. Quoted in Oury, *L'abbaye Sainte-Anne*, 130.
16. F, July 6, 1946, A. le B. Coll.
17. F, June 11, 1940, A. le B. Coll.
18. F, August 1, 1944, A. le B. Coll.
19. F, January 21, 1945, A. le B. Coll.
20. F, June 30, 1944, A. le B. Coll.
21. F, September 23, 1940, A. le B. Coll.
22. To his sisters, June 16, 1944, A. le B. Coll.
23. F, end of 1944; precise date uncertain.
24. F, December 18, 1943, A. le B. Coll.
25. Ibid.
26. F, October 13, 1946, A. le B. Coll.

27. Ibid.

28. F, July 25, 1946, A. le B. Coll.

29. Ibid.

30. F, July 27, 1946, A. le B. Coll.

31. F, July 7, 1946, A. le B. Coll.

32. F, September 9, 1946, A. le B. Coll.

33. F, August 24, 1946, A. le B. Coll.

Chapter 4: Another Irresistible Vocation

1. Louisette, September 24, 1946, A. le B. Coll.

2. Louisette, January 31, 1945, A. le B. Coll.

3. *Meeting*, 104.

4. *Life*, 8.

5. *Amour et Sagesse*, manuscript written for his mother in 1942; quoted in *Life*, 8.

6. Ibid.; quoted in *Life*, 9.

7. E-mail from Canon Lemarié to author, December 26, 2001.

8. F, August 22, 1947, A. le B. Coll.

9. F, July 21, 1946, A. le B. Coll.

10. Louisette, December 27, 1944, A. le B. Coll.

11. L, September 22, 1973, *Life*, 12.

12. L, March 13, 1967, *Life*, 13.

13. Fr M, August 18, 1947, *Life*, 17.

14. Quoted to Louisette, October 11, 1945, A. le B. Coll.

15. Louisette, December 27, 1945, A. le B. Coll.

16. Louisette, January 3, 1947, A. le B.Coll.

17. Ibid.

18. F, January 11, 1947, A. le B. Coll.

19. Louisette, January 1, 1947, A. le B. Coll.

20. F, February 2, 1947, A. le B. Coll.

21. F, June 9, 1945, A. le B. Coll.

22. Lousiette, January 12, 1947, A. le B. Coll.

23. L, Easter Tuesday, 1947, A. le B. Coll.

24. F, February 2, 1947, A. le B. Coll.

25. Undated, no recipient named, probably May 1947, A. le B. Coll.

26. Ibid.

27. To his sisters, May 28, 1947, A. le B. Coll.

28. Dr. Biot; quoted in *SPAA*, 99-100.

29. Monchanin to H. Le S., August 7, 1947, *Life*, 16.

30. To his sisters, August 8, 1947, A. le B. Coll.

31. Monchanin, August 8, 1947, *Life*, 18.

32. Ibid., 19.

33. Ibid.

34. Ibid.

35. Ibid.

36. Ibid.

37. Monchanin to H. Le S., January 29, 1948, *Life*, 23.

38. F, December 27, 1947, A. le B. Coll.

39. Louisette, January 14, 1948, A. le B. Coll.

40. F, March 13, 1948, A. le B. Coll.

41. To father, Louisette, and Georges, June 3, 1948, A. le B. Coll.

42. Interview with author.

Chapter 5: The Promised Land

1. F, August 15, 1948, *Life*, 23.

2. Ibid.

3. F, August 21, 1948, *Eyes of Light*, 154.

4. Ibid.

5. Ibid.

6. August 16, 1948, *Life*, 24; quoted in *J. Monchanin*, ed. Siauve, 184.

7. F, August 21, 1948, *Eyes of Light*, 157.

8. November 22, 1948, *Lettres*, 28.

9. F, August 21, 1948, *Eyes of Light*, 156-57.

10. F, December 29, 1950, *Life*, 26.

11. F, November 9, 1949, *Life*, 27.

12. RW, December 6, 1950, Kergonan Archives.

13. F, July 18, 1949, *Life*, 31.

14. RW, December 6, 1950, Kergonan Archives.

15. F, August 29, 1949, *Life*, 36.

16. F, August 1, 1949, *Life*, 29.

17. Ibid., 28.

18. *Life*, 28-29.

19. L, November 22, 1948, *Lettres*, 27-28.

20. F, November 9, 1949, *Life*, 37.

21. F, February 26, 1950, *Life*, 38.

22. F, January 15, 1949, *Life*, 28.

23. February 21, 1948, *Diary*, 11.

24. AMS, August 3, 1971, *Life*, 10.

25. Ibid., 11.

26. F, December 29, 1950, *Life*, 25.

27. L, November 22, 1948, *Lettres*, 28-29.

28. Ibid.

29. Ibid.

30. L, February 10, 1952, *Lettres*, 35.

31. F, September 16, 1948, *Life*, 32.

32. September 17, 1948, *Life*, 32; quoted in *J. Monchanin*, ed. Siauve, 185.

33. L, November 22, 1948, *Lettres*, 31.

34. RW, December 6, 1950, Kergonan Archives.

35. F, September 16, 1948, *Life*, 32.

36. L, November 22, 1948, *Lettres*, 31.

37. F, September 16, 1948, *Life*, 32.

38. *A Benedictine Ashram*, 14.

39. Ibid., 16-17.

Chapter 6: Arunachala

1. Quoted in *The Secret of Arunachala*, introduction.

2. Siauve; quoted in *Life*, 33.

3. Arthur Osborne, *Ramana Maharshi and the Path of Self-Knowledge* (York Beach, Me.: Samuel Weiser, 1995), 144-45.

4. Ibid., 17.

5. Ibid., 18.

6. Ibid., 18-19.

7. *Secret*, 17.

8. *Talks with Sri Ramana Maharshi* (3 vols.; Tiruvannamalai: T. N. Ventaraman, Sri Ramanasramam, 1972), 302-3.

9. *Secret*, 8.

10. Ibid., 9.

11. Ibid., 11.

12. Ibid., 13.

13. Ibid., 23.

14. Ibid.

15. Ibid., 25.

16. March 29, 1952, *Diary*, 25.

17. *Secret*, 28.

18. March 31, 1952, *Diary*, 28.

19. F, April 1, 1952, *Life*, 61.

20. L, April 29, 1952, *Lettres*, 52.

21. March 29, 1952, *Diary*, 26.

22. *Secret*, 30.

23. April 6, 1952, *Diary*, 37.

24. Ibid.

25. *Secret*, 30.

26. L, July 11, 1952, *Lettres*, 60.

27. Ibid.

28. *Secret*, 49.

29. L, June 11, 1952, *Lettres*, 58.

30. *Secret*, 105.

31. *Secret*, 107.

32. *Secret*, 52.

33. *Secret*, 53-54.

34. MT, July 7, 1952, *Life*, 63.

35. March 31, 1952, *Diary*, 28.

36. March 13, 1953, *Diary*, 64.

37. June 8, 1952, *Diary*, 44.

38. June 12, 1952, *Diary*, 46.

39. Ibid.

40. June 8, 1952, *Diary*, 43.

41. Ibid.

42. July 15, 1952, *Diary*, 49.

43. July 17, 1952, *Diary*, 49.

44. July 19, 1952, *Diary*, 50.

Chapter 7: A Pioneering Experiment

1. F, January 21, 1951, *Life*, 51.
2. March 23, 1950, Siauve, 198; quoted in *Life*, 41.
3. F, June 2, 1950, *Life*, 42.
4. Ibid.
5. *SPAA*, 28.
6. *Benedictine Ashram*, 17.
7. *SPAA*, 36.
8. Ibid., 37.
9. Ibid.
10. *SPAA*, 35-36.
11. Ibid., 16.
12. *Benedictine Ashram*, 46.
13. *Life*, 44.
14. Ibid.
15. *Benedictine Ashram*, 71.
16. F, December 13, 1950, *Life*, 49.
17. Bede Griffiths, "The One Mystery," *The Tablet*, March 9, 1974.
18. L, March 18, 1952, *Lettres*, 41.
19. Ibid., 44.
20. F, June 2, 1950, *Life*, 41-42.
21. L, November 22, 1948, *Lettres*, 29.
22. L, March 18, 1952, *Lettres*, 41.
23. *Benedictine Ashram*, 4.
24. F, October 1951, *Life*, 52-53.
25. *SPAA*, 47; quoted in *Life*, 53.
26. F, March 4, 1951, *Life*, 51.
27. L, February 10, 1952, *Lettres*, 35.
28. *Benedictine Ashram*, 2.
29. *SPAA*, 33.
30. Jacques Dupuis, S.J., introduction to *Intériorité et révélation: Essais théologiques*, trans. James Stuart (Sisteron: Editions Présence, 1982).
31. F, April 29, 1950, *Life*, 45.
32. F, August 21, 1950, *Life*, 47.
33. Ibid.
34. *SPAA*, 62-63.
35. Anthony Kalliath, *The Word in the Cave: The Experiential Journey of Swami Abhishiktananda to the Point of Hindu-Christian Meeting* (New Delhi: Intercultural Publications, 1996), 64.
36. Ibid., 65.
37. L, March 18, 1952, *Lettres*, 42.
38. F, September 24, 1950, *Life*, 48.
39. Quoted in *Life*, 58.
40. Raimon Panikkar, "Letter to Abhishiktananda," *Studies in Formative Spirituality* 3, no. 3 (1982): 447.
41. L, April 29, 1952, *Lettres*, 52.
42. March 30, 1953, *Diary*, 70.

43. Sten Rodhe, *Jules Monchanin: Pioneer in Christian-Hindu Dialogue* (Delhi: ISPCK, 1993).

44. July 24, 1952, *Diary*, 51.

45. *Lettres à son mère* 1913-1957; quoted in Rodhe, *Jules Monchanin*, 47.

46. July 24, 1952, *Diary*, 52.

47. *Lettres à son mère*, quoted in Rodhe, *Jules Monchanin*, 47.

48. L, January 22, 1948, *Lettres*, 29.

49. L, February 2, 1952, *Lettres*, 35-38.

50. L, August 1, 1953, *Life*, 73.

51. *Lettres à son mère*; quoted in Rodhe, *Jules Monchanin*, 43.

52. L, February 10, 1953, *Lettres*, 68.

53. *SPAA*, 66-67.

Chapter 8: Christianity and *Advaita*

1. F, December 29, 1950, *Life*, 25.

2. Bettina Bäumer, "Abhishiktananda and the Challenge of Hindu-Christian Experience," *Monastic Interreligious Dialogue* (MID) Bulletin 64 (May 2000).

3. L, February 10, 1952, *Lettres*, 36-37.

4. September 7, 1970, *Diary*, 319.

5. *Secret*, 81.

6. Ibid., 82.

7. Ibid., 84.

8. March 14, 1953, *Diary*, 64.

9. *Secret*, 84-85.

10. Ibid., 85.

11. L, April 29, 1953, *Lettres*, 72.

12. April 5, 1952, *Diary*, 35.

13. L, November 1, 1952, *Lettres*, 63.

14. March 23, 1953, *Diary*, 66-67.

15. May 16, 1958, *Diary*, 213.

16. March 29, 1953, *Diary*, 67.

17. Ibid.

18. L, April 29, 1953, *Lettres*, 71.

19. September 27, 1953, *Diary*, 75.

20. October 22, 1970, *Diary*, 321.

21. OB, September 9, 1971, *Life*, 282.

22. Bettina Bäumer in conversation with author, 2004.

23. March 23, 1953, *Diary*, 66.

24. *Secret*, 86.

25. L, February 10, 1952, *Lettres*, 36.

26. Bettina Bäumer in conversation with author, 2004.

27. July 24, 1971, *Diary*, 331-32.

28. F, April 8, 1951, *Life*, 51.

29. MT, August 22, 1952, *Life*, 65.

30. F, December 26, 1951, *Life*, 56.

31. L, June 17, 1954, *Life*, 79-80.

32. September 25, 1953, *Diary*, 73.

33. March 8, 1953, *Diary*, 62.
34. September 19, 1953, *Diary*, 73.
35. September 27, 1953, *Diary*, 74.
36. February 22, 1953, *Diary*, 59.
37. RP, July 15, 1966, *Life*, 204-5.
38. L, February 17, 1958, *Lettres*, 202.
39. L, April 29, 1953, *Lettres*, 72.
40. Ibid., 70.
41. Ibid., 73.
42. Ibid.
43. Ibid., 76.
44. July 17, 1952, *Diary*, 49.
45. L, December 8, 1953, *Lettres*, 94.

Chapter 9: Spiritual Crisis

1. September 5, 1955, *Diary*, 124.
2. L, August 27, 1967, *Lettres*, 351.
3. http://www.gandhiserve.org/information/chronology_1944/chronology-19444.html
4. August 3, 1955, *Diary*, 113.
5. July 27, 1955, *Diary*, 107.
6. July 28, 1955, *Diary*, 108.
7. Ibid.
8. Ibid., 109.
9. Ibid.
10. July 29, 1955, *Diary*, 110.
11. November 27, 1953, *Diary*, 77.
12. July 27, 1955, *Diary*, 106-7.
13. August 2, 1955, *Diary*, 113.
14. August 3, 1955, *Diary*, 114.
15. August 27, 1955, *Diary*, 118.
16. September 5, 1955, *Diary*, 124.
17. November 16, 1955, *Diary*, 130.
18. January 6, 1956, *Diary*, 136.
19. July 29, 1955, *Diary*, 109.
20. Ibid., 110.
21. August 2, 1955, *Diary*, 113.
22. July 31, 1955, *Diary*, 111.
23. Ibid.
24. Ibid.
25. Ibid.
26. August 30, 1955, *Diary*, 120.
27. August 26, 1955, *Diary*, 117.
28. September 3, 1955, *Diary*, 121.
29. September 18, 1955, *Diary*, 126.
30. Ibid.
31. November 16, 1955, *Diary*, 130.

32. July 31, 1955, *Diary*, 112.

33. August 26, 1955, *Diary*, 117.

34. February 17, 1958, *Life*, 124.

35. January 10, 1956, *Diary*, 138.

36. L, October 24, 1960, *Life*, 147.

37. *Life*, 64.

38. S. Siauve, ed., *Jules Monchanin: Mystique de l'Inde, mystère chrétien* (Paris: Fayard, 1974), 269–73; quoted in Abhishiktananda, *Intériorité et révélation: Essais théologiques* (Sisteron: Editions Présence, 1982), 39.

39. *Initiation à la spiritualité des Upanishads* (Sisteron: Editions Présence, 1979), 1. "The Grace of India," 44.

40. Ibid., 47.

41. *Life*, 83.

42. January 1955, *Diary*, 101.

43. March 8, 1968, *Life*, 223.

44. L, September 22, 1963, *Life*, 178.

45. L, March 4, 1955, *Life*, 87.

Chapter 10: Total Immersion in Hinduism

1. MT, March 25, 1956, *Life*, 102.

2. *The Upanishads,*trans. Juan Mascaro (London: Penguin Books, 1965), 58.

3. *The Further Shore: Three Essays* (Delhi: ISPCK, 1984), 12.

4. April 3, 1952, *Diary*, 31.

5. *Guru*, 29.

6. Ibid., 25.

7. Ibid.

8. Ibid., 26.

9. Ibid., 27.

10. Ibid., 29.

11. Ibid.

12. Ibid., 30.

13. Ibid., 47.

14. F, March 19, 1956, *Life*, 101.

15. Ibid.

16. MT, March 25, 1956, *Life*, 152.

17. December 25, 1955, *Life*, 131.

18. L, March 14, 1956, *Life*, 100.

19. Ibid., 101.

20. February 5, 1956, *Diary*, 142.

21. *Guru*, 51.

22. Ibid., 52.

23. March 5, 1956, *Diary*, 145.

24. MT, June 24, 1956, *Life*, 106.

25. *Guru*, 116.

26. Ibid., 79.

27. Ibid., 40.

28. Ibid., 46.

29. Ibid., 126-27.
30. Ibid., 87.
31. Ibid., 87-88.
32. March 6, 1956, *Diary*, 146.
33. *Intériorité et révélation*, "Esseulement" 134; quoted in Edward T. Ulrich, "Swami Abhishiktananda: An Interreligious Hermeneutics of the Upanishads" (Ph.D. diss., The Catholic University of America, 2001), 123.
34. March 5, 1956, *Diary*, 145.
35. January 14, 1956, *Diary*, 139.
36. March 5, 1956, *Diary*, 145.
37. Ibid., 146.
38. March 6, 1956, *Diary*, 146.
39. March 8, 1956, *Diary*, 147.
40. *Guru*, 103.

Chapter 11: A Month in Solitude

1. December 7, 1956, *Diary*, 195.
2. October 31, 1956, *Life*, 110-11.
3. Ibid.
4. November 9, 1956, *Diary*, 158.
5. November 13, 1956, *Diary*, 161.
6. November 14, 1956, *Diary*, 162.
7. November 13, 1956, *Diary*, 161.
8. November 30, 1956, *Diary*, 185.
9. November 15, 1956, *Diary*, 162.
10. November 24, 1956, *Diary*, 175.
11. December 1, 1956, *Diary*, 191.
12. November 11, 1956, *Diary*, 159.
13. November 15, 1956, *Diary*, 164.
14. November 24, 1956, *Diary*, 174.
15. Ibid., 170-71.
16. November 30, 1956, *Diary*, 188.
17. November 24, 1956, *Diary*, 171.
18. December 1, 1956, *Diary*, 190.
19. November 14, 1956, *Diary*, 162.
20. TJ, May 27, 1961, *LS&T*.
21. Bettina Bäumer in conversation with author, 2004.
22. *Prayer*, 108.
23. April 4, 1952, *Diary*, 33-34.
24. MT, August 1, 1955, *LS&T*.
25. F, August 23, 1958, *Life*, 128.
26. *Intériorité et révélation*, "Esseulement," 128 (translator unknown).
27. Ibid., 135.
28. November 13, 1956, *Diary*, 161.
29. November 17, 1956, *Diary*, 164-65.
30. April 4, 1952, *Diary*, 34.
31. Ibid.

32. Ibid.

33. L, April 29, 1953, *Lettres*, 78.

34. Foreword, *Life*, x.

35. June 5, 1958, *Diary*, 217.

36. Ibid.

37. November 7, 1956, *Diary*, 156.

38. November 9, 1956, *Diary*, 158.

39. November 10, 1956, *Diary*, 159.

40. November 21, 1956, *Diary*, 166-67.

41. November 22, 1956, *Diary*, 169.

42. December 6, 1956, *Diary*, 194.

Chapter 12: The Other Side of Silence

1. MT, July 3, 1957, *Life*, 118.

2. Murray Rogers in conversation with author, 2004.

3. L, June 20, 1955, *Lettres*, 132.

4. L, May 27, 1957, *Life*, 116.

5. Bettina Bäumer in conversation with author, 2004.

6. Michael Barnes, "From Ashrams to Dalits: The Four Seasons of Incultura-tion," *The Tablet*, January 2001.

7. Father Mahieu in conversation with author, 1994.

8. L, April 29, 1953, *Lettres*, 79.

9. L, March 28, 1955, *Lettres*, 130.

10. L, July 18, 1955, *Lettres*, 134.

11. F, July 16, 1955, *Life*, 90.

12. L, July 18, 1955, *Lettres*, 134.

13. August 27, 1952, *Diary*, 53.

14. L, April 29, 1953, *Lettres*, 76.

15. L, July 18, 1955, *Lettres*, 135.

16. L, November 8, 1955, *Lettres*, 138.

17. L, December 24, 1955, *Lettres*, 142.

18. L, January 20, 1956, *Life*, 99.

19. L, October 31, 1956, *Life*, 110.

20. April 11, 1957, *Diary*, 203.

21. April 8, 1957, *Diary*, 202.

22. April 12, 1957, *Diary*, 204.

23. April 14, 1957, *Diary*, 205.

24. L, May 27, 1957, *Lettres*, 175.

25. MT, July 3, 1957, *Life*, 118.

26. L, August 28, 1957, *Lettres*, 189.

27. *Life*, 120.

28. L, October 13, 1956, *Life*, 110.

29. L, January 17, 1958, *Life*, 123.

30. *SPAA*, 71.

31. L, December 29, 1957, *Lettres*, 197.

32. MT, November 21, 1958, *Life*, 129.

Chapter 13: A Very Active Hermit

1. L, March 18, 1961, *Life*, 151.
2. SA, 1966, *LS&T*, 150.
3. FT, December 29, 1959, *LS&T*, 131.
4. F, June 21, 1958, *Life*, 126.
5. L, June 16, 1960, *Life*, 145.
6. F, August 23, 1958, *Life*, 128.
7. October 29, 1959, *Diary*, 128.
8. May 16, 1958, *Diary*, 214.
9. May 17, 1958, *Diary*, 215.
10. *Diary*, 211.
11. April 12, 1957, *Diary*, 203.
12. August 19, 1959, *Diary*, 221.
13. March 30, 1957, *Diary*, 201.
14. MT, March 19, 1959, *Life*, 130.
15. TJ, November 23, 1959, *LS&T*, 139.
16. MT, August 21, 1960, *LS&T*, 129.
17. This story is told in *The Tablet*, April 21, 2001.
18. Murray Rogers to author, 2001.
19. Murray Rogers to author, 2001.
20. AMS, June 17, 1959, *Life*, 133.
21. L, September 9, 1959, *Life*, 136.
22. MT, December 17, 1964, *Life*, 190.
23. TJ, November 23, 1959, *LS&T*, 139.
24. *Mountain*, 6.
25. Ibid., 25.
26. L, June 3, 1959, *Life*, 132-33.
27. Ibid.
28. MT, July 16, 1959, *Life*, 134.
29. Ibid.
30. L, August 18, 1959, *Life*, 136.
31. *Mountain*, 23.
32. Ibid., 23-24.
33. Ibid., 25.
34. L, September 20, 1959, *Lettres*, 230.
35. FT, October 26, 1959, *Life*, 137.

Chapter 14: Pioneers in Dialogue

1. Sara Grant, Foreword to Abhishiktananda, *Hindu-Christian Meeting Point: Within the Cave of the Heart* (Delhi: ISPCK, 1983), viii.
2. See chapter 9 above.
3. *Contacts: revue française de l'orthodoxie*, Ier trimestre (1963): 41-51.
4. *Intériorité et révélation: Essais théologiques* (Sisteron: Editions Présence, 1982); *Initiation à la spiritualité des Upanishads* (Sisteron: Editions Présence, 1979).
5. L, December 19, 1961, *Lettres*, 272.
6. Murray Rogers in conversation with author, 2004.

7. MT, February 6, 1961, *Life*, 149.

8. L, March 18, 1961, *Life*, 153-54.

9. AMS, May 12, 1961, *Life*, 154.

10. *Meeting*, 12-13.

11. Ibid., 13.

12. Ibid., 14.

13. TJ, November 23, 1959, *LS&T*, 140.

14. *Meeting*, 16.

15. *Swami Abhishiktananda: The Man and His Message* (Delhi: ISPCK, 1993), 28-29.

16. Abhishiktananda, "Christians Meditate Together on the Upanishads, 25 April 1964," *Informations catholiques internationales*, no. 221-22 (August 1964): 11-17.

17. Ibid.

18. Ibid.

19. Ibid.

20. MT, February 5, 1964, *Life*, 178.

21. Ibid.

22. MR, undated, *Life*, 177.

23. Abhishiktananda in conversation with MR. Date unknown.

24. L, November 19, 1962, *Life*, 167.

25. "Christians Meditate on the Upanishads."

26. Ibid.

27. Dr. Cuttat to Ilse Friedeberg and Rev. Murray Rogers, July 8, 1972, MR Coll.

28. Bettina Bäumer to author, July 12, 2004.

29. MR to author, 2003.

30. TJ, November 23, 1959, *LS&T*, 139.

31. AMS, January 25, 1969, *Life*, 235.

32. MR, September 2, 1973.

33. *Meeting*, 9.

34. Ibid.

35. *Life*, 163.

36. *Saccidananda*, xi.

37. RP, May 18, 1966, *Life*, 202.

38. *Saccidananda*, viii.

39. No. 80 (1966).

40. *Clergy Supplement*, vol. 8.

41. RP, July 15, 1966, *Life*, 205.

Chapter 15: To the Source of the Ganges

1. *Mountain*, 13. There are two English translations of this book. The one used here was published by ISPCK in 1990.

2. L, April 29, 1961, *Life*, 151.

3. FT, January 14, 1962, *LS&T*, 134.

4. November 13, 1962, *Diary*, 246-47.

5. L, July 15, 1962, *Life*, 164.

6. TL, November 23, 1961, *Life*, 159.
7. AMS, August 3, 1971, *Life*, 11.
8. Ibid.
9. AMS, August 3, 1971, *Life*, 10.
10. MC, April 4, 1973, *Life*, 328.
11. *Mountain*, 46.
12. *Secret*, 120.
13. Ibid.
14. *Secret*, 123.
15. http://www.thewaterpage.com/ganges.htm
16. *Mountain*, 6.
17. MT, June 12, 1963, *Life*, 171.
18. *Mountain*, 11.
19. Ibid., 58.
20. Ibid., 59.
21. Ibid.
22. MT, June 28, 1964, *Life*, 182.
23. Ibid.
24. Ibid.
25. Ibid.
26. *Mountain*, 27.
27. Ibid., 29.
28. Ibid., 31.
29. L, July 12, 1964, *Lettres*, 303-4.
30. *Mountain*, 32.
31. Ibid., 27.
32. Ibid.
33. *Prayer*, 110.
34. Ibid., 111-12.
35. Ibid., 116.
36. Ibid., 120.
37. Bede Griffiths, *The Golden String*, new ed. (Tucson, Ariz.: Medio Media, 2003), 170.
38. *Prayer*, 113.
39. December 1, 1956, *Diary*, 189-90.
40. June 26, 1964, *Diary*, 274.

Chapter 16: Overcoming Opposites

1. OB, January 5, 1968, *LS&T*, 164.
2. *Life*, 213.
3. MT, December 26, 1966, *Life*, 211.
4. RP, December 5, 1969, *Life*, 249.
5. L, March 13, 1967, *Life*, 214.
6. L, May 15, 1967, *Life*, 214.
7. AMS, February 2, 1967, *Life*, 213.
8. RP, May 18, 1966, *Life*, 202.
9. BB, September 16, 1966, *LS&T*, 153.
10. FT, October 10, 1963, *LS&T*, 137.

11. FT, Ibid., 138.

12. AMS, January 29, 1966, *Life*, 198.

13. RP, October 29, 1966, *Life*, 209.

14. L, January 24, 1969, *Life*, 235.

15. L, November 14, 1968, *Life*, 233.

16. L, November 22, 1966, *Life*, 211.

17. SA,1967, *LS&T*, 151.

18. RP, June 21, 1968, *Life*, 227.

19. *The Church in India: An Essay in Christian Self-Criticism* (The Christian Literature Society, 1969).

20. RP, June 21, 1968, *Life*, 227.

21. Sara Grant, *Lord of the Dance* (Bangalore: Asian Trading Corporation, 1987), 57.

22. *All India Seminar: The Church in India Today, Bangalore 1969* (New Delhi: CBCI Centre), 79.

23. RP, June 25, 1969, *Life*, 239.

24. Sara Grant, "Swamiji—the Man," *Clergy Monthly* 38, no. 11 (1974): 487-88; quoted in *Life*, 238-39.

25. *Church in India*, 24.

26. Ibid., 62.

27. Ibid., 64.

28. OB, May 31, 1968, *LS&T*, 164.

29. MT, September 25, 1966, *Life*, 207.

30. *Life*, 216.

31. MT, October 2, 1968, *Life*, 228.

32. MC, October 4, 1971, *Life*, 353.

33. MR to author, 2002.

34. OB, August 24, 1969, *Life*, 245.

35. L, July 20, 1969, *Life*, 241.

36. MT, December 17, 1968, *Life*, 233-34.

37. OB, January 23, 1969, *Life*, 234.

38. RP, February 24, 1970, *Life*, 252.

39. RP, December 11, 1969, *Life*, 250.

40. *Message*, 25.

41. TJ, December 14, 1970, *LS&T*, 147.

42. MT, December 18, 1972, *Life*, 315.

43. TJ, February 22, 1966, *LS&T*, 145.

44. MT, May 11, 1970, *Life*, 250.

45. MC, April 12, 1973, *Life*, 330.

46. FT, October 25, 1962, *LS&T*, 134.

47. L, December 22, 1965, *Life*, 196.

48. JL (a priest friend), May 9, 1965, *LS&T*, 159.

49. L, October 24, 1965, *Life*, 195.

50. MT, May 11, 1970, *Life*, 259.

51. OB, July 11, 1969, *LS &T*, 167.

52. TL, February 16, 1967, *Life*, 213.

53. TJ, March 18, 1970, *LS&T*, 146.

54. TL, March 18, 1970, *Life*, 258.

55. M, March 4, 1970, *Life*, 256.
56. TL, March 18, 1970, *Life*, 257.
57. OB, September 13, 1967, *LS&T*, 163.
58. OB, November 9, 1969, *LS&T*, 168.

Chapter 17: A True Disciple

1. M, November 13, 1970, *Life*, 267.
2. Abhishiktananda, *The Further Shore: Three Essays* (Delhi: ISPCK, 1984), 13.
3. *The Upanishads*, Mundaka Upanishad, Mascaro, 77.
4. Abhishiktananda, *The Eyes of Light* (Denville, N.J.: Dimension Books, 1983), 102.
5. M, November 13, 1970, *Life*, 267.
6. *Eyes of Light*, 102.
7. Unpublished excerpt from journal, August 25, 1972, *Eyes of Light*, 178.
8. MT, August 18, 1961, *Life*, 155.
9. Th, May 21, 1961, *Life*, 155.
10. Th, July 14, 1961, *Life*, 155.
11. L, May 25, 1963, *Life*, 171.
12. OB, November 3, 1971, *Life*, 288.
13. L, October 8, 1966, *Life*, 208.
14. OB, November 3, 1971, *Life*, 288.
15. Bettina Bäumer to author, July 2004.
16. L, June 10, 1969, *Lettres*, 370.
17. MC, September 29, 1969, *Life*, 245.
18. MC, March 4, 1970, *Life*, 255.
19. MC, October 16, 1970, *Life*, 265.
20. *Guru* [2000], 28-29.
21. *Life*, 286.
22. MC, April 18, 1973, *Life*, 331.
23. Quoted in Odette Baumer-Despeigne, "The Spiritual Way of Henri Le Saux, Swami Abhishiktananda," *La Vie Spirituelle*, no. 691 (September-October 1990): 22.
24. Ibid.
25. MC, December 6, 1971, *Life*, 287.
26. Baumer-Despeigne, "Spiritual Way," 22.
27. MC, December 6, 1971, *Life*, 291.
28. MC, January 14, 1972, *Life*, 293.
29. MC, December 17, 1971, *Life*, 291.
30. FT, November 16, 1961, *LS&T*, 133.
31. MT, August 21, 1960, *LS&T*, 129.
32. MC, December 17, 1971, *Life*, 291.
33. OB, January 7, 1972, *Life*, 290.
34. MC, January 8, 1972, *Life*, 292.
35. December 11, 1971, *Diary*, 333.
36. MT, January 29, 1972, *Life*, 294.
37. AF, June 8, 1972, *LS&T*, 157.
38. December 24, 1972, *Diary*, 336.

39. *Swami Abhishiktananda: The Man and His Message: Papers Read at an Abhishik-tananda Week (Dec. 1985)*, ed. Vandana Mataji (Delhi: ISPCK, 1986).

40. Ibid., 8.

41. Ibid., 12 (emphasis in original).

42. Ibid., 17.

43. Ibid., 52.

44. Ibid., 67.

45. Told to the author by Bettina Bäumer.

46. Baumer-Despeigne, "Spiritual Way," 22.

47. May 28, 1972, *Diary*, 351.

48. Ibid.

49. Baumer-Despeigne, "Spiritual Way," 23.

50. See Bettina Bäumer, in *Message*, 52-56.

51. May 11, 1972, *Diary*, 348.

52. Svetasvatara Upanishad, 8; see *The Vedic Experience: An Anthology of the Vedas for Modern Man and Contemporary Celebration*, ed. Raimon Panikkar with N. Shanta, M. A. R. Rogers, B. Bäumer, and M. Bidoli (London: Darton, Longman & Todd, 1977), 734.

53. Baumer-Despeigne, "Spiritual Way," 22.

54. Anne-Marie Stokes, "Recollections of Abhishiktananda" (unpublished), quoted in *Life*, 324.

55. May 28, 1972, *Diary*, 351.

56. *Life*, 300.

57. OB, May 28, 1972, *Life*, 300.

58. May 28, 1972, *Diary*, 351.

59. OB, May 8, 1972, *Life*, 301.

60. MC, June 9, 1972, *Life*, 304.

61. Ibid.

62. *Further Shore*, 50.

63. MR, July 3, 1973.

64. Baumer-Despeigne, "Spiritual Way," 23.

65. MT, July 6, 1973, *Life*, 340.

66. July 3, 1973, *Diary*, 382-83.

Chapter 18: The Final Explosion

1. TL, November 24, 1973, *Life*, 360.

2. MR, August 6, 1993, *Life*, 346.

3. Murray Rogers to author, June 2004.

4. July 3, 1973, *Diary*, 383.

5. July 5, 1973, *Diary*, 384.

6. MT, March 5, 1960, *Life*, 143.

7. September 11, 1973, *Diary*, 386.

8. Jean Sulivan, *Le plus petit abîme* (Paris: Editions Gallimard, 1965), quoted in *Life*, 337.

9. *Life*, 342.

10. Odette Baumer-Despeigne, "The Spiritual Way of Henri Le Saux, Swami Abhishiktananda," *La Vie Spirituelle*, no. 691 (September-October 1990): 23.

11. Ibid., 23-24.

12. Ibid., 24.

13. Ibid.

14. MR, September 10, 1973, *Life*, 350.

15. Baumer-Despeigne, "Spiritual Way," 24.

16. September 11, 1973, *Diary*, 385.

17. Ibid.

18. *Life*, 344.

19. Quoted in letter from Sister Sara Grant to Heather Sandeman, December 24, 1973.

20. September 11, 1973, *Diary*, 386.

21. Ibid.

22. MT, August 9, 1973, *Life*, 347.

23. To Christian Belle, quoted in Odette Baumer-Despeigne, "The Spiritual Journey of Henri Le Saux, Abhishiktananda," *Cistercian Studies Quarterly* 18, no. 4 (1983): 310-29.

24. September 11, 1973, *Diary*, 386.

25. MT, August 9, 1973, *Life*, 347.

26. L, September 22, 1973, *Lettres*, 418.

27. MR, September 2, 1973, *Life*, 348.

28. OB, July 23, 1973, *LS&T*, 171.

29. TL, November 24, 1973, *Life*, 360.

30. To a German couple, November 13, 1970, *LS&T*, 162.

31. BB, July 2, 1970, *LS&T*, 153.

32. February 17, 1956, *Diary*, 144.

33. MC, January 28, 1972, *LS&T*, 57.

34. March 8, 1972; Raimon Panikkar, "Letter to Abhishiktananda," *Studies in Formative Spirituality* 3, no. 3 (1982): 429-51.

35. MR, September 2, 1973.

36. MR, October 4, 1973.

37. MR, September 2, 1973.

38. Ibid.

39. Th to MT, January 18, 1974, Kergonan Archives.

40. Ibid.

41. Ibid.

42. FT, November 11, 1973, *Life*, 361.

43. OB to the abbot of Kergonan, 1974, Kergonan Archives.

44. Baumer-Despeigne, "Spiritual Way," 24.

45. Th to MT, January 18, 1974, Kergonan Archives.

46. Baumer-Despeigne, "Spiritual Way," 24.

47. Th to Father Dominique; see Baumer-Despeigne, "Spiritual Way," 25.

48. Th to MT, January 18, 1973, Kergonan Archives.

49. Ibid.

50. Father Gratian Aroojis to MR, December 12, 1973, MR Coll.

51. Francis Acharya, *Swamy (sic) Abhishiktananda—A Memorial Tribute* (Kurisumala, 1974).

52. September 12, 1973, *Diary*, 388.

Glossary

acharya	Master, teacher, head of an ashram
acosmic	Literally, denial of a universe distinct from God
advaita	From Sanskrit *a-* and *dvaita*, literally, "not two"—nonduality
advaitin	One who lives by advaita
aham	I, myself
ahamkāra	The sense of oneself as an individual
ākāśa	Empty space
anamnesis	(Greek) memory or memorial
ānanda	Joy, bliss
ananya	The not-other
añjali	Greeting with the palms together
antarātman	Inner self
anubhava	Direct experience, knowledge derived from immediate spiritual insight
arati	Worship offered by the waving of lights
arunāchala	*aruna*, "color of dawn"; *achala*, "mountain"
ashram	A place of retreat, the abode of a guru and his disciples
ātman	The Self, the ultimate ground at once in the human being and in the universe
bhakta	Worshiper, devotee
bhakti	Love of God
bheda	Separation, distinction
bhikshā	Begging for food by a monk
Brahman	The Absolute Being, omnipresent and transcendent
Buddha	The illuminated one, the awakened one
darshan	A blessed seeing sought by a devotee visiting a holy man, a temple or a holy place
dhoti	A strip of cloth around the waist covering the lower part of the body
dhyāna	Meditation, contemplation
dīkshā	Initiation
guhā	Cave, the cave of the heart, the heart regarded as a spiritual place, where the mystery is hidden
Guhāntara	The one who dwells within the cave, a pseudonym of Abhishiktananda
hrid	Heart, the spiritual center
jnanic	From *jñani*—a sage, one who has awakened to reality
karma	Action, work, the result of actions done in a previous life
kāvi	The saffron-colored cloth worn by monks
kenōsis	(Greek) emptying, stripping

keshī	The hairy one, acosmic ascetic of the Vedas
kevala	Applied to one who has attained to unity in total isolation; Abhishiktananda also called it "the solitude that has no name."
Krishna	The cowherd God, incarnation of Vishnu
kutiya	(Hindi) hut
līlā	The creation as divine play
linga	The phallic symbol of Shiva everywhere venerated
mahāvākya	One of the great sentences which sum up the teaching of the Upanishads, e.g., "thou art that, *tat tvam asi*"
mandir	(Hindi) temple
mantra	Sacred word, formula of prayer
mauna	Silence
māyā	The undefinable condition of the world of manifestation, which cannot be called either real or unreal
muni	An ascetic who is vowed to silence, in Tamil *munivar*
nāmajapa	The prayer of the name, repetition of the divine name
nāma-rūpa	Name and form, the external manifestation of reality
namaskāram	Greeting with joined hands, prostration
neti neti	"Not this, not that"
nirvāna	"Extinction," total liberation in Buddhism
nitya	Permanent, eternal
OM tat sat	An Upanishadic mantra, "indeed That (*brahman*) is the Real."
OM, AUM	The sacred syllable, means also "so be it" (cf. *amen*).
Paramātman	The supreme Self, God
prasāda	Grace, blessed food which is offered to God
pūjā	ritual worship offered to an image, with light, flowers, and incense
purusha	The primordial, archetypal man
rishi	Vedic seer
saccidananda	From Sanskrit *sat*, "being," *cit*, "awareness," and *ananda*, "bliss"
sad-guru	The true guru, master
sādhanā	Spiritual practice, discipline
sādhu	A wandering monk, renouncer, ascetic
sannyāsa	The life of total renunciation
sannyāsi	Renouncer, a Hindu monk
satori	(Japanese) illumination, realizations in Zen
shakti	The active power of God, often personified as a feminine principle
Shiva, Śiva	Supreme God of Hindus, the model of renouncers and yogis
swami	Lord, Master, title of a *sannyāsi* (like Dom or Father)
swamiji	Familiar form of swami
tundu	(Tamil) a strip of cloth thrown over the shoulder
Upanishads	Sacred texts, regarded as the completions of the Vedas
Veda	The sacred scriptures of Hinduism
Vishnu	One of the principal Gods in Hinduism

Resources

SELECTED BIBLIOGRAPHY

Primary Sources

Books by Abhishiktananda

Amour et Sagesse. 1942 (unpublished typescript). Abhishiktananda Society Archives.

Ascent to the Depth of the Heart: The Spiritual Diary of Swami Abhishiktananda. Edited by Raimon Panikkar. Translated by David Fleming and James Stuart. Delhi: ISPCK, 1998.

The Church in India: An Essay in Christian Self-Criticism. Madras: Christian Literature Society, 1969.

Ermites du Saccidânanda: Un essai d'intégration chrétienne de la tradition de l'Inde (with Father Monchanin). Tournai/Paris: Casterman, 1956.

The Eyes of Light. Denville, N.J.: Dimension Books, 1983.

The Further Shore: Three Essays. Reprinted with extra material. Delhi: ISPCK, 1984.

Guhantara: au sein du fond. Written 1953-54. Only extracts published so far.

Guru and Disciple: An Encounter with Sri Gnanananda, a Contemporary Spiritual Master. Delhi: ISPCK, 1970. First published in English, London: SPCK, 1970.

Hindu-Christian Meeting Point: Within the Cave of the Heart. Delhi: ISPCK, 1983.

An Indian Benedictine Ashram (with Father Monchanin). Tiruchirapalli: St. Joseph's Industrial School Press, 1951. New edition entitled *A Benedictine Ashram.* Douglas, Isle of Man: Times Press, Ltd., 1964.

Initiation à la spiritualité des Upanishads: "Vers l'autre rive." Sisteron: Editions Présence, 1979.

Intériorité et révélation: Essais théologiques. Sisteron: Editions Présence, 1982.

The Mountain of the Lord: Pilgrimage to Gangotri. New edition. Delhi: ISPCK, 1990.

Prayer. New edition. Delhi: ISPCK, 1999.

Saccidananda: A Christian Approach to Advaitic Experience. Delhi: ISPCK, 1997.

The Secret of Arunachala: A Christian Hermit on Shiva's Holy Mountain. Revised edition. Delhi: ISPCK, 1979.

In Spirit and Truth: An Essay on Prayer and Life. Delhi: ISPCK, 1989.

Swami Abhishiktananda: His Life Told through His Letters. Edited by James Stuart. Delhi: ISPCK, 1989.

Swami Parama Arubi Anandam (Fr. J. Monchanin) 1895–1957: A Memorial. Saccidananda Ashram, 1959.

Correspondence

Henri Le Saux: Lettres d'un sannyasi chrétien à Joseph Lemarié. Paris: Editions du Cerf, 1999.
Letters Spiritual and Theological 1953–1973. Unpublished typescript from the Kergonan Archives.
Family Letters 1928–1948. Photocopies from the collection of Agnès le Bris.

Secondary Sources

Books about Abhishiktananda

Conio, Caterina. *Abhishiktananda: Sulle frontiere dell'incontro cristiano-indù.* Assisi: Cittadella Editrice, 1984.
Davy, M.-M. *Henri Le Saux, Swami Abhishiktananda, le Passeur entre deux rives.* Paris: Editions du Cerf, 1981.
Grant, Sara. *Lord of the Dance: Swamiji—The Man.* Bangalore: Asian Trading Corporation, 1987.
Hackbarth-Johnson, Christian. *Interreligiöse Existenz, Spirituelle Erfahrung und Identität bei Henri Le Saux (O.S.B) Swami Abhishiktananda (1910–1973).* Frankfurt a. M.: Peter Lang, 2002.
Kalliath, Anthony. *The Word in the Cave: The Experiential Journey of Swami Abhishiktananda to the Point of Hindu-Christian Meeting.* New Delhi: Intercultural Publications, 1996.
Rogers, Murray, and David Barton. *Abhishiktananda: A Memoir of Dom Henri Le Saux.* Oxford: Sisters of the Love of God, 2003.
Swami Abhishiktananda: The Man and His Message. Delhi: ISPCK, 1993.
Ulrich, Edward T. "Swami Abhishiktananda: An Interreligious Hermeneutics of the Upanishads." Unpublished doctoral thesis, 2001.
Visvanathan, Susan. *An Ethnography of Mysticism: The Narratives of Abhishiktananda, A French Monk in India.* Shimla: Indian Institute of Advanced Study, 1998.

Related Material

All India Seminar: Church in India Today, Bangalore, 1969. New Delhi: CBCI Centre.
Barnes, Michael, S.J. *Theology and the Dialogue of Religions.* Cambridge: Cambridge University Press, 2002.
Cuttat, Jacques-Albert. *The Spiritual Dialogue of East and West.* New Delhi: Max Mueller Bhavan Publications, German Cultural Institute, 1961.
du Boulay, Shirley. *Beyond the Darkness: A Biography of Bede Griffiths.* London: Rider, 1998.
Dupuis, Jacques. *Toward a Christian Theology of Religious Pluralism.* Maryknoll, N.Y.: Orbis Books, 1997.

Jules Monchanin (1895–1957) As Seen from East and West. 2 volumes. Delhi: ISPCK; Delhi, Saccidananda Ashram, 2001.

Mataji, Vandana, ed. *Christian Ashrams: A Movement with a Future?* Delhi: ISPCK, 1993.

Osborne, Arthur. *Ramana Maharshi and the Path of Self-Knowledge*. York Beach, Me.: Samuel Weiser, 1970.

Osborne, Arthur, ed. *The Collected Works of Ramana Maharshi*. London: Rider, 1959.

Oury, Guy-Marie. *L'abbaye Sainte-Anne de Kergonan: Un siècle d'histoire*. Paris: Sarment/Fayard, 1997.

Panikkar, Raimon, ed., with N. Shanta, A. M. S. Rogers, B. Bäumer, and M. Bidoli. *The Vedic Experience: An Anthology of the Vedas for Modern Man and Contemporary Celebration*. London: Darton, Longman & Todd, 1977.

Reymond, Lizelle. *To Live Within: The Story of Five Years with a Himalayan Guru*. London: George Allen & Unwin, 1972.

Rodhe, Sten. *Jules Monchanin: Pioneer in Christian-Hindu Dialogue*. Delhi: ISPCK, 1993.

Siauve, S., ed. *J. Monchanin: Mystique de l'Inde, mystère chrétien*. Paris: Fayard, 1974.

Talks with Sri Ramana Maharshi. 3 volumes. Tiruvannamalai: T. N. Venkataraman, Sri Ramanasramam, 1972.

Trapnell, Judson B. *Bede Griffiths: A Life in Dialogue*. Albany: State University of New York Press, 2001.

The Upanishads. Translated from the Sanskrit by Juan Mascaro. London: Penguin Books, 1965.

FILM

Swamiji. Un voyage intérieur. Film by Patrice Chagnard, Paris, 1984. English version video, *Swamiji. An Interior Journey*. 86 minutes, color, PAL.
Distributor/ Order: Inner Quest, 75860 Paris, P.B. 29, CEDEX 18
Internet: www.inner-quest.org/Videos_4.htm

CONTACTS

Abhishiktananda Society
Brotherhood House
7 Court Lane
Delhi 110054 - India
Web Site: www.abhishiktananda.org

Related Organizations
Association Jules Monchanin - Henri Le Saux (France)
President: Mme Francoise Jacquin
Address: 31, place Bellecour, F-69002 France
Web Site in French: monchaninlesaux.lyon@wanadoo.fr

Centro Interreligioso Henri Le Saux (Milano, Italy)
The Centro Le Saux was founded in 1974 by Prof. Dr. Caterina Conio. After her
death Dr. Elvira Bernareggi became the Director.
Address: Centro Interreligioso Henri Le Saux, Via Carroccio 4, I-20123 Milano
(Italy).

Saccidananda Ashram, Shantivanam
Founded in 1950 by H. Le Saux and J. Monchanin, guided by B. Griffiths
(1968–1993)
Address: Saccidananda Ashram, P.O. Thannirpally 639 107, Kulithalai, Dist.
Karur, Tamil Nadu, India
E-mail: saccidananda@hotmail.com

Bede Griffiths Sangha
Beech Tree Cottage
Selling, Faversham,
Kent ME13 9RH UK
bg.sangha@btinternet.com

Index